IN THE NAME
OF GOD...

WHO KNEW WHAT WHEN?

Christine Dolan

IN THE NAME
OF GOD...

WHO KNEW WHAT WHEN?

Foreword by Fr. Tom Doyle

VINDICTA

Vindicta Publishing

Las Vegas ♦ Chicago ♦ Palm Beach

Published in the United States of America by Histria Books
7181 N. Hualapai Way, Ste. 130-86
Las Vegas, NV 89166 U.S.A.
HistriaBooks.com

Vindicta Publishing is an imprint of Histria Books and a joint venture of Histria Books and Creative Destruction Media. Titles published under the imprints of Histria Books are distributed worldwide.

Library of Congress Control Number: 2024931050

ISBN 978-1-59211-423-8 (hardcover)
ISBN 978-1-59211-440-5 (eBook)

This book is dedicated to all child abuse survivors globally, including those betrayed by the Roman Catholic Church.

I also dedicate this book to the loving memory of Thomas J. Dolan, our beloved late father, whom we all called "Buddy." He gave my siblings and me the most cherished, loving, and protective childhoods. My siblings, extended family, friends, and I were particularly inspired by his courage to take on Cardinal Law in Boston in 2002. His moral compass, clarity, tenacity, and faith were contagious. He firmly believed that it was the duty of all adults to protect all children.

Contents

Foreword

It is vitally important that the focus be kept on the church because of the responsibility the Catholic Church has, and other churches have for moral leadership and for taking care of and watching out for the welfare of the most vulnerable and marginalized people in our society. In this case, we are speaking of children and young adolescents throughout the world, who are sexually exploited by sexual abuse, sexual torture, pornography rings, and much more.

This is a vital time because there is the continuation of the groundswell and it is a time when we can break down the societal apathy not just in the churches but in society in general, toward the issue of the sexual exploitation of children.

I think that this book and the whole impetus behind it, point to the fact that this is a worldwide problem!

IT'S NOT SMALL...IT'S HUGE!

It is not just inappropriate touches or temporary lapses of judgment as some churchmen would have you believe. We ARE talking about things like rape, sexual torture, selling kids for reasons of pornography - as serious, and drastic as you can imagine, and then some.

This is a time when the churches of course, and the secular society in general, can jump on this bandwagon and do something. Talk is cheap when it comes to protecting children. It does not do any good to issue guidelines, or statements, or apologies.

What is important is action - and what is needed is not just action by the leaders, but a breaking through of the apathy and the denial of the rank and file of society in general to wake up to the fact that this is not just a serious problem, but a critical problem.

We are talking about our future and the future of a society that purports to be enlightened and have the greatest respect for individuals…if we do not take it and apply it to the most marginalized - the most helpless individuals then we live in a society of hypocrisy!

Fr. Tom Doyle
Washington, D.C. 2002

Introduction

In 2000, the International Centre for Missing and Exploited Children commissioned me to investigate the exploitation of children emanating from the Balkans Crises – a conflict I had covered in the 1990s.

During that summer, I crisscrossed western and eastern Europe, and the Balkans, interviewed as many players as possible – both good and bad – and victims who agreed to speak with me.

Having been trained as a criminal investigator while in law school, I approached this investigation as I would have any investigation of a complex racketeering and conspiracy nature. I attempted to connect a series of seemingly random dots to arrive at a complete picture based upon facts.

It was almost like an artist painting a canvas having no idea how the creativity would evolve before the portrait came to fruition.

The stories I heard initially seemed frighteningly implausible. What law enforcement officials told me and showed me was horrifyingly evil and exploded my reality. What I digested convinced me of the need for this subject to be investigated globally.

War correspondents assume and witness evil in war zones. As I began to learn about human trafficking what dawned on me was that this evil was "among" the so-called civilized world. Once I saw this evil, it became very difficult to unsee it and was very different than in a war zone on a scale that later revealed itself in plain sight.

It forced me to ask the question, "How did we in the mainstream media, which I had been a part of for decades, miss a story of this magnitude?"

The curse of human trafficking is a global phenomenon. Slavery at the cusp of the 21st Century did not just appear overnight. Child sex abuse is rampant and buried within industries.

The numbers were absolutely staggering in 2000 according to experts then –
two to four million new victims annually. Moreover, as Queen Silvia of Sweden
said at the time, they were shocking.

"The ages are frightening," exclaimed the Queen.

Infants, toddlers, and incredibly young children and adolescents were then,
and still are today, at risk of sexual violence that is nothing short of sexual torture.

The sexual demand for these children was, and still is, extremely high and con-
stantly growing because of the internet. Those who were, and are still today, engaged in this obscene trade were and are often part of international, transnational,
and trans criminal syndicates, which have engulfed even friends and family members as traffickers and child rapists, who are close to victims.

The result of my first investigation is a book released in July 2024, **Shattered
Innocence – A Shared Global Shame** covering over 24 years of investigating human trafficking in 140 countries. The first findings were originally released as a
report at the National Press Club on May 4, 2001. [1]

---

[1] "Christine Dolan's report is one of the finest works of investigative journalism I have seen in my
25 years in network television news. Her groundbreaking undercover journey is truly the first peek
behind the evil curtain of the underworld of the Have Nots…and into the fractured lives of their
most vulnerable commodity - the children. Christine's clear presentation of the patterns, the players,
and the problems faced by law enforcement from country to country was an eye opener that provides
great insight into the *current war against terrorism.* Every news organization and politician needs to
read *Shattered Innocence.* Dolan puts her finger on the pulse of this phenomenon more squarely
than anyone. She saw it first-hand," stated Patrick Roddy, Television Executive and former
Executive Producer of ABC's Good Morning America.

"Dolan's Investigation and Report is riveting and the most valuable investigation for law enforcement
worldwide," endorsed Inspector Paul Holmes, the former head of the Metropolitan London Police
Department division charged with the responsibility over Vice and Clubs, and the then Chair of
Interpol's Committee on Human Trafficking in 2001.

"I was blown away. I suggest it to everyone. *Shattered Innocence* connects the dots like no other
intelligence piece of information I have ever seen," said Dutch Investigator Jola Vollebreght and
Deputy Director of Interpol's Committee on Human Trafficking in 2001.

"When I read *Shattered Innocence*, it became clear to me that apparently, humanity's capacity for
evil is bottomless. I can empathize with Christine as she chose what level of graphic detail to include.

Homayra Sellier, President of Innocence in Danger, invited me to speak at the United Nations in Geneva, Switzerland in 2001. While there, I was presented with something so horrifying and of such urgency that I expanded my body of work deeper into the internet as a journalist.

I was shown 20 CD-ROMS filled with child pornography, which had not been fully investigated by European law enforcement authorities. These images were of unimaginable cruelty – such as pictures of babies' vaginas pierced with needles, and more horrifying images.

After seeing these images, I thought I had heard and seen it all until Sharon Girling, a member of Scotland Yard's National Crime Squad, and one of the world's leading experts on internet child pornography, told me that her office had confiscated an image of a sexually abused newborn infant still attached to an umbilical cord.

I had no desire to see that image and never did.

Then through a hunch and a guess, and what some of my colleagues at the time thought initially was a "whacked theory," we discovered that some of the children pictured on the CD-ROMS were in fact, among the 1,263 then still unidentified victims in the 1998 Operation Cathedral/Wonderland international internet child-pornography investigation that Girling oversaw at Scotland Yard.

At the time, Operation Cathedral/Wonderland was the largest and most successful international law enforcement crackdown of any internet pedophile ring. Over thirty international law enforcement agencies joined forces to bust this ring. Despite its success, however, the sad fact remained that even up to 2001, 1,263 young victims whose images had been circulated around the internet had still been unidentified.

I am sure the haunted images of the sexually abused children across Europe, as in the other areas of the world where her research has taken her, will be forever seared in her mind and her conscience. Pressure must be brought on governments to cooperate and bring this issue higher up their radar screens. There is no short cut to the painstaking work of the kind that Christine Dolan brings to this issue. I urge you to support her in this most noble cause because she is talking about our future and the quality of the lives of our children who should be able to enjoy today and tomorrow. Thank you, Christine, for being a voice for the voiceless. You deserve all our commitment and support.," said Ambassador Richard Sezibera, Rwandan Ambassador to the United States in 2002.

Several victims we were able to cross-reference and find successfully turned out to be children of European women Homayra and I had interviewed.

These were women who had been engaged in vicious custody battles in French courts. They had found themselves hamstrung in their efforts to legally protect their children from further abuse at the hands of their children's fathers and the fathers' friends (men and women, who were pedophiles) by an anachronism of Napoleonic laws. Minors were not allowed to testify in court. These were incredibly young children under the age of 10 years of age.

Because these children were automatically considered incompetent to speak on their own behalf in the French courts, their horror stories had to be told by the doctors who treated them once they were free of their abusers.

In turn, those doctors and psychologists were attacked legally by the accused predators as a group – something akin to the North American Man Boy Love Association (NAMBLA) in the United States. [2]

The French doctors and psychiatrists were at risk of losing their medical licenses if they testified. It was a vicious circle.

Even more astonishing, the presiding French judges, for reasons that remain inexplicable even today, had ruled as if they believed that the mothers' testimonies were false, baseless, unsubstantiated, and no more than ruses concocted to retain custody of their children.

As a result, these mothers, who were trying to shield their children from further sexual abuse, sexual torture, and pedo-criminality, found themselves being abused legally, financially, psychologically, and emotionally.

Yes, this was very dark, but my instincts told me that there was something else at play here.

The legal system was a blockade from the truth.

Overtime, I also came to acknowledge a myth that I had been holding – women would naturally protect children. I had believed that there were few female child sexual predators.

---

[2] The best book on NAMBLA was authored by my friend, Bob Hamer, who is a retired undercover FBI agent. *The Last Undercover: The True Story of an FBI Agent's Dangerous Dance with Evil* was published in 2008. It covers his infiltration of NAMBLA circa 2003.

I was not only wrong but, I was dead wrong.

One-third of the predators in the images in the Operation Cathedral/Wonderland case were female sexual predators.

Sharon Girling of Scotland Yard allowed me to view these women's images to assess whether they looked like models or those who crawled out of gutters. The ages, looks, and ethnicities spanned the spectrum.

We also came across considerable evidence of sex rings, pedophile rings, and ritual abuse torture of children by adults in groups, who inflicted pain for their own pleasure.

In pursing this part of the investigation 25 years ago, I discovered that nowhere in the world then was a single one-stop depository of confiscated internet child pornography images for law enforcement officials to examine if a child's image had been circulated over the internet.

When I asked why a one-stop depository and image-bank did not already exist, I was told that, even though it was commonly agreed that a single, centralized storehouse of images collected worldwide would be of great and significant value, it was infeasible legally because it would require the participation of multiple nations and there were too many legal hurdles to overcome.

This would create, the experts said, a major problem of conflicting laws from the cooperating nations, with none entitled to more deference than another.

Remember – this was 2000 – 2001 – at the beginning of when the internet was being introduced to mainstream society. This is well before where the internet has evolved today.

Each nation, for example, had different standards for protecting personal privacy and other civil liberties, different rules governing evidence and prosecutorial actions, different financial and political restrictions, and so forth.

Given the overwhelming need for a one-stop depository, I did not believe that such legal technicalities should prevent its creation, so I asked how much money it would take to set up an image bank and equip it with the software tools needed to make it functional if none of the legal impediments were an issue. The answer was $5 million.

That was a drop in the bucket to protect children from pedo-criminality over the internet and to create tools for law enforcement to save children and hold the bad actors accountable.

In addition to image storage, financing was needed to finish the ongoing work on a new computer program that not only could "age" a victim's face, but which could also remove the victim's image from a picture to compare the details in the background of one picture with another to advance investigations. Cross-referencing image details is a heightened skill for computer programs that enhance those comparisons.

Partly, or, because I was raised in the Roman Catholic Church faith and educated by the Madams of the Sacred Heart and Jesuits, and because my first trafficking investigation took place in Europe in 2000, where the Church [3] played a major role, I took a particular interest then of the Church's position on the issue of trafficking. I continually monitored the Church's activity in response to its own sex scandals.

I knew nothing of the Catholic Church's sex scandals in 2000, but I heard a lot of whispers in Europe in 2000, and I was intrigued from an institutional perspective.

How can someone who claims to believe in God create a fertile ground for child rape and how can the Church coverup for any of these insidious crimes?

But admittedly, in 2000, I was not equipped to digest the information before me. It seemed too incongruent to the Teachings of Jesus of my heritage.

As my trafficking research expanded, I became increasingly puzzled by the Church's clear lack of moral leadership in responding to their own simmering crisis.

So, by October 2001, I decided to take on the Roman Catholic Church – my heritage even thought I had never been raped, abused and neither had my siblings.

In November 2001, I officially launched an investigation into the Roman Catholic Church sex scandals globally.

---

[3] Note that throughout this book I will use the terms "Roman Catholic Church" and "Church" interchangeably.

We never imagined how timely this work would prove to be considering the avalanche of revelations about the sexual torture by members of the Roman Catholic clergy that imploded by early 2002 in Boston.

That was my place of birth and where my Catholic family on both sides was entrenched in our faith. Those connections within our family were not limited to Boston. They expanded not only across the U.S. but, across the globe.

The subject matter of this book is the sexual exploitation of children within the Roman Catholic Church, although it is not the only religious institution whose clergymen and nuns, in this case, have betrayed the special trust placed in them.

Enormous amounts of information concerning abuses by spiritual leaders within every other faith are available for anyone.

I chose to focus on my heritage – the Roman Catholic Church.

This investigation is not intended to denigrate the fundamental institution that the Church stands for, or to deny the good it has accomplished throughout its 2000-year history, or to move anyone to call his or her faith into question, or to doubt that incalculable benefit of faith to billions who believe in the *Teachings of Jesus*.

The reader must, however, distinguish between the divine teaching that is the foundation of the Church and the fact that as an institution, it is a creature of this world – one that is run by people, who, no matter what their stature and strengths remain subject to the same frailties and weaknesses as every other human being, and sometimes they embrace the devil. Brokenness is a fact of life. We see it alive and well in the 21st century.

Accordingly, I am specifically focusing on the intentional crimes, errors, and failings of those charged with the protection of children and the preservation of the Church as an institution. That does not call into question the value or validity of the institution itself, or the *Teachings of Jesus*.

We should challenge our political leaders without ever questioning the value of governments, and we should challenge leadership in our places of worship and not be fearful of wrath and blowback when it comes to the protection of children.

In my profession, investigating corruption is what investigative journalists do, and sometimes it hits home as this investigation has done.

By virtue of its age, organizational structure, and global reach, the Catholic Church is a particularly apt illustration of the most important point of this book – **the need for a profound paradigm shifts in the manner with which it defines and responds to child sexual abuse, slavery, and human trafficking institutionally**.

We must understand that children are trafficked for sexual torture not only by international mobs, perverts, maggots, terrorist organizations, and safe clubs like the Boys Club, but by Catholic priests, nuns, members of Catholic orders, and sometimes their criminal acts are covered up by the Church's hierarchy – all the way up the ladder to the popes.

The crime of trafficking and child sexual abuse occurs in our religious institutions that lie at the core of society – even at the level of the church and the family.

As a result, I urge the readers of this book to think **'OUTSIDE THE BOX'** when examining the evidence of the Roman Catholic Church's involvement in the trafficking of human beings, their predators and their institutionalization of child abuse and protracted denials and coverups not just in the recent decades, but over centuries.

Over time, we have allowed the clergy and the hierarchy of the Catholic Church to believe their roles place them closer to God and as such, they are entitled to special deference or preferential treatment, or that somehow the laws that govern the rest of us do not apply to them. We have been encouraged to believe this.

Let me be truly clear –

A priest or nun who rapes a child should be no more immune from the law of the State than anyone else. A bishop who has shuffled a rapist priest from parish to parish to prevent his discovery of rape merits no different treatment than any other individual who participates in the concealment of a crime.

It is extremely hard to say that one type of child sexual predator is worse than another because they are all bad actors.

But there seems to be a special type of evil at work here when the trust of innocence is betrayed by one whom we are taught to put our trust in because of his or her special role as an intermediary with the divine.

What the predator/cover-up priests and hierarchy do and what their superiors have allowed to be done to children in the Name of God is obscene and it is criminal; what has taken place within the Catholic Church meets the definition of human trafficking institutionally.

I hope that ***In the Name of God…Who Knew What, When?*** will offer some insight into the notion of human trafficking and slavery in the 21st Century institutionally within the Roman Catholic Church.

We need to examine how sadistic predators operate, how the Catholic Church has been a participant by its own institutional rules of canon law, and how the hierarchy's deliberate and conscious choices have defined the difference between how the Church has traditionally viewed its actions and how society at large must see the institution now. The Vatican still has not fully addressed and dealt with this scandal over 20 years since I first began this investigation and that is an understatement because I have gone back to the beginning of my investigation and re-investigated some of the same cases and what has surfaced is more complicity in institutional crimes.

Who Knew What, When? is of utmost importance when analyzing what has happened since the Boston diocese imploded in January 2002.

The Church's first reaction then was one of denial and deflection. The Church hierarchy claimed that they did not understand and had no grip on the extent of their sex scandals. That was a fallacy then as it is a fallacy today.

They all knew from the top down in a diocese and from the top down in a religious order and all the way from the top down in the Vatican hierarchy, including the popes. The Catholic Church's internal documents prove it.

In early January 2002, my late Father asked me to meet with some prosecutors in Boston.

"They are negotiating with Cardinal Law's lawyers for documents. You know more than some of these prosecutors. Tell them about the "historical secret archives."

I met with three prosecutors. They claimed they did not know of the "historical secret archives."

I told them to stop negotiating with Cardinal Law's lawyers.

They had a way forward to break their investigation wide open.

I explained to them that all they had to do was use a search warrant and ignore canon law arguments because canon law does not supersede common law. That was the argument the diocesan lawyers used as an excuse not to turn over the Church documents to the prosecutors.

The Church lawyers were arguing that the documents that the prosecutors wanted could not be turned over because those documents were protected under 'confidentiality' under canon law.

I forewarned them that the diocesan lawyers would use that argument as long as they could. These lawyers held conferences on how to protect those documents from secular society. And, despite the prohibition of the Statute of Limitations with some of these documents, the seized "historical archives" documents would give the prosecutors the roadmap to understand *who knew what when* and establish the evidential trail of deception and fraud.

The truth is they all knew.

I predicted that the next legal hurdle would be the Church would want to keep those documents under seal. I felt strongly knowing what I knew at that point in time in January 2002 from sealed documents given to me. The strength of the argument to unseal these documents would rest upon the public's interest.

This was a coverup the magnitude of which would expose the evil mired in the Roman Catholic Church.

The next hurdle would be who was the presiding judge who would make the decision to unseal them.

Judge Constance Sweeney in Boston proved that justice would prevail. She unsealed the documents.

This is the story of the coverup, and who knew what when and how insidious the coverup has been for centuries by one of the oldest religious institutions on the planet.

For anyone to conclude that the Roman Catholic Church has done its best to clean up their crimes is not dealing with reality.

We know so much more today than we did over 20 years ago. These sexual attacks on children were not lapses in judgment. These rapists consciously and without a conscience targeted children and their families.

As an institution, theses coverups were consciously, deliberately, and elaborately orchestrated. It engulfed not just the rapists and the leaders of the institution to protect the church's image, but also their enablers and the lawyers, without whom these coverups would not have been so successful for so long, especially leading into the 21st century.

The enablers excused their coverup actions. They justified to themselves they were taking such steps to preserve an institution they believed in - *In The Name of God.*

I profusely and profoundly disagreed with their overblown justifications when I first embarked upon this investigation, and still do today.

One Catholic Church priest, who is an exorcist, contacted me in 2002 when he learned I was investigating the Church. I met him in the 1980s when I was CNN's Political Director. The late Cardinal John O'Connor of New York and I were friends. He introduced us. He prayed for me every day and called me several times a week until he died.

"God will protect you. I am praying for you, and know you will be tested," he repeatedly told me.

I was.

"You need to read **Ephesians 6** every day," the priest told me.

I still do because I have no doubt that those who harm children and cover up this evil are cowards.

What I have learned is truth cancels cowardice and evil.

EVIL **spelled backwards is** *LIVE.*

We must never forget that.

We must push forward to LIVE.

That is how we move the dime on humanity.

Commodifying any human being by way of lies, coercions, fraud, force, or mandated policies that inflict harm upon children is the antithesis to living freely.

Those who want to distort reality and lie should be fully exposed.

I want to give credit to Bishop Accountability. It serves as a great resource of naming and shaming not just the perverts but those in the church hierarchy who have covered up these crimes. This organization has been relentless since 2003.

There are many faces of human trafficking and slavery in the 21st Century, even on the institutional level. Nearly 25 years ago, I created the first FACES of HUMAN TRAFFICKING model to simplify and educate audiences to the notion that globalization, the Fall of Communism and the internet had contributed to the fact that slavery never died but morphed into a new phase on the cusp of the 21st Century. I did not have to argue whether slavery was moral or immoral. We all knew it was immoral. What I had to do was prove it was alive and well.

Here is my basic model of the different faces of Human Trafficking to date:

1. Sex Trafficking (brothels, pedophile rings, families, cults, gangs, migrations).

2. Labor Trafficking (domestic slaves, camel jockeys, street beggars, even government contractors in Third World countries).

3. Internet Trafficking (using ads online, tourism offers, exchange of pictures via dark web, LIVE streams, etc.).

4. Sex Tourism (when a pervert travels overseas with the intention of buying a minor child).

5. Child Soldiers (i.e., Kony, head of LRA in Africa, terrorists).

6. Organ Trafficking (your kidney or eyes have a higher price depending upon the market).

7. Skin Trafficking (body parts are used in voodoo to solidify a contract).

8. Medical Trafficking (fraudulent science and medical experiments – no informed consent).

9. Ritual Abuse Torture (think cults and intergenerational abuse).

10. Institutional Trafficking (churches, organizations, cults).

    If one lies, coerces, defrauds, deceives, or forces a human being for any one of these faces of human trafficking and all their subset categories for money, that is legally the short version of what criminally defines human trafficking.

Roman Catholic Church Historical Archives

"But if anyone causes one of these little ones who believe in me to sin, it would be better for him to have a large millstone hung around his neck and to be drowned in the depths of the sea."

— Matthew 18:16

Repeatedly, the Roman Catholic hierarchy had claimed that they were not "experienced" or "did not know how to address" or "deal with" or "comprehend" the severity of sodomizing, torturing, and raping children as the sexual abuse scandals were rocking the Church in early 2002 as the Boston diocese was imploding with the revelations of child sex abuse cases.

The church's talking points to the public and media were intellectually dishonest and not only false statements, but they were intentional lies and attempts to further cover up the breadth and depth of their crimes.

For centuries, the Church has known about sexual crimes against children among its clerics.

The Vatican and the Catholic Church diocesan hierarchy minimized child sexual torture by claiming that these "crimes" were "pastoral problems," and protected under the tutelage of "canon law." Those arguments are fallacies both in fact and history.

Canon law is not law in any legal sense of the word. Canons have to do with church structure and internal discipline. It has no authority within the secular world. It has no influence within civil and criminal law anywhere in the world other than Vatican City, which is an independent city-state within Rome. Canon law's only importance has to do with the fact that church leaders have invoked it to serve their means to their ends much like a monarchy for a Royal Priesthood.

Canon law has had absolutely nothing to do with the sexual torture of minors in criminal and civil cases in the secular world. The Vatican Curia and Catholic Church hierarchy have repeatedly invoked canon law for confidentiality use to withhold documents to coverup their institutional complicity in their institutional crimes. Hence, it is imperative for the public to understand how the Church has misused it intentionally for a very long time.

Civil law and criminal law supersede canon law in the secular world. The Vatican has used canon law as a ruse in court proceedings and public relation campaigns. It has been used as a tool by bishops, the Vatican Curia, and their representatives and attorneys for courtroom obfuscation and as a mechanism for stalling, deflecting, and thwarting discovery in civil and criminal investigations and as a basis for demanding the voluminous non-disclosure agreements for settlements for decades.

The Church's lawyers used the confidentiality of canon law documents as an excuse to hold onto the internal Church documents about perverts throughout their institution globally.

The coverup goes up the ladder all the way up to the Dicastery for the Doctrine of the Faith, which used to be called Congregation for the Doctrine of the Faith (CDF), underneath the power of the pope. This office is the Vatican office whose duty is to promote and safeguard the doctrine of the faith and morals within the Catholic Church globally.

Too often, canon law was used as a tool for hiding, denying, and delaying, and supporting the Church hierarchy's monarchical structure of power with top-down control enabling the Church leaders to cover up crimes against children worldwide. And to make matters worse, it was used inconsistently by church leaders from one country to the next, and it was used as a diversionary tactic in church scandals.

"The [Canon] Code ascribes to the papal office the authority of a virtually absolute Monarch while affording minimal expression to Episcopal collegiality," wrote author and canon law professor, James A. Coriden.[4]

The Roman Catholic Church historical records have been steeped in references to sexual abuse among the clergy and laity. Church documents go back centuries. Sexual abuse has been stipulated in the actual church canons.

"The church's leadership has recognized from the earliest centuries that sexual abuse of minors is a heinous crime, so much so that guilty clerics have been, at various times, excommunicated, removed from the clerical state, and/or cut off from all financial assistance. In short, the destructive nature of child sexual abuse is clearly not a new issue for the church. The only "official" sources which are derived from church authority, are the legal/canonical texts," writes Father Tom Doyle. [5]

"Both versions of the Code of Canon Law (1917 and 1983) contain canons that criminalize several examples of illicit or immoral clergy behavior. These include punishing illegal disposal of church property (canon 1377); profiting from offerings for Masses (canon 1385); solicitation for sexual favors by priests hearing confession (canon 1387); violation of the seal of confession (canon 1388); abuse of authority by clerics (canon 1389); and sexual exploitation of minors (canon 1395). All these canons are grounded in ecclesiastical legal or disciplinary documents that reach back to the Middle Ages," Doyle further notes.

"The present Code of Canon Law contains a canon (c.1395) that specifically names sexual contact with a minor by a cleric as an ecclesiastical crime. This canon repeated a similar law in the 1917 Code. The prior Code included sexual abuse of minors as a specific canon or law because the problem existed at the time the Code

---

[4] Coriden, James A., *Canon Law as Ministry – Freedom and Good Order for the Church*, Paulist Press, New York/Mahwah, N.J., 2000.

[5] Thomas P. Doyle, O.P., J.C.D., *Roman Catholic Clericalism, Religious Duress, and Clerical Sexual Abuse*, September 2002, p. 4.

was being compiled (1903-1917). Not only was it a problem at that time, witnessed by the simple fact that it was included as a specific crime in the Code, but it had been officially acknowledged as a problem for centuries," adds Doyle. [6]

The early and medieval church was concerned with homosexual acts regardless of age. The term used historically was "sodomy." At that time, there was little distinction in the church between pedophilia, ephebophilia, or adult homosexual acts. Same gender sex was considered sodomy.

"This is because the same-sex interplay in the ancient world was 90% adult-adolescent or pederastic as opposed to adult-infant, or pedophilic. This trend probably continued into the late middle ages or even beyond. Consequently, when medieval ecclesiastical literature refers to clerics committing sodomia it is most probable that the reference is to sexual relations with young adolescent boys. There is no reference in the literature reviewed to sex with infants or "pedophilia" as we call it today," writes Doyle. [7]

Because Christianity is primarily Judaic in origin – meaning early Christians consisted of those from the Jewish religious culture - and the Judaic tradition equated sodomy with murder, early Christians adopted a view of what we would today call homophobia.

As early as 177 (Bishop) Athenagoras characterized adulterers and pederasts as foes of Christianity, subjected them to excommunication, then the harshest penalty the church could inflict. The Council of Elvira (309 CE) severely condemned pederasts. Canons 16 and 17 of the Council of Ancyra (314) inflicted lengthy penances and excommunication for male homosexuality. [8]

During the Council of Elvira, canons specifically confronting clerical behavior included:

---

[6] Ibid, p. 5.

[7] Ibid, p. 6.

[8] Ibid, p. 6; Warren Johansson and William Percy, "Homosexuality" in <u>Handbook of Medieval Sexuality</u> (New York, garland Publishing Company, 1996), PP. 158-159.

1. Canon 18 punished any bishop, priest, or deacon discovered to be a sexual offender and deprived him of Holy Communion at the time of death.

2. Canon 71 condemned sex between adult men and young boys: "Men who sexually abuse boys shall not be given communion even at the end."

Dating from the 7th century and continuing into the late medieval time (13th century), and even further evidenced until the 16th century, was penitential literature. The clerics used the handbooks while hearing confessions. Initially confessions consisted of group confessions. Later, the practice of confession was changed to individual confessions. These confessional books listed sins and the accorded penances, including those bestowed upon the hierarchy – the bishops and cardinals.

Several of the more prominent Penitential books refer to sexual crimes committed by clerics against *young boys and girls*. The Penitential of Bede, dating from England in the 8th century, advises that clerics who commit sodomy with children be given increasingly severe penances commensurate with their rank. Laymen who committed such crimes were excommunicated and ordered to fast for three years; clerics not in holy orders, five years; deacons and priests seven and ten years respectively; and bishops who sexually abused children were given 12 years of penance.[9]

Historical legal texts referenced sodomy among the clergy as well.

The earliest records were the Visigothic laws of Spain (7th and 8th centuries), which contained legislation against homosexuality with a specific canon providing for the degradation of clergy guilty of sodomy.[10]

Because a cleric's body was specially consecrated to God, an offense of sacrilege was added to the severity of sodomy. As the centuries evolved, more stringent measures were taken by the Church.

---

[9] Ibid, p. 7, "There are examples of such crimes in the *Penitential of Columban* (c.600AD), the *Penitential of Theodore* (c. 668-690) and the *Penitential of Cummean* (c. 650)."

[10] Ibid, p. 7.

The Third Lateran Council (1179), a medieval equivalent to the Vatican Council II, decreed that clerics who commit sins against nature be confined to a monastery for life or leave the church. After 1250, the penalties became much harsher with sodomy often linked to heresy. There is even some indication that sodomy was commonly identified with clerics in the popular mind. The sacral offense entered secular law, and offenders were subjected to severe punishments including fines, castration, exile, and death. The church added an additional penalty, "infamy of fact."

"This amounted to a perpetual exclusion of the offender and even his family from the Christian community. In effect this amounted to a civil death with complete ostracization and economic boycott. This penalty was imposed on clerics as well as on lay men. "[11]

A canon from the *Rule for the Monastery of Compludo* (11th century) states, "A cleric or monk who seduces youths or young boys or is found kissing or in any other impure situations is to be publicly flogged and lose his tonsure. When his hair has been shorn, his face is to be foully besmeared with spit, and he is to be bound in iron chains. For six months, he will languish in prison-like confinement and on three days of each week shall fast on barley bread in the evening."

"After this, he will spend another six months under the custodial care of a spiritual elder, remaining in a segregated cell, giving himself to manual work and prayer, subject to vigils and prayers. He may go for walks but always under the custodial care of two spiritual brethren, and he shall never again associate with youths neither in private conversation nor in counseling them."[12]

By the Fourth Lateran Council in 1215 every Catholic was mandated to confess their sins to a priest at least once a year. Only bishops and priests could administer this sacrament. By the Council of Trent (1545-63), the confessional was made part of the ritual creating a barrier between the confessor and the religious.

---

[11] Ibid, p. 7.

[12] Barlow, C.W., *Rule for the Monastery of Compludo* in *Fathers of the Church*, Volume 63 (Washington, DC).

Unfortunately, the privacy led to documentation of clerics taking advantage of those who repented, and records included intercourse, oral and manual sex, solicitation of sex without the act, and sadomasochistic sex.

The first recording of solicitation of sex was first recorded by Peter Damian in his *Book of Gomorrah* during the Gregorian era.

The earliest diocesan legislation referencing solicitation of sex in confession occurred in Spain in the sixteenth century, but four centuries before during the Council of Treves in 1227, the priests or bishops violating confessional sex could lose their office and be excommunicated. It mattered not whether the confessor was an adult or a child. Overall, the act was considered a spiritual breach as serious as spiritual incest because of the balance of power. It did not matter over time when the act occurred as the Church did not enforce the statute of limitations to enforce its punishments.

Depending upon the century and the state of the Church's scandals and impact upon the church, different proclamations and rules were advanced.

"In 1568, Pope Pius V issued a public decree called "Horrendum illud scelus," which literally means "This horrendous crime" which required that clergy abusers of boys be degraded, stripped of their source of income, and then turned over to the secular arm for punishment and this punishment could include decapitation."[13]

Roman Catholic Historical Dateline:

I.   1st-6th Centuries:

60   Didache – early Christian moral manual for churches

309   Council of Elvira

439   Theodosian Code (church constitutions)

530   Digest of Justinian

533   Institutes of Justinian

---

[13] Doyle Email to Author, October 21, 2002.

II.   7th-11th Centuries:

600   Penitential of St. Columban

650   Penitential of Cummean

690   Penitential of Archbishop of Canterbury St. Theodore

700   Penitential of St. Bede

1012 Decretum of Bishop Burchard of Worms

1051 St. Peter Damian's *Book of Gomorrah*

III.   12-15th Centuries:

1139 Lateran Council II

1140 *Decretum Gratiani* of Gratian

1179 Lateran Council III

1215 Lateran Council IV

1234 *Decretals of Gregory IX*

1449 Council of Basle (1431-1449) – Church canons until 1917

IV.   16-19th Centuries:

1514 Papal Constitution, Leo X (May 5, 1514)

1563 Council of Trent (1545-1563)

1561 Cum sicut nuper of Pope Pius IV (April 16, 1561)

1566 Cum primum of Pope Pius V (April 1, 1566)

1568 Horrendum of Pope Pius v (August 30, 1568)

1622 Universi dominici gregis, Pope Gregory XV

1726 Lavellana, Sacred Congregation (July 6, 1726)

1741 Sacramentum poenitentia, Pope Benedict XIV

1742 Etsi pastorales, Pope Benedict XIV

1745 Apostolicae muneris, Pope Benedict XIV

1775 Ad Cochinchia

1866 Instruction by Holy Office (February 22, 1866)

1869 Apostolicae Sedis, Pope Pius IX

1890   Instruction by Holy Office (July 20, 1890)

V.   20ᵗʰ-21ˢᵗ Centuries:

1917   Code of Canon Law

1922   De Modo Procedendi in Causis Sollicitationis - (confessions)

1962   De Modo Procedendi in Causis Sollicitationis – (confessions)[14]

1965   Vatican Council II (1962-1965)

1975   Human Persona, Declaration on Sexual Ethics

1983   Code of Canon Law revised

1985   Sexual Molestation Manual by Doyle, Mouton, and Peterson

1990   Canada's Archdiocesan Commission Into Clergy Sex Abuse

1993   Pope John Paul II's Letter to U.S. Bishops

1994   U.S. Catholic Bishop Conference – Restoring Trust, Vol. I

1995   U.S. Catholic Bishop Conference - Restoring Trust, Vol. II

1996   U.S. Catholic Bishop Conference – Restoring Trust Vol. III

---

[14] Although this document was never publicized in the official Vatican legal bulletin, the Acta Apostolicae Sedis was distributed to every bishop and major religious order globally. The document was ordered to be kept in the diocesan and order secret archives, not published or commented by anyone. The 1922 and 1962 documents bear the same titles. The document refers to any report of sexual abuse of a minor by any cleric is to be referred to the Congregation for the Doctrine of the Faithful (CDF) and that any disposition of cases even for past incidents can only be resolved by the CDF. The specifics of the document lays out the procedural secretive process to maintain confidentiality of all parties involved. Cardinal Joseph Ratzinger, later Pope Benedict XVI, ran CDF from 1981 – 2005 under Pope John Paul II, followed by U.S. Cardinal William Joseph Levada, 2005 -2012 under former Cardinal Ratzinger then Pope Benedict XVI. The CDF position was then filled by German Cardinal Gerhard Ludwig Muller, 2012-2017 under Pope Francis, followed by Spanish Jesuit Luis Francisco Ladaria Ferrer, 2017-2023 under Pope Francis. Now, the CDF head position is held by Argentine Prelate Victor Manuel Fernandez beginning in 2023 and still under Pope Francis. These are the men, who have overseen the sex abuse scandals depositories globally for the Vatican in recent times.

2001   Sacramentorum Sanctitatis Tutela, Pope John Paul II [15]

2001   De Delictis Garavioribus (May 18, 2001)

2002   U.S. Cardinals at the Vatican (April 2002)

2002   Charter for the Protection of Children, USCCB (June 2002)[16]

There were some major multi-million-dollar settlements in 1990s in the U.S. At the beginning of 2002, when the Boston sex scandals were imploding, reported in the media, and investigated by prosecutors not only in Boston, but, in New Hampshire, New York, and beyond, the Catholic hierarchy and the Vatican's public statements were one of bewilderment and ignorance about child sex abuse among the Church's religious rank and file.

The Church was losing credibility daily because many of the Auxiliary Bishops in Boston had been reposted to New Hampshire, New York, Connecticut, and other dioceses, where coverup tactics were further duplicated and implemented as business as usual.

The Church hierarchy knew about their institutional abuse of children for centuries.

They also knew from their own evidence within their own *historical secret archives, which were sent to the Vatican and retained in the diocesan and religious orders' vaults.*

The diocese hierarchy knew about the scandals from the evidence contained in their own paperwork when the decisions were made to move priests from parish to parish and across national borders to avoid scandals.

---

[15] This document includes much of the procedures outlined in the 1962 document, but there were significant developments: Bishops and superiors were to send complaints to the Vatican; canonical age of a minor was raised from 16 to 18; Statute of Limitations was extended to 10 years. If a minor, the Statute of Limitation began when the minor was 18 years of age; only priests could be involved in processing cases; completed files at local level were to be sent to the Vatican for retention; Pontifical Secret was imposed on all officials involved. There was no recommendation in this document or any other from the 18th century up to this document requiring the report of child sex scandals to civil authorities. The intent of the process by the Church was intentional institutional secrecy.

[16] Partial list from Sex, Priests, and Secret Code, The Catholic Church's 2,000-Year Paper Trail of Sexual Abuse, Thomas P. Doyle, A.W.R. Sipe, Patrick Wall, 2006.

They knew from their own documentation and correspondence exchange with the medical professional when psychiatrists entered the picture in the 20th century and sexual clinics were created. Not only were American priests sent to those clinics in the U.S. as early as late 1950s, but priests from other countries were sent to these American psycho-sexual retreat centers. The paperwork on those transfers alone is voluminous within the *historical secret archives* that the Church wanted to keep confidential under the auspices of canon law. Protecting the "reputation" of the clergy superseded the protection of the children.

Decisions were based upon the justification that the hierarchy wanted to preserve the image of the priesthood and hence, the Church as an institution.

What the Church accomplished was hiding its evil in a cloak of secrecy, sacrificing children and families for its own self-serving gains, and creating an institutional model for the exploitation of sexually abusing children. The outcomes of these intentional actions inflicted pain upon victims and their families. Church officials misled law enforcement and covered up these crimes while minimizing them to the public. Some believe the hierarchy only wanted to protect the royalty of the priesthood alone. Their objectives were far more insidious. They wanted to hide their institutional crimes so that their pews would not be empty, and their financial coffers would not dry up.

And, in the end, the church operated like a mafia cult.

The Roadmap in Plain Sight

Pope John Paul II died in April 2005. The Dean of the College of Cardinals, Cardinal Joseph Ratzinger, succeeded him as Pope Benedict XVI.

Cardinal Ratzinger was previously appointed by Pope John Paul II in late 1981 as head of the Congregation for the Doctrine of the Faith (CDF), the very office which received the complaints on perverted catholic clergy.

This office was originally established in 1542 by Pope Paul III. It is the oldest department in the Roman Curia. It was then called the Supreme Sacred Congregation of the Roman and Universal Inquisition. The department's mission followed in the footsteps of the Medieval Inquisition in 1184, the Spanish Inquisition in 1478, and the Portuguese Inquisition in 1536.

The purpose of these Catholic Inquisitions was to prosecute those these tribunals deemed guilty of various criminal acts against Catholic law and doctrine. They prescribed penalties for those they adjudged to be heretics of both clergy and laity.

In 1908, the Supreme Sacred Congregation of the Roman and Universal Inquisition was renamed the Supreme Sacred Congregation of the Holy Office. By 1965, the department was named the Congregation for the Doctrine of Faith (CDF). Since 2022, it is named Dicastery for the Doctrine of the Faith. It is often referred to as the Holy Office.

Buried within this church office were documents under canon law that allowed these sexual acts to remain secret and hidden from the laity and law enforcement.

The historical evolution of documents within this department is important for the public to understand how this scandal happened in plain sight. The legal loopholes in canon law allowed the clerical perverts to roam free without consequences for a very long time even though the Catholic hierarchy was fully aware.

The 1917 Code of Canon law called for those clergy who engaged in the sexual abuse of minors, sodomy, incest, and other sexual deviant behavior to be "declared infamous."

C. 2359 § 2 of the 1917 Code of Canon Law states:

"If [clerics] engage in a delict against the sixth precept of the Decalogue with a minor below the age of sixteen, or engage in adultery, debauchery, bestiality, sodomy, pandering, [or] incest with blood-relatives or affines in the first degree, they are suspended, *declared infamous*, and are deprived of any office, benefice, dignity, responsibility, if they have such, whatsoever, and in more serious cases, they are to be deposed."

Five years later, that law was secretly changed to conceal these criminal offenses.

In 1922, a secret Vatican document titled *Crimen Sollicitationis* was published making it an excommunicable offense for any bishop to reveal the criminal offenses of pedophiles, homosexuals, and those who engage in bestiality. The document primarily deals with priests who solicit the penitent to engage in illicit or immoral acts, and in dealing with such cases, paragraph 11 of the document states:

11. Since, however, in dealing with these causes, more than usual care and concern must be shown that they be treated with the utmost confidentiality, and that, once decided and the decision executed, they are covered by permanent silence (Instruction of the Holy Office, 20 February 1867, No. 14), all those persons in any way associated with the tribunal, or knowledgeable of these matters by reason of their office, are bound to observe inviolably the strictest confidentiality, commonly known as the secret of the Holy Office, in all things and with all persons, under pain of incurring automatic excommunication, ipso facto and undeclared, reserved to the sole person of the Supreme Pontiff, excluding even the Sacred Penitentiary. Ordinaries are bound by this same law , that is, in virtue of their own office; other personnel are bound in virtue of the oath which they are always to swear before assuming their duties; and, finally, those delegated, questioned or informed [outside the tribunal], are bound in virtue of the precept to be imposed on them in the letters of delegation, inquiry or information, with express mention of the secret of the Holy Office and of the aforementioned censure.

Toward the end of *Crimen Sollicitationis*, the entire procedure in dealing with priests accused of solicitation is extended to clerics accused of homosexuality, pederasty, pedophilia, and bestiality.

71. The term crimen pessimum ["the foulest crime"] is here understood to mean any external obscene act, gravely sinful, perpetrated or attempted by a cleric in any way whatsoever with a person of his own sex.

72. Everything laid down up to this point concerning the crime of solicitation is also valid, with the change only of those things which the nature of the matter necessarily requires, for the crimen pessimum, should some cleric (God forbid) happen to be accused of it before the local Ordinary, except that the obligation of denunciation [imposed] by the positive law of the Church [does not apply] unless perhaps it was joined with the crime of solicitation in sacramental confession. In determining penalties against delinquents of this type, in addition to what has been stated above, Canon 2359, §2 is also to be taken into consideration.

73. Equated with the crimen pessimum, with regard to penal effects, is any external obscene act, gravely sinful, perpetrated or attempted by a cleric in any way with pre-adolescent children [impuberes] of either sex or with brute animals (bestialitas).

This document made it impossible for any bishop, priest or even victims to report such grave sexual abuses to civil authorities or even to warn others of the criminal behavior of these priests, even after the priest had been found guilty. And so, what was once a law to declare priests who committed these abysmal crimes "infamous," became an impenetrable secret just five years later. To make matters worse, this document was to be kept in the "secret archive" and never written about or spoken of publicly, including in canon law commentaries, thereby making the secret concealing of perverse crimes a secret in and of itself.

Over the course of the last sixty years, this secret change in the Code of Canon Law has slowly been made known, and while certain restrictions were lifted, the central problem persisted.

In 1962, Crimens Solicitationis was reissued and reintroduced under Secretaire Continaire in 1982. By 2001 Pope John Paul II lifted some restrictions allowing

U.S. and European bishops to report to law enforcement officials "if required by law."

In 2019, Pope Francis allowed bishops anywhere in the world to report "if required by law," but what is missing is the acknowledgement that these insidious acts are in fact, crimes and that the church must come clean not just on current crimes, but their own institutional complicity of covering up these crimes while simultaneously, claiming for years that the church was not aware.

The Few, the Brave, the Naive

In late 2001, I was ignorant of the extent of these historical secret historical archives and the church canon documents detailing cleric abuse and policies going back centuries, but I was able to examine and write about what was known to me at the time by early 2002 after I told the Boston prosecutors about the historical secret archives in January 2002.

By 2002, my focus was on the Paraclete Center in Jemez Springs, New Mexico. This is one treatment center where bishops sent priests with psychosexual and alcoholic issues. Much later, I discovered the depth and breadth of so many other treatment centers and *who knew what when* about them.

The following is an excerpt of an article I wrote for *The Washington Times' Insight Magazine* in spring 2002 while church officials publicly were denying how much they and the Vatican knew about the child sex abuse scandals.

…But the sad fact is that the American Catholic hierarchy, as well as the Vatican, have known for more than 40 years that pedophile priests are incurable and a threat to society.

According to a New Mexico attorney who has represented victims of clerical molestation, high officials in the church were aware of the predator-priest problem more than 50 years ago.

In 1947, the Rev. Gerald Fitzgerald of the Archdiocese of Boston received $25,000 from Cardinal Francis Spellman of New York to open a center in Jemez Springs, New Mexico, to treat priests with emotional problems, including alcoholism and pedophilia. It was first called Via Coeli; today it is called the Paraclete Center.

According to legal documents filed by Rhode Island attorney Tim Conlon in <u>Heroux v. Carpentier</u>, Fitzgerald wrote to Archbishop Ed Byrne of Santa Fe, N.M., warning him not to send any more pedophile priests to the center.

"Experience has shown us that it would be best not to offer hospitality to men who have seduced or attempted to seduce little boys or girls," Fitzgerald wrote. "These men are devils, your Excellency, and the wrath of God is upon them, and if I were a bishop, I would tremble when I failed to report them to Rome for involuntary laicization [removal from the priesthood]."

In 1960, Fitzgerald wrote a second letter urging the immediate removal of a pedophile priest from the facility and urged the Paraclete Superior to put that priest in "protective custody."

According to a New Mexico attorney, in the 1950s Fitzgerald purchased an island in the Caribbean as a permanent residence for pedophile priests whom he considered "incurable." The idea was to isolate the clerics, thus protecting children. In 1965, Fitzgerald was called to Rome and ordered to sell the island; in 1966, priests with sexual problems were reassigned to the Paraclete Center.

Later, "since the archdiocese in New Mexico was short on priests, some of these priests were assigned to parishes," where they raped children and had oral, anal, and vaginal sex with their victims in the seventies and eighties, says Dr. Michael Daughter, a New Mexico psychologist who has treated sex offenders at the Paraclete Center...[17]

Complainants continued to report, but they were dismissed and disbelieved. If the complainants posed a problem, only the hierarchy and their most trusted advisors handled the matter, and never were these child sexual abuse cases reported to law enforcement. If law enforcement was involved, the hierarchical powers of persuasion were called forth to deflect the crimes and silence the victims and their families.

I later discovered more letters that Father Gerald Fitzgerald wrote. On September 12, 1952, Fitzgerald wrote to Bishop Robert J. Dwyer of the Reno, Nevada diocese.

In reference to a priest named Edmund Boyle, who was a patient at Paraclete, Father Fitzgerald was quite blunt and advised Bishop Dwyer that it may be best for Dwyer to revert to "secular activity."

---

[17] Dolan, Christine, "Pontiff Should Demand Cardinal Law's Resignation," in *Insight Magazine*, Spring 2002.

"We find it quite common, almost universal with the handful of men we have seen in the last five years who have been under similar charges – we find it quite universal that they seem to be lacking in appreciation of the serious situation. As a class they expect to bound back like tennis balls on to the court of priestly activity. I myself would be inclined to favor laicization for any priest, upon objective evidence, for tampering with the virtue of the young…," wrote Fitzgerald. [18]

On May 7, 1963, Father Fitzgerald expressed his concern to Bishop Vincent J. Hines of the Norwich, Connecticut diocese regarding an unnamed priest.

"…I am very much of the opinion that when a padre has fallen into the classification of this young man, he needs a very solid jolt to attempt (if this be possible) to achieve the realization of the gravity of his offence. Personally, I would want to spend the rest of my life on my knees asking God's Mercy for I know of no more terrible threat than the words of Our Lord: those who tamper with the innocence of the innocents – "it was better that they had never been born…," wrote Fitzgerald. [19]

Seven months later in December 1963, Bishop Hines wrote to Father Fitzgerald about Father Bernard Bissonnette.

"Father Bissonnette's serious faults are common knowledge among all the clergy and well-known also to many of the laity of our diocese. Since our diocese is so compact it would be impossible for me to give him an assignment here where his past faults would be unknown…I have learned from the priests of the diocese who were with him in the Seminary that he had this moral fault even as a seminarian. Fellow seminarians reported it to the Superior, but evidently it was never reported to my predecessor. I am sure that if it had been he would never have been ordained…If Father Bissonnette can find a benevolent bishop, I would have no objection, but in conscience, I could not give him a recommendation. If he cannot

---

[18] September 12, 1952, Letter to Bishop Robert J. Dwyer of Reno, Nevada from Father Gerald Fitzgerald of Via Coeli: Monastery of the Servants of the Paraclete.

[19] May 7, 1963, Letter to Bishop Vincent J. Hines of Norwich, Connecticut to from Father Gerald Fitzgerald of Via Coeli: Monastery of the Servants of the Paraclete.

resume active work in a diocese, he would have only two alternatives; to stay indefinitely at Via Coeli, if you can keep him, or to request the Holy See to reduce him to the lay state..." wrote Bishop Hines. 20

Bernard Bissonnette was born in 1931 and ordained in 1958. He had been moved from parish to parish in the Norwich, Connecticut diocese in the 1960s as noted above because he had sexually abused multiple minors. He was then sent to Paraclete and to Minnesota parishes and onto New Mexico parishes where he sexual abused even more minor children. It took the church to finally laicize Bissonnette in 2005. He died in 2008.

In 2015, Bissonnette was accused of sexual abuse in lawsuits filed in New Mexico. By late 2015, he was included on the official list of the clergy credibly accused of child sexual abuse by the Diocese of Duluth, Minnesota. 21

What should have rolled into a public snowballing of revelations about child sexual abuse in the church had become little more than whispers in parishes through the years because of the Catholic hierarchy's denials and coverup. The church hierarchy successfully transferred predatory priests and nuns to new unsuspecting parishes, dioceses, states, and countries, resulting in thousands of new victims.

By 1984, the dam was about to break beyond how the church had been handling these secrets.

The Father Gilbert Gauthe sexual abuse case in Louisiana started to reveal the depravity of American Catholic Church's sexual abuse scandals.

Jason Berry, a fellow Georgetown University graduate, got wind of the Gauthe case. By 1992, Berry published his findings in his book, *Lead Us Not Into Temptation.*

While the full nature of the horror had never been fully exposed until Jason Berry wrote the book, Gauthe's Louisiana case led to a collaboration of three men: canon lawyer Father Tom Doyle, who is quoted in earlier chapters, attorney Ray Mouton, who was hired by the church to defend Gauthe, and Father Michael

---

[20] December 19, 1963, Letter to Father Gerald Fitzgerald of Via Coeli from Bishop Vincent J. Hines of Norwich, Connecticut.

[21] www.bishop-accountability.org

Peterson, who was a psychiatrist and the head of St. Luke's Institute, a sex abuse treatment center that was opened in Suitland, Maryland in 1981. [22]

These three men were determined to help the church by creating a manual for dioceses with specific guidelines to deal with the predators and help the victims. Their collaborative efforts in 1984-85 were enlightening. The American bishops had tried to turn deaf ears and blind eyes to bury their efforts. These three men stood their ground and then some to the dismay of the bishops.

Herein lies the story of their "manual" as told to me by Father Tom Doyle in 2002.

The "Manual" in its original form consisted of about 100 pages of text prepared by Mouton, Peterson, and me. This treated various aspects of medical, civil law, canon law, insurance, and pastoral aspects of the problem.

As part of the manual Fr. Peterson included copies of several clinical articles about the nature of pedophilia, its treatment, curability etc. The Manual was not commissioned by nor assigned by anyone in any position, official or otherwise. It was an entirely private venture, undertaken by Peterson, Mouton, and Doyle as a response to what they believed was quickly developing into a very serious problem for the Catholic Church.

The case of Fr. Gilbert Gauthe of Lafayette LA had become a public issue by the late fall of 1984. Fr. Gauthe was facing serious criminal charges, and the diocese hired Mr. Mouton to act as his defense. A civil suit had already been initiated by one of the families (Glen and Faye Gastal) whose son had been abused by Gauthe. The idea for some sort of instrument about how to deal with cases of priest pedophilia first came into being in Jan. 1985 at a meeting between myself, F. Ray Mouton, and Fr. Mike Peterson. Mouton was in Washington to meet with Fr. Peterson about the possibility of sending Fr. Gilbert Gauthe to St. Luke Institute (located in Suitland, Maryland) for evaluation and possible treatment.

Peterson was founder and director of St. Luke Institute, a health care facility for priests and religious. I had put Peterson and Mouton in touch with each other. I had never met Mouton, but Peterson was a friend and collaborator.

---

[22] Friends in the Knights of Malta in the Washington, D.C. area told me in 2002 that they had raised money for St. Luke's Institute for years, but they were told it was an alcoholic treatment center for priests. They were never told this was a center for clergy child sex abuse rapists.

I was, at the time, canonist at the Vatican embassy and charged with monitoring the correspondence on the Gauthe case. Shortly after the New Year (1985) Fr. Peterson informed me that Mr. Mouton planned a visit to Washington to discuss the situation of Fr. Gauthe. The day after Mouton arrived, Fr. Peterson called and stated that it was urgent that Mouton meet and speak with me.

We decided to have the meeting at the Dominican House of Studies rather than at the Nunciature (Vatican Embassy in Washington DC). Mouton indicated that there were several other priests in Lafayette who had been involved in sexual abuse of children and that the Diocese was covering them up and thus hurting his chances of a decent defense for Gauthe. He had hoped to reach a plea bargain for Gauthe which would enable him to be hospitalized or otherwise confined to a secure facility where he would receive treatment for his problem. This discovery of the other priests would make this plan risky if not unworkable in light of the fact that the District Attorney, Nathan Stansbury, would not be able to treat the case lightly.

During our conversation, Peterson indicated that he knew from confidential sources that there were many other priests around the country who had sexually abused children. I informed Archbishop Laghi of the gravity of the situation. Fr. Peterson spoke with Archbishop Laghi a few days later. The archbishop then called Archbishop Hannan of New Orleans and informed him that there would be a meeting in the Washington area at which Bishop Frey, Archbishop Hannan, their lawyers, Fr. Peterson and I would be present. The purpose of the meeting was to attempt to clarify the issues especially those of the other priests.

The meeting was held on Feb. 8 in a hotel in Arlington. Present were Hannan, Frey, Alex Larroque, Bob Wright and Thomas Reyer as well as Fr. Peterson and me. After the meeting, and after conversations with Mouton and Peterson, I suggested to Archbishop Laghi that a bishop be delegated to go to Lafayette to assist in managing the crisis. I selected Bishop A.J. Quinn, auxiliary of Cleveland because of his legal background. Archbishop Laghi agreed with my suggestion and the appropriate communications were had with the Holy See to secure the appointment.

The three of us believed now that the Gauthe case had become public and received so much publicity from coast to coast, the entire issue would no longer be able to be contained by Church leaders. I was also aware of other cases of sexual abuse that had quickly become public throughout the country. Also, for the first time, a family was starting a civil suit against a diocese (_Gastal v. Lafayette_) for failure to take proper precautions when warned about Gauthe.

When the civil suit was filed, the district attorney in the area also brought criminal charges. Fr. Gauthe had in fact been reported to the bishop several times since 1972 and before long, it was discovered that he had abused scores of young children. All were young boys with one exception. In the end, he pleaded guilty to 39 counts and was sentenced to twenty years in prison.

We decided on our own, to try and write something to give to the bishops to assist them in dealing with cases that we predicted would start to appear with increasing regularity. We discussed various approaches with different people including several bishops who were receptive to the idea. We had several conversations with Bishop Quinn. Bishop Quinn suggested that whatever was composed be done in such a format that it be based on a set of questions that would respond to as many different angles and aspects of the issue as could be conceived of.

Within a short time, we had decided to collect information and put together a manual or book that would be set up in a question-and-answer format. The full edition would also contain copies of several medical articles about pedophilia. Most of these were taken from medical journals and several were authored by Dr. Fred Berlin of the Johns Hopkins University Hospital Sexual Disorders Clinic. Along with the manual, we also proposed that the NCCB sponsor a committee (or project) that would supervise detailed research into the various areas of the problem: civil and criminal law, insurance, canon law, medical, pastoral. The research would be made available to the bishops to assist in making enlightened decisions about the problem.

The third part of the proposal involved a crisis intervention team which would consist of legal, medical, and canonical/pastoral resource persons who would be available to any bishop who requested their services in assisting in dealing with specific cases. A key aspect of the manual and proposal included a method of uniform case management or at least case following.

Within a few months after the Gauthe case, i.e., by the middle of 1985, there were several civil court actions involving priests and dioceses. Over the years since then there have been hundreds. There has been no uniform case management or following by any Church agency. Hence there has been no way of determining the development of civil law jurisprudence, of tracking the nature and amount of settlements, of studying legal strategies etc.

On the negative side, the lack of following has given rise to rumor and innuendo about the monies spent, judgments of courts etc. The original idea for a crisis intervention team was Ray Mouton's (cf. letter of Feb. 22, 1985). The notion of a research committee was essentially mine but quickly concurred with by Mouton and Peterson. The nature of the entire proposal was presented to Archbishop Laghi. Indeed, I had been briefing him on the overall situation daily.

The original idea was to compose a manual containing information about the issue from different approaches: canon law, civil law, criminal law, insurance, pastoral practice, medical. The manual would be given to the NCCB in hopes that they would take some kind of action. We were not commissioned to write it and did so entirely on our own with no backing, financial or otherwise, from anyone. Drafts of sections were composed by the three of us.

In the meantime, I was speaking informally to the Vatican ambassador (Archbishop Pio Laghi) and to a number of bishops and cardinals about the project. I had support from all to whom I spoke. This support extended to the research and crisis intervention aspects of the overall proposal. Conversations with bishops indicated that they were certainly alerted to and worried about the problem. Fr. Peterson called Cardinal Krol (Philadelphia) in May to ask for a private meeting. Such a meeting was arranged and took place in the office of the director of the National Shrine in May 1985.

Just prior to the meeting I had sent the cardinal a copy of the canonical section of the report which I had drafted. At the meeting, the Cardinal praised the draft section and promised support for the entire project. He stated that he would speak to Cardinal Law and Bishop Quinn.

He subsequently wrote to me on June 11, 13, and 29 about his efforts and support of the project. Cardinal Law (Boston) stated that he would get the project into the NCCB by creating a special ad hoc committee of his own committee on research and pastoral practices.

The final draft was completed on May 14, 1985. That same month the three of us had met with Archbishop Levada, secretary to Cardinal Law's committee. He was positive about progress. A short time later he phoned me and stated that the project had been shut down because another committee of the NCCB was going to deal with it and the duplication of efforts would not make the other committee look good. No more was said about the project to me or anyone else.

I heard informally that the NCCB Committee on Priestly Life would be looking into the issue but never heard or saw anything that had been done. Nevertheless, we proceeded and contacted auxiliary Bishop Quinn of Cleveland (then an ally) who would take several copies of the manual to the NCCB June [1985] meeting in Collegeville, Minnesota. This he did.

The president of the NCCB announced after an executive session, at which there was discussion of the problem of priest-pedophilia, that a committee to work on the issue was formed, headed by now retired Bishop Murphy of Erie, Pennsylvania. At the meeting three presentations were made in an executive session. One each by Wilfred Caron (civil law), Bishop Kenneth Angell and Dr. Richard Issel (psychology).

The reports about the session from bishops were that the psychologist was excellent and the lawyers mediocre at best. This sentiment was stated in a letter from Cardinal Krol to me. I learned later in June from Bishop Anthony Bevilacqua of Pittsburgh (now Cardinal of Philadelphia) that there was no committee, and no action was planned. It was merely a Public Relations move to announce it.

I later learned that the Committee of Priestly Life was supposed to consider the issue. If it did, nothing ever came of consideration. At the press conference held by Bishop Malone, he specifically stated that such a committee existed. Yet in a deposition given in 1993, Sr. Euart, associate secretary general of the NCCB stated that the first committee ever to exist was that headed by Bishop Kinney and created in 1993. Nothing was ever said to Peterson, Mouton, or me about the manual. We never knew what happened to it on the NCCB level.

Some sources from that agency stated that the manual was never properly submitted for consideration by the conference. Its existence was well known. The internal procedures of the NCCB were not known to any of the three authors nor did anyone ever suggest the procedures to be followed.

In later years, after the manual had been circulated around (we sent a copy to every diocese at our own personal expense) and had become well known to attorneys and others involved in the issue, people, especially reporters, would often ask bishops or officials at the NCCB whether they knew about it or had it and if so, why had no action been taken either at the time or since.

These questions engendered a variety of answers, none of which accurately reflected the truth. The general response from the NCCB, almost always through the office of their general counsel (Mark Chopko), was that the NCCB already knew everything that was in the manual, that the NCCB had already taken appropriate action, that the idea of a special committee and ad hoc team of experts was not appropriate. He stated the latter, saying that the NCCB could not bind other dioceses, that it would cost too much, that Mouton, Peterson, and I were in this only to sell the idea to bishops and thus make money off the problem.

He also stated that there were problems with the content of the manual. As one of the authors, it is my contention that the original motivation for composing the manual and submitting the action proposals was grossly misunderstood or perhaps understood but intentionally misconstrued by the officials at the NCCB. It has occasionally crossed the minds of the two remaining authors that officials at the NCCB/USCC who have consistently made derogatory comments about the project are in fact, trying to shift the onus of responsibility from themselves to someone else, or at least conjure up some sort of excuse for failure to act in the face of explicit warnings about the problem, its extent and probable consequences.

At no time since then (1985 to the present) has any contact made between anyone in the NCCB and either Mouton, Peterson, or me. In December 1985, a copy of the manual was sent to each diocesan bishop in the United States through St. Luke Institute. There was no response from anyone to this gesture. Some bishops, when asked by the press, indicated that they had found it helpful.

The NCCB, however, never acknowledged its existence nor have they ever contacted Mouton or me in relation to any of the meetings which they have had concerning the issue since that time. I have received only one letter from the NCCB (Oct. 1992) and that was a response to a letter I had sent to the president after the first VOCAL conference of victims in Chicago in Oct. 1992.

The bishops' conference has discussed the issue in plenary meetings at least five or six times, the first one being in June of 1985 (already alluded to above). Speakers at that meeting included a psychologist (Dr. Richard Isell, Chicago), an attorney (Wilfred Caron, NCCB), a bishop (Bishop Kenneth Angell, Providence RI). The bishops' conference has also issued at least five statements on the subject and sent several memos from the general counsel to all diocesan bishops.

The early suggestions for a research committee as well as a crisis intervention team never went anywhere. It was not until very recently (Oct. 1993) that the NCCB appointed a committee of bishops, headed by Bishop John Kinney of Bismarck, to study the issue. This committee has had some meetings but to date has done nothing more than issue a report.

*The original version of the manual contained four major sections: **civil law, criminal law, canon law, insurance, and medical considerations.** To these were added photocopies of articles about the medical/psychological dimensions of pedophilia. Fr. Peterson composed and attached an "Executive Summary" to the manual during the summer of 1985. At that time, the canonical section was also revised to reflect the change in belief that accused priests are not canonically suspended during the initial investigation but rather that they be placed on administrative leave.*[23]

Translated into layman's terms - the U.S. Bishops wanted a public relations spin to maintain their power and control, and assurance of the complete protection of the Royal Priesthood's public image.

In 1986, Bishop William Levada was elevated to Archbishop of Portland, Oregon. By 1987, Father Michael Peterson died of AIDS. Ray Mouton closed his law practice and authored a book about bullfighting. Father Tom Doyle lost his job as a Catholic University professor and his job at the Apostolic Nunciature in Washington, D.C. He was well on his way to insulating himself from the clerical political arena by becoming the U.S. Air Force Chaplain at the U.S. Air Force base in Ramstein, Germany.

Through the next decades, Doyle devoted his personal time and energy as an advocate for survivors worldwide, advising Catholic hierarchy from New Zealand to Australia to Ireland to Canada and the United States and beyond.

Punishing the messengers like Doyle, Mouton, and Peterson went well beyond to the victims and their parents, who came forward. How the church responded was demonically revealing.

Some diocesan attorneys would not pass up the chance to savage not only the abused survivors, but also their parents. One such infamous diocesan lawyer was James A. Serritella. He was a hefty man known for browbeating the opposition

---

[23] Email to Author, 2002. In 2006. Father Tom Doyle released the original document in *Sex, Priests, and Secret Codes.*

and referring to them as "the enemy." Serritella was referred to in some circles as the Chicago diocesan's legal "pit-bull."

When Serritella died in 2021, the *Chicago Catholic* published a notice of his death, which was massively misleading.

"Mr. Serritella is credited with helping develop the Archdiocese of Chicago's 1992 policies for preventing and responding to clerical sexual abuse, policies that later became the basis for 2002 U.S. Conference of Catholic Bishops Charter for the Protection of Children and Young People, but he was also instrumental in the development of civil law and public policy relating to religious organizations," reads the *Chicago Catholic* article.

So, what were those policies?

On April 27, 1987, Serritella, delivered a paper at the 23rd National Meeting of Diocesan Attorneys. His own words resonate the way the game was supposed to be played by his side of the table representing the Catholic Church regarding the privacy of diocesan "historical secret archive files." These historical secret archive files were material evidence. They exhibited the unquestionable paper trail of crimes within the Catholic Church.

"If there is information that is and will be relevant to the assignment of a priest for his entire career, it should be kept for his entire career in some form… Let us begin by describing, at least generally, what may be included among clergy personnel records. There may be seminary files, assignment files, files containing letters of praise or accusation, health files, and perhaps evaluation files. In some diocese there may be more; in others, there may be less. In all dioceses these files may be divided among and located in several different offices," reads a paper that Serritella wrote. [24]

In Serritella's opinion, the constitutional argument of confidentiality was worthy of discussion.

"Even if [the constitutional argument of disclosing confidential information would be an exercise of the rights of the clergyman or the church] not specifically

---

[24] Serritella, James A. *Confidentiality and the Church*, A Paper Delivered at the Twenty-third National Meeting of Diocesan Attorneys, April 27, 1987, pp. 29, 17.

protected by church law, the resulting injury would be greater than the benefit thereby gained for the correct disposal of the litigation," he further noted.[25]

Serritella was vigilant about protecting his client – the Church and the perverted clergy. He justified the means to the end of protecting his clients by even filing slanderous causes of actions against parents who went to the church hierarchy to right the wrongs of the priests and/or nuns, who abused their own children. All the parents wanted was accountability and for the abuse to stop.

In one case, Serritella counterclaimed against the parents for slander, and successfully won motions to not have the "historical secret archives" opened for discovery and won motions to prevent the consolidation of cases that would have corroborated the victimized children's claims.

"This guy would stoop so low and stop at nothing. Chicago would make the scene today in Boston look like the minor leagues. Cases were rigged all the time," said one Chicago attorney in 2002.

During the May 1-2, 1989, 25th National Meeting of Diocesan Attorneys, Bishop Adam Joseph Maida of Green Bay, Wisconsin, who became Archbishop of Detroit in 1990, and was elevated to Cardinal in 1994, and was a canon and civil attorney, wrote the statement, "The Selection, Training, and Removal of Diocesan Clergy."

"Let us move to the area of pedophilia and the process a bishop can invoke when he deals with a question of this seriousness. In these areas there is high profile conduct on the part of the priest. It is usually notorious and always extremely serious. How does a bishop deal with this on a practical level? In the canonical penal process, there must be three judges involved, evidence from witnesses, and the opportunity for counsel for the accused. Also under our penal process, when a priest expresses sorrow, it derails the process," wrote Maida.

"If he seeks reconciliation, in canon law we may give him absolution and say, "sin no more." But every civil lawyer knows that what is between God and his conscience does not satisfy either the victims (or the potential victims) or the civil law. In canon law, we are limited because a diocese cannot proceed to a final determination of laicizing a priest, which is the ultimate way of bringing about that

---

[25] Ibid, pp. 20.

excardination and severing the legal bond between bishop and priest. I am worried about the legal issues, and I am worried about money, but in these cases where we receive massive newspapers coverage I am more worried about the image of the priesthood," Maida emphasized. [26]

By 1992, Cardinal Bernard Law of Boston publicly "had called down heaven's wrath on the media…for reporting and exposing a decade of deception, deceit and cover-up" related to sexual abuse by priests.[27]

That same year in Australia, Brother Barry M. Coldrey authored a report for the Congregation executives of the Christian Brothers, a Catholic order. It was called, "Reaping the Whirlwind: Sexual Abuse from 1930 to 1994."

The report detailed not just abuses in orphanages but used terms like "sex rings" and a "sex underworld." The report found a "serious, even pervasive" problem of sexual abuse since the 1920s. Several of the Catholic Order leaders' correspondence acknowledged a clear comprehension of the abuse in Australia. The predators even targeted intellectually challenged children.

For decades, Catholic bishops knew there were sexual abuse scandals simmering just waiting to explode globally. Their primary avenues of information were the files, other diocesan priests, their pit-bull lawyers, clerical colleagues, but that was just the beginning. Vatican Intelligence watched priests coming up the ranks for years and built their own files.

The hierarchical focus was on protecting the image of the priesthood. But just what was the basis of the image of the priesthood? How was this clerical society transformed into 'us' versus 'them' — 'clerics 'versus 'laity?' There was no mystery to their information. The mysterious cloud of ignorance fell upon the Catholic laity who never understood the secrecy of the clerical world, or for that matter, clericalism itself.

---

[26] Maida, Adam Joseph Bishop, *The Selection, Training, and Removal of Diocesan Clergy,* 25th National Meeting of Diocesan Attorney, May 1-2, 1989

[27] Anderson, Jeffrey, *When Clergy Fail Their Flock – Innovative Strategies for Prevention, Healing and Justice,* 2003.

Clericalism

To fully understand the issue before us, it is imperative that the Catholic laity and the public understand the cloak of clericalism.

"Catholicism is a religious force and a way of life. It is also a complex socio-cultural reality and a world-wide political entity. It touches the spiritual, moral, emotional, psychological, and economic aspects of the lives of its members. It even impacts the lives of non-members. In the minds of many Catholics and non-Catholics alike, the church is identified with the clergy. The clergy hold all important positions of power in the church. The mistaken belief that the members of the clergy are a spiritual elite, superior to the average lay person and in closer touch with the Almighty leads to clericalism. Clericalism has always had a pejorative connotation and has been a negative force in the church and in society," wrote Father Tom Doyle. [28]

Doyle has agreed with the retired New Zealand Bishop Peter Cullinane's definition.

"Clericalism is a term used to describe an attitude about the clergy that they themselves have caused to happen by fostering the false assumption that the clerical state is of divine origin. It is easiest to understand clericalism by seeing what it is about. Much of it is about power. Power seeking, power sharing and power keeping are part of the clerical mind set but they are not part of the Gospel understanding of authority," wrote Cullinane. "The other commodities that have high value to the clerical world are the prestigious autocratic social status that accompanies the priesthood and/or the bishopric and the money or funding for the comfortable lifestyle, fond of by many high-ranking clerics." [29]

---

[28] Ibid, p. 21.

[29] Ibid, p. 23; Bishop Peter Cullinane, "Clericalism: Avoidable Damage to the Church, <u>Australian Catholic Review</u> 1997. p. 187.

"Clericalism was deeply entrenched in the pre-Vatican church and in the secular culture as well. The mind set assumes that clerics are meant to be the dominant elite in the church, responsible for all aspects of governance and direction. Laity is meant to be a subservient mass. The Clerics were the essence of the pre-Vatican II church defined as the "perfect society." Although certain manifestations of clericalism have changed over the years, as a religious and social phenomenon it is still firmly entrenched," added Cullinane. [30]

So why is clericalism so important? Because that is how the laity relates to the church, and this overflows to how people react to the child sexual torture by clerics and nuns within the Church. For insane reasons, clericalism fosters a belief system of sorts that religious clerics, especially priests are ontologically different than the laity. That too is intellectually dishonest.

"To understand the complex dynamics of clergy sexual abuse one must also understand clericalism because clericalism is directly related to the reasons why victims/plaintiffs remain silent about the abuse at the time it happens and why they often remain silent for so many years thereafter. It also helps to explain why the contemporary institutional church reacts to reports of abuse with denial, scapegoating, and blame-shifting," writes Doyle.

Clericalism helps us to understand why secular institutions such as law enforcement agencies, the press or the judiciary sometimes defer to the institutional church when dealing with sex abuse cases, protecting the image of the institutional church and its leaders at the expense of true justice for the victims, "adds Doyle.[31]

Jeffrey Anderson, a lawyer representing victims, who has confronted church lawyers like Serritella for decades, gave a layman's version of what clericalism is.

The churches that are exclusively male-run hierarchical organization are also the institutions that have been trusted by Western culture to operate onto themselves — the Roman Catholic, the Mormon church now known as the Church of Latter-Day Saints and the Jehovah Witnesses. Each of these hierarchical organizations decree religious belief policy and practice from a male dominated patriarchy. The congregational

---

[30] Ibid, pp. 23, 24.

[31] Ibid, p. 25.

churches that are more open and inclusive in practice and principle permit more mechanisms for openness, accountability, and change.

In short, the hierarchical churches have been allowed to operate under the same practices and principles formulated centuries ago. The courts and lawmakers have abstained from interference in religious practices and policy. The net result is children remain seriously imperiled by church law and custom. For example, in the Church of Latter-Day Saints, the belief in "repentance" and "forgiveness" results in the widespread practice by the church leaders of returning known pedophiles to lay ministry after they have "repented" their sins.

The Jehovah Witnesses profess the belief and employ the practice that a report of child sexual abuse is not "believable" unless witnessed by another person or admitted by the molester (often a lay minister or church elder). When a victim reports to the hierarchy (the Watchtower and Bible Tract Society) they are not believed, rather they are routinely shunned, if not excommunicated from their church, family, and community.

The Catholic church is the most striking and powerful clerical culture of secrecy and insularity. We allow it to operate under the canon law which adheres to principles that protect the church against "scandal," while protecting known predators. The Vatican has refused to remove offending priests from the clerical state and therefore has permitted if not required the Bishops to participate in a pattern of shuttling pedophiles from parish to parish, state to state, and in some cases country to country to avoid detection and "scandal."

The Vatican in the Code of Canon Law (Revised 1983) Canon 489 specifically provides that the Bishop maintain a "sub secreto" archival file of any material that could subject the church to "scandal." The effect is that any data or evidence of child molestation by priests is secreted away by church authorities.

How successful has this shroud of secrecy been to date?

The U.S. criminal justice system is impotent for criminally prosecuting church leaders as are other international criminal justice systems. Very few church bishops, archbishops, or cardinals have been criminally prosecuted for aiding and abetting or failing to report sexual crimes of children considering the scope of these crimes and coverups worldwide, but there have been exceptions.

In France, Abbot Rene Bissey was a parish priest in Monsignor Pierre Pican's diocese. Pican was Bishop of Bayeux and Lisieux in Normandy, France. Father Bissey confessed to Monsignor Pican he had molested children. Pican chose not to report Bissey's crimes to law enforcement. He justified his position because Pican was told of the crime during Bissey's "confession." Later, Bissey was convicted and sentenced to 18 years in prison in October 2000 for his sexual crimes against children.

The abuses occurred between 1987 and 1996. Bissey repeatedly raped one boy and abused 10 other minor children. The bishop knew of Bissey's crimes for two years before Bissey was arrested. In 1996, Pican removed Bissey from his parish work and sent him to a home to rest for 6 months. Pican then reassigned Bissey to another parish.32 French prosecutors indicted Pican for not going to French law enforcement. Pican maintained that since he heard the crimes in confession, he could not breach that confidentiality.

Father Stanislas Lalanne, Spokesperson for the French Bishop's Conference, stated on Vatican Radio that when Bishop Pican first learned of Bissey's criminal acts, Bissey was on the verge of suicide and that is why Pican did not go to the police. He believed that Bishop Pican exercised "freedom of conscience."

When Pican took the stand during Bissey's trial, he refused to answer the question whether he knew of Bissey's criminal acts. At his own trial, it was acknowledged that Bishop Pican learned of Bissey's offenses from the Vicar General of Normandy in 1996.

Pican claimed that he did not know the extent of Bissey's crimes. Bishop Pican was convicted for failing to blow the whistle on the pedophile priest in his parish. The judge sentenced him to a three-month suspended prison term and ordered him to pay one franc to each of the four victims as a symbolic gesture. Pican's conviction was the first time in more than 150 years that a high-ranking clergyman in France was found guilty of a crime. 33

---

[32] www.ireland.com, *Bishop to be Tried for not Denouncing Child Abuse, April 22, 2001.*

[33] Zenit.org – Paris, *Prosecutor Says Secrecy of Confession Is No Excuse – Wants Bishop Imprisoned for Failing to Denounce Pedophile,* June 17, 2001.

In the U.S. and in Vatican circles, rumors had persisted for years that U.S. Cardinal Theodore McCarrick of the Archdiocese of Washington, D.C., and earlier in New Jersey and New York, had molested seminarians.

It was only after the 2018 New York diocese review board found credible evidence that McCarrick had sexually abused a 16-year-old altar boy in New York in the 1970s that McCarrick resigned from the College of Cardinals. He was later exposed for sexually abusing an 11-year-old victim and several more minor boys.

On July 27, 2018, Pope Francis ordered McCarrick to observe "a life of prayer and penance in seclusion." He was laicized in 2019 after his abuse of more minors was reported. Later, criminal investigations followed. By 2021, McCarrick was charged with sexually assaulting a 16-year-old in Massachusetts in 1974.

By early 2023, McCarrick's lawyers stated that his cognitive decline was significant. A state-appointed forensic psychologist confirmed "deficits of his memory and ability to retain information."

By April 2023, McCarrick was charged in a different case with one count of fourth-degree sexual assault during a 1977 incident that allegedly occurred multiple times.

By August 2023, the court ruled that McCarrick was incompetent to stand trial.

Over the last two decades that I have investigated the Catholic Church scandals, there have been tens of thousands of cases reported of abusing, molesting, and raping children all over the world going back decades. Some settlements have been reached. Some dioceses have even filed for bankruptcies to thwart additional payouts to the victims even after massive restitutions had been made. The church has paid billions to the victims, but it has not been a moral windfall for any victims and their families because of the institutional deception and coverup.

There is no doubt that the Church hierarchy paid lip service and wanted their congregations and the public to believe they were cleaning up the perversion. In the end, the hierarchy consciously and without consciences put the institution and themselves above the protection of children and their families.

Tools of Deception

"When you look at this scandal, there is one common factor - all of them involve an abuse of power! The hierarchy lies, guilts, and stalls. Church officials tell the police that they will take care of it. Instead, they promote and cover up for perverts. They move them and give them new fertile grounds to abuse more victims."

— A Female Abuse Victim from Kansas City

In some church circles, it is well known that church leaders loathe the media for reporting on these scandals. In recent times, the hierarchy even has blamed the media for exposing their sex scandal stories worldwide. The church falsely has accused the media of turning *their* scandals into a media sensationalism blame-game, instead of publicly acknowledging their responsibility for not forcefully and courageously addressing the issue decades earlier when they were encouraged to face their own irrefutable evidence – their own **"historical secret archives."**

The keys to their vaults and safes, where these sordid documents are kept in dioceses are restricted to the head of the abbeys and the bishops and their vicars and the like. Although it is the responsibility of prosecutors to seize these documents and make them public sometimes the prosecutors even have protected these church's documents.

One U.S. judge professed frustration about the alliance between the church and state prosecutors for not being transparent. On the one hand, the prosecutors were claiming the victims were their top priorities and they hoped to get justice for them, but simultaneously, the prosecutors agreed to keep the church's secret historical archives under seal.

A Connecticut Superior Court Judge even accused his state prosecutors of a longstanding complicity with the Diocese of Bridgeport, Connecticut for hiding the extent of clergy sexual church "cover-up." The judge said that complicity was at "the heart of the scandal."

In a 2002 written opinion, Judge Robert F. McWeeny criticized what he called: "a judicial model of cooperation with the Diocese [of Bridgeport, Connecticut] in endlessly delaying litigation, sealing files and coercing victims into non-disclosure settlements."

In extraordinary language aimed at the Connecticut Appellate court, which had delayed the judge's order to make public seven boxes of secret documents, Judge McWeeny declared that it is "indefensible morally as well as legally" to keep the documents under court seal. Even the delay, he said, "precludes any timely vindication of any public right to access this compelling information."

The Bridgeport Diocese, he continued, "though unsuccessful in nearly every legal claim it has asserted, has nonetheless for years shielded these materials from public review. Connecticut courts have facilitated this process in the following manner: sealing the files over the objections of the victims; delaying the trials; thus, encouraging the plaintiffs to enter into settlement agreements containing confidentiality and non-disclosure provisions; and preventing any timely adjudication of the merits of legal efforts to make the records public."

McWeeny had ordered the release of the documents after receiving motions from *the New York Times, Boston Globe, Hartford Courant*, and *Washington Post*. Those motions were filed after the *Courant*, which obtained some documents, reported in February 2002 that, while a bishop, Cardinal Edward Egan had covered up allegations of abuse against priests and allowed known child molesters to continue in positions that placed children at risk.

Stephen Gillers, a New York University School of Law ethics specialist, said McWeeny's opinion was unusual for a trial-level judge. He was not supposed to challenge the system but was supposed to follow the rules that are laid down.

"Judge McWeeny obviously feels that the nature of the case requires him to put himself on the line, to throw down a gauntlet and say to his fellow judges, we have misbehaved, and we ought to clean this up," said Gillers. [34]

---

[34] *Boston Globe* staff, 6/14/2002

Judge McWeeny could not have been more correct in his assessment of the Bridgeport diocese's coverup, but it would take nearly 17 years for the proof.

The Bridgeport, Connecticut diocese was created in 1953. Pope John Paul II appointed Bishop Egan as the third bishop of the Diocese of Bridgeport in 1988, where he served until 2000. Bishop Edward Egan was a canon lawyer.

Within the U.S. Conference of Catholic Bishops (USCCB), Egan served as chair of the board of governors of the Pontifical North American College and of the Committee on Science and Human Values. He was also a member of the Committee on Canonical Affairs, the Committee on Education, the Committee on National Collections, and the Committee on Nominations, and served on the USCCB administrative board.

Pope John Paul II appointed Egan as archbishop of the Archdiocese of New York in 2001 a week after Cardinal John O'Connor died. By early 2001, Pope John Paul II elevated Bishop Egan to Cardinal Egan. In 2002, Pope John Paul II named Egan and five other cardinals to the Supreme Tribunal of the Apostolic Signature, the Roman Catholic Church's highest court of Canon Law.

In June 2003, Egan was accused of covering up for pedophile priests but was found not guilty by the Church. He presided over the New York diocese until 2009. Cardinal Egan died in 2015.

In 2018, Bishop Frank Caggiano of the Bridgeport diocese commissioned an investigation into the sex scandals in his diocese going back to 1953. The investigation was conducted by the law firm of Pullman & Comley and a report was released in 2019.

The 2019 investigation found that 71 priests in the Bridgeport diocese abused 281 individuals as far back as 1953. Nearly all the cases involved minors. Ten priests were responsible for 60% of the reported cases. No reports of abuse had been reported since 2008. All reports were in violation of state laws. Bishops presiding over the Bridgeport diocese were found to have kept poor records and actively destroyed some records. Bishops, including Egan, transferred predatory priests from parish to parish, refused to meet with victims and their families, did not establish policies for mandatory reporting to law enforcement or removing the priests from ministry.

The Bishops, including Egan, were found to have put the diocese's reputation and assets over justice, transparency, and accountability. The report found Egan to be "dismissive, uncaring, and at times threatening attitude toward survivors and survivors' advocates." The investigation concluded that Egan "followed a scorched-earth litigation policy" that "re-victimized survivor plaintiffs."

The investigation revealed a 1993 letter that Bishop Egan authored whereby he concluded that taking canonical action against a perverted priest or seeking to have him removed from ministry would be worse for the Church than the abuse itself.

"There can be no canonical process either for the removal of a diocesan priest from his priestly duties or for the removal of a priest from his parish when there is a serious reason to believe that the priest in question is guilty of the sexual violation of children, and especially when he has confessed," wrote Egan. "For the bishop who would countenance such a process would be opening the way to the gravest of evils, among them financial ruin of the dioceses which he is to serve."

Egan was more worried about the finances and reputation of the church than the sodomizing and raping of children.

This 1993 Egan letter was sent to the Vatican concerning a notorious priest named Raymond Pcolka, who had molested 16 children, both boys and girls. One of the male victims' father gave a deposition in the 1990s, when Egan was the presiding Bishop of Bridgeport, Connecticut. The father testified that his son, who was one of Pcolka's altar boys, told him that Pcolka tied him to a bed, covered the backside of the boy with shaving cream, and anally raped him.

Egan was informed of this at the time. Yet, Egan, who was later elevated by Pope John Paul II to a cardinal and assigned to the New York diocese, believed it would be a graver evil to remove Pcolka because it would put the diocese at financial risk.

The Pcolka cases cost the Bridgeport diocese $11 million.

With the intentional goal of keeping the Catholic faithful in the dark and in the pews and selling the notion that these sexual acts were isolated, reactions were over blown, and to consciously counterattack the swell of public outrage, Church leaders and their lawyers used *well-chosen words to intentionally minimize these horrific acts of torture against children worldwide.*

In early February 2002 from the pulpit of Holy Cross Cathedral in Boston just prior to his Mass homily, Cardinal Bernard Law, who oversaw the Archdiocese of Boston, stated that the cardinal was "not a CEO or politician" – rather "the head of a family" and that the family "was hurting" and he was not going to "abandon" the family.

Pressure had been building for Cardinal Law to resign. He rejected that notion at the height of the church sex scandals' exposure in Boston at that time. He was not going to accept responsibility for moving known rapist priests from parish to parish, diocese to diocese, and across state lines. He was not going to accept responsibility for not chastising a known perverted priest who had promoted the infamous North American Man Boy Love Association's (NAMBLA) mantra that sex between minor children and adults was *normal* human behavior.

Father Paul Shanley of the Boston Archdiocese was arrested in 2002 in California, extradited to Massachusetts, and indicted for sexually abusing children. Shanley had been promoting NAMBLA for years. [35]

After Mass in the vestibule of the cathedral that Sunday, one woman cried out to Cardinal Law, "Why can't you face the fact that these are rapes we are talking about?" [36]

Law ignored the question and turned to another question. By March 2002, Law was still referring to his acts of omission of not addressing the diocese's sex scandals as "grave mistakes."

That language seemed to be a repetitive talking point among the hierarchy.

By April 2002, Cardinal Roger Mahony of Los Angeles, whose diocese was also imploding, followed suit.

"I take responsibility for making *a mistake*," stated Cardinal Mahony after it was revealed that he had transferred Father Michael Wempe to work in a hospital without telling the institution the man was alleged to have abused children. [37]

---

[35] It should be noted that Rev. Paul Shanley and Rev. Jack White, classmates at St. John's Seminary, went to Thailand before Shanley was arrested in California. As one source stated, "We know that they were not there looking for rice paddy opportunities."

[36] Author's attendance at Mass, Sunday, February 10, 2002.

[37] Los Angeles Times, April 14, 2002.

During the July 2002 Papal visit to Canada, the *National Globe and Mail* newspaper reported that the head of the Catholic Church in Sydney, Australia, Archbishop George Pell told 500 young delegates at the World Youth Day forum in Toronto that "abortion was a worse moral scandal than priests sexually abusing young people because it's [abortion] always a destruction of human life."[38] Pell's remarks followed his denial the month before that as an auxiliary bishop in Melbourne that he covered-up the child sexual abuse of Father Kevin O'Donnell, one of Australian's most notorious pedophile priests. O'Donnell was sentenced to prison for 15 years for sexual offenses against 21 children. Pell was accused of offering money to the victims in exchange for silence. Initially, Pell denied the accusation, but then publicly admitted it on television when presented with a copy of a letter sent on his behalf.

"I offered them 50 grand (US$30,000) in compensation according to the publicly acknowledged procedure. They chose not to accept it," said Pell.

The parents of two victims, who were children when Father Kevin O'Donnell raped them, claimed that lawyers, acting on Pell's behalf, had warned them that if they did not "accept" the money that the Church would be "strenuously defended" if any legal actions were filed. Pell denounced any notion of this hush money.

Pell also denied offering a bribe to hush another victim. David Ridsdale had claimed that he approached Archbishop Pell in 1993 after his uncle, Father Gerald Ridsdale, sexually abused him

David Ridsdale claimed that Pell stated to him, "I want to know what it will take to keep you quiet." Gerald Ridsdale was sent to jail for abusing children.[39] He was a notorious abuser. He was even sent to the Paraclete in the U.S. for rehabilitation, which was a disastrous failure.

Cardinal Francis George of Chicago held a press conference and made a hypothetical statement on national television that seemed to clearly suggest that priests

---

[38] News.com.au, *Pell's Comments Spark Fury,* July 30, 2002.

[39] BBC News, *Bishop Admits Abuse Money Offer,* June 3, 2002; www.yahoo.com, *Catholic Church in Australia Under Fire over Sex Abuse Remarks,* July 30, 2002

having sex with minor (under 18) girls was excusable behavior on the part of a priest, especially if the priest "had too much to drink."

Cardinal Anthony Bevilacqua of Philadelphia had claimed that "the reason for a higher incidence of pedophilia amongst American clergy was partly because U.S. laws consider a minor to be anyone eighteen and under, while many countries it's fifteen and under." [40]

One of the more extraordinary interviews I conducted in April 2002 was with 47-year-old Tom Smolich, S.J., who was the head of the Jesuit Provincial of the Western Province in Los Gatos, California. He had been sharing a house with some priests near Santa Clara. One of them was a registered sex offender and crossdresser, who was caught by law enforcement in a car with a minor.

I had been investigating claims that two older disabled men living in the boiler building on the provincial property under Smolich's charge had been abused for years at the Sacred Heart Jesuit Center in Los Gatos, California by known perverted priests. Although the men were in their fifties they were mentally arrested near 14 years of age.

I met the men and was given a tour of their bedrooms in the boiler building. They were an odd couple. One was messy; one was very neat. Each had their own themed collection from trains to Elvis Presley.

Across the hall from their stark bedrooms was the rape room where perverted priests who lived on the grounds had sexually abuse them. The Sacred Heart Jesuit Center in Los Gatos was a dumping ground of perverted priests over the years, but I did not know the full extent well after 2002 when I was first on the Jesuit property.

The disabled men's cases were horrifying. When Smolich agreed to meet with me, I asked him about their cases. Naturally, he was defensive. How he then tried to deflect the situation was intellectually offensive and devoid of compassion.

Smolich asserted the victims "were not children." [41]

I leaned across the table and looked deep into his eyes.

---

[40] Mason, Warren, *Zero Tolerance is the least we should expect!* October 2002.

[41] Interview with Author, Los Gatos, California, Spring 2002.

"Have you read the California Disability Act," I asked barely able to contain myself.

Smolich claimed he had not.

He was unaware I had met with the victims, had seen their rooms, entered the room across the hall from their bedrooms where there were raped and had spoken with several people who were trying to help these men.

I found Smolich's response dismissive and detached from the situational reality of harm. Or he did not care. He was asserting these men as non-victims. This was a very difficult interview. Both of my older brothers graduated from Jesuit high schools and universities. I was a graduate of Georgetown University, another Jesuit college.

One of the priests under Smolich tutelage was Brother Charles Leonard Connor. The year before our interview, Connor was convicted of committing a lewd act on one of the victims. He was free after six months of home detention. Another Jesuit, Father Edward Thomas Burke, admitted to his superior in 2000 that he had engaged in "sexual misconduct" with one of the victims. Connor and Burke were among four of the Jesuits named as defendants in a civil case filed on behalf of these two disabled men. The defendants were accused of repeated acts of sodomy, molestation, and false imprisonment.

The initial lawsuit was filed in June 2001. The complaint alleged that the two disabled men were "sexually abused" for 30 years.

One of the disabled men was 56 years of age and had contracted polio as a child. He was put in foster care and then moved to the Jesuit Sacred Heart Center in 1969 at the age of 24. He was an Elvis Presley fan.

The other man was born in Germany and adopted from an orphanage as a toddler. His parents divorced when he was 10 years of age. He never attended school and spent his teenage years in a state mental institution and arrived at the Jesuit Sacred Heart Center at the age of 19 in 1970.

Both men were diagnosed with cognitive disabilities and were employed as dishwashers for the Jesuits. Initially, they were paid a monthly stipend of $150, which was raised to $1,000 a month salary with expenses deducted for room and board by the time their lawsuit was filed in 2001. Police reports and internal memos revealed that the Jesuits received warnings well before the suit was filed, which was followed by a reluctance to notify law enforcement.

Three other Jesuits under Smolich's supervision were registered sex offenders in Northern California. They had been convicted for raping two seven-year-old girls. Some of them were later suspected of molesting the disabled men.

The lawyer representing the Jesuit Province had claimed that the Jesuit higher-ups did not know that the abuse of the disabled men had occurred. However, that was not true. An acquaintance of the disabled men had alerted the Jesuit superiors as early as 1995. By 1997, Santa Clara County sheriff deputies had even visited the Jesuit Center based on a tip.

When Smolich was asked why the Jesuits were housing these Jesuits who sexually molested victims, his response was stunning.

"Diocesan priests have retirement accounts. They can leave and take care of themselves. Men who have spent their lives in the Jesuit Order have nothing. We are not able to throw them out. I would not do it," said Smolich.

When I left Smolich office, I was so disgusted and morally outraged with him, I called the victims' lawyer and encouraged him not to settle for anything short of seven figures.

The suit filed on behalf of these two disabled men was settled for $7.5 million in August 2002.

Sometime later, Smolich moved on to head up the Jesuit Refugee program overseas.

Also, in the spring of 2002, I caught wind of a settlement in a child molestation case in northern California. Father Patrick Dooling, pastor of St. Joseph's Parish in Capitola, California, had denied to his parishioners that he knew the rapist of a teenager in his parish. He had lied to his parishioners.

The priest was a homosexual. He was known to smoke pot allegedly for medicinal purposes and had been arrested for possession of child pornography. The priest had trafficked a teenager in Dooling's parish to the Catholic shrine of Medjugorje in Bosnia where he raped the teenager in a visionary's home. [42]

---

[42] Interview with Tom Alperin, *Esquire*, California, April 2002.

Dooling's public statement to his parishioners was that he did not know anything about this rapist and that he too had been fooled when the priest showed up at St. Joseph's parish.

Dooley's public statements were in direct contradiction to his own words. Under oath in a June 18, 2001, deposition, Father Dooling stated that he not only knew that the rapist was a homosexual, smoked pot, and had been arrested for possession of child pornography, but that he chose not to disclose any of this information to the parents of the teenager when they inquired of Dooley whether it was safe for their child to go to Bosnia with this priest. [43]

Father Dooling's June 18, 2001, deposition is self-explanatory.[44]

Question: Well, when the parents of [victim's name redacted] were talking with you about their concerns about their son going away with this man, it did not occur to you to pass on this information?

Dooling: They did not present – they did not present the questions they asked me as being concerned. They were curious about what type of person this is. They wanted to ask me in a very light-hearted manner, "What do you think about this guy?"

Question: And knowing what you knew, you told them none of these things, none of the facts relating to the fact that he was a homosexual, the fact that he had been arrested for child pornography, the fact that you'd had a conversation with him in which you were questioning whether he was in fact a religious or not. You did not tell them any of those things.

Mr. Gaspari: Mischaracterizes his testimony.

(Gaspari is the lawyer in this case. He also represented the Jesuits in the disabled men's case circa 2001-2002).

Dooling: Yes, those are not what I said.

---

[43] Deposition of Father Patrick Dooling, June 18, 2001.

[44] John DOE, a minor, et al., vs. Diocese of Monterey, et al., No. CV 138321, Deposition of Rev. Patrick J. Dooling.

Paul Gaspari of Tobin & Tobin law firm in San Francisco, California represented four of the defendants in the case: Father Dooling, St. Joseph's Parish,
Bishop Sylvester Ryan, and the Monterey diocese.

Dooling reported to Bishop Ryan. Hence, it was fair to conclude that when
Dooling had made these statements to his parishioners after the settlement that
Ryan was aware of the rapist's proclivities and that Dooling's denial to his parishioners was false. His actions seemed to fall in line with just protecting the image
of the priesthood and the church.

When this story broke about the child being trafficked to Bosnia and the facts
surfaced that this teenager was raped in a visionary's home, the reaction in Bosnia
was also minimized.

In August 2002, Father Svetozar Kraljevic, pastor of St. James Church in Medjugorje, Bosnia, referred to the trafficking and sexual torture of this American
teenager over international borders (drugged, sodomized, and raped) as something
"akin to a car accident." [45]

Prior to the April 2002 U.S. National Conference of Catholic Bishops meeting
with Pope John Paul II at the Vatican, but published after their meeting, the
presses were churning at La Civilta Cattolica ("Catholic Civilization"), the Vatican
owned and sponsored media publication.

Father Gianfaranco Ghirlanda, a very influential Vatican adviser to six Vatican
agencies and the Vatican's Appeals Court, and Dean of the Canon Law faculty at
the prestigious Pontifical Gregorian University, asserted in a May 18, 2002, article
that *canon law still superseded civil law.*

The Church hierarchy was still pushing that canon law ruled in the secular
world. The Church's intellectual arguments and legal gymnastics were nonsensical.

In the article, Ghirlanda asserted that a bishop should not refer an abuse allegation to law enforcement until he has first "reached moral certainty" that a priest
was guilty. He further argued that the "moral certainty" should and would only
be attained through internal church legal procedures.

---

[45] Interview with Author, Bosnia, August 2002.

Ghirlanda further asserted that an accused and/or guilty priest's past should not be revealed if he is reassigned to another parish because in so revealing the priest's past, *his right to a "good reputation" under canon law would be violated and discredit his ministry.* That decision would be dependent upon the bishop believing that the priest would not abuse again.

With further twisted logic, Ghirlanda argued that a priest could not be required by a bishop to undergo psychological testing because that *would be an infraction of his right to privacy.*

But the icing on the cake was Ghirlanda's statement that church leaders have no responsibility either morally or legally if a priest abuses a child. He insisted that church leaders must protect the "good" name of their priests. Ghirlanda was not alone.

Both Archbishop Julian Herranz, President of the Canon Law Council, and Archbishop Tarcisio Bertone, the second highest ranking official in the Doctrine office at that time agreed. They were both opposed to automatic reporting of allegations to secular law enforcement authorities. Again, elevating canon law above common law for crimes against children in the secular world.

One needs to keep in mind that the Vatican had released a statement in December 2001 stipulating *that all allegations would be reported to Rome*, that there would be *trials* and that they would be held in *secrecy*. That was the gist of the Vatican's position prior to the implosion of the Catholic Church sex scandals in January 2002 when the Boston diocese sex scandals were an avalanche of news.

At the time, Monsignor Francis Maniscalco, spokesman for the U.S. Conference of Catholic Bishops, got defensive and even dismissed Ghirlanda, Herranz, and Bertone's positions.

"He's a canon lawyer, not a civil lawyer, and our [U.S.] bishops do have to obey the laws of our country," said Maniscalco. [46]

Months after interviewing Jesuit Tom Smolich in Los Gatos, California in spring 2002, I went online to the Jesuit website's bulletin board where anyone can ask a question about St. Thomas Aquinas or Teilhard de Chardin, or the like.

---

[46] Ostling, Richard N., The Associated Press, *Will Vatican OK Reforms?*, May 23, 2002.

I chose a different topic.

"What in the world is Tom Smolich, the head of the Western Jesuit Province in the United States, doing living with a convicted sex offender and cross dresser in the Provincial house across the street from the University of Santa Clara?" I asked.

Smolich had been then overseeing approximately 436 Jesuits in a five-state area. Although his office was at the Sacred Heart Center in Los Gatos, he lived with about seven Jesuits at this other location.

Angelo Mariano, S.J. was a convicted sex offender, who lived in that house with Smolich. Mariano was listed on the Santa Clara Police Sex Registry.

Mariano had gone on the internet and posed as *Kim* – a woman from Hawaii. One night, just before midnight in a residential area, the local police received a phone call because two suspicious cars were parked on the street. Two individuals were in one car and another person occupied a second car.

The police responded. As they approached the vehicle with the two individuals, Mariano, aka *Kim, whipped off a wig, smeared his makeup, pulled out false boobs from his shirt, and ripped the spiked- heels off his feet*. Mariano's car was registered to the Jesuit Sacred Heart Center in Los Gatos. Mariano was also one of the suspects in the disabled men case.

After Mariano's criminal proceedings in that case, he returned to the Sacred Heart Jesuit Center. Later, he was moved to the Santa Clara residence he shared with Smolich.

During the civil suit filed on behalf of the two mentally challenged men under Smolich's charge, Mariano was subpoenaed for a deposition. He pled the Fifth Amendment even when asked where he lived.

It was so frustrating that Bob Tobin, who was the disabled men's attorney in that civil case, made Mariano a defendant in the case. The plaintiffs had mentioned a "Father Angel" as one of their predators. Later, although three Jesuits were indicted and convicted for molesting the disabled plaintiffs, Mariano was dropped as a defendant in the civil case. This was one of the terms of the civil case settlement for the $7.5 million in August 2002.[47]

The following Monday morning after I posted that question on the Jesuit website, I received an email from Father Quinn, who was one of the Jesuit webmasters who happened to be working in Washington, D.C. at the Jesuit Conference Center.

He informed me he was "ordered" to remove my question. We exchanged several emails and then we spoke on the phone. I learned he reported directly to Smolich.

The most amazing impression I had during our conversation was that he, just like Smolich, was devoid of reality.

Quinn either sincerely did not "understand," or was instructed to act like there was nothing wrong with a middle-aged convicted sex offender and cross-dresser wearing a priest's collar and living in a Catholic clergy's house, literally, sharing a house with a Head of a Jesuit Provincial.

My mind was absolutely blown as a Catholic and a graduate of a Jesuit university. Furthermore, as a television producer and political journalist, I was completely taken aback how the Jesuits studiously and intentionally missed the significance of that optic.

Father Gary Hayes, a priest in Kentucky, had been abused while he was a high school freshman in New Jersey. His predator plied him with alcohol, molested him, and then threatened him. Hayes told the local bishop. Hayes claimed that church officials acknowledged the priest's behavior, and yet, did not remove him from ministry. The priest continued his abuse and eventually the 12-year-old Gary Hayes told his parents. The priest was convicted and died in prison.

For years, many people told Hayes to "get over his abuse."

Instead, Hayes spoke out and advocated for victims to keep talking until someone acted.

In 2002, I learned of one of the more insidious tactics of suppressing information from the Catholic laity and the public at large. There were voluminous

---

[47] Interview with one of the plaintiff's guardians, 2002.

non-disclosure gags orders that diocesan lawyers coerced Catholic victims and their parents to sign.

The number of gag orders in the U.S. alone was stunning. These non-disclosure agreements, otherwise known as NDAs, were calculated to protect the church and the image of the clergy.

Another red flag was the number of cases where judges denied the admission of irrefutable evidence in one case that would have been corroborating evidence in another.

When one connects the dots from the evidence from one case to another, it is clear the assumption that predators only prey upon one or two victims is false.

Predator/priests always have numerous victims and the hierarchy, the church lawyers, and the psychiatrists hired by the Catholic Church have known this for decades.

The Church is shameless about covering up their institutional crimes. Since 2002, Catholics laity, victims/survivors and their families and the public have become outraged and have demanded that the Catholic Church hierarchy be transparent.

Under Pope Francis, who is also a Jesuit, the Catholic Church hierarchy still refuses to come clean when challenged even though prosecutors know more today than they did since 2001 when I first started my investigation into the church sex scandals.

It is no secret that the church has kept copious notes on their internal transgressions for centuries. Yes, some of the hierarchy has destroyed documents, but there are enough historical secret archives that have proven *who knew what when*. The church hierarchy has painted a very deceitful, immoral, and ugly portrait.

Granted it has been like pulling teeth to get to the truth, but the overall pressure has pushed transparency in the right direction however slow and painful the process has been for victims and their families.

The truth is we know more in 2024 than the Church ever admitted in 2002.

When I sat across the table from Jesuit Tom Smolich in 2002, and he dismissed the two mentally challenged men whom he knew were abused at the Jesuit Provincial headquarters for decades, I had a very difficult time getting over his arrogance. It was a pivotal moment for me as a non-victim because I realized how difficult it must be for victims, survivors and families who were treated even worse.

Smolich had downplayed the dumping ground of perverts on the Sacred Heart Jesuit property at that time. What I did not know then was the extent of that Jesuit Provincial being used as a dumping ground for perverts.

Nearly 15 years after that 2002 interview with Smolich in Los Gatos, California at the Jesuit West of the Society of Jesus, as they call that province today, both California and the Oregon provinces had been combined into Smolich's provincial by 2017.

This Jesuit Provincial headquarters now comprises all Jesuits in Arizona, Alaska, California, Hawaii, Idaho, Montana, Nevada, Oregon, Utah, and Washington.

In 2018, the Jesuit West Provincial released a list of Jesuits "with credible claims of sexual abuse of a minor or vulnerable adult, dating back to 1950," ostensibly "as part of our provinces' ongoing commitment to transparency and accountability," reads their publicized statement. They also boasted that by releasing the list they claimed, "a significant reform in how the Church and religious orders like ours handle claims of sexual abuse."

All sounds acceptable on the surface, but the findings were remarkably shocking.

This 2018 Jesuit West list published 133 names of Jesuits who had abused minors or vulnerable human beings.

Why did it take the Jesuits this long to come clean?

"The list contains the names of Jesuits who are or were members of Jesuits West Province, the former California, and the former Oregon Provinces, against whom a credible claim of sexual abuse of a minor (under the age of 18) or a vulnerable adult has been made. Also included are the names of Jesuits from other provinces against whom there are credible claims resulting from their work while assigned to Jesuits West or the California or Oregon Provinces; and Jesuits of the former Oregon Province with credible claims already published as part of the Oregon bankruptcy filing. Finally, the list includes Jesuits listed in the diocesan bankruptcies or listed by other dioceses," reads their public statement.

The statement was obviously written by the Jesuits' attorneys because of the following sentences.

"Inclusion in this list [which is detailed] does not imply that the claims are true or correct or that the accused individual has been found guilty of a crime or liable for civil claims. In many instances, the claims were made several years or decades after the alleged events and were not capable of an investigation and determination," the statement notes. "Many claims were received after an accused priest was deceased. In those instances, the accused was unable to defend himself or deny the charges. The Province was unable to undertake a thorough investigation. Deceased individuals are included in this list based upon the fact that an accusation was reported."

This is a classic legal *"Cover Your Ass"* statement made by the oldest Catholic Order in the Roman Catholic Church.

They all knew, and the mere fact that it took the Jesuits this long to gather this information to make this public is breathtaking.

The Jesuit West list of predator priest perverts is listed here. [48]

Priests mentioned in this chapter, who raped the two disabled men living at the Jesuit Sacred Heart Center are mentioned on this list.

In 2001, the late Richard Sipe, Author of *Celibacy: A Way of Loving, Living and Serving,* who was an advocate for victims, survivors, and justice, just like Father Tom Doyle, wrote,

"One reality that gives the problems recorded a special urgency and force is missing from all the accounts. One word is never mentioned. Crime. Rape (sexual abuse and harassment, too) is a crime. Collusion to cover up crime is itself negligent and reprehensible. So is conspiratorial silence; so is the failure to protect the endangered and warn the innocent. Church authorities cannot plead ignorance, nor innocence." [49]

Amen!

---

[48]   https://www.jesuitswest.org/wp-content/uploads/sites/10/2023/06/JW_List_1207_EnglishR14.pdf

[49] Sipe, A.W. Richard, National Catholic Reporter, Problems Cry Out for Reform, April 6, 2001.

Intimidation Tactics

There are roughly 1.39 billion Catholics worldwide. In 2024, there are roughly 400,000 priests globally consisting of diocesan and religious order priests plus 700,000 religious nuns. Those numbers also represent approximately 2500 different Catholic orders of priests and nuns.

The Roman Catholic Church structure is organized into dioceses worldwide, which consist of local parishes. Each parish is assigned a pastor, each diocese a Bishop, and each Archdiocese, an Archbishop, or a Cardinal.

The religious priest orders consist of Jesuits, Benedictines, Franciscans, Dominicans, Opus Dei, Christian Brothers, Augustinian, Redemptorists, and the like.

The nuns' orders consist of Sacred Heart, Little Sisters of the Poor, Notre Dame, Ursuline, St. Benedict, Visitation, and the like.

In the U.S. in 2024, there are approximately 37,000 priests. One-third of them belong to religious orders. The number of nuns range around 45,000.

While all these diocesan and religious orders have separate structures with their own rules, the organizations' rules of following their leaders and not rocking the boat are matters of survival and advancements.

When it comes to addressing sexual predators within these religious orders, despite all the public hand wringing by hierarchy and priests, my investigation found plenty of proof that in private "Leave Well Enough Alone..." had been the order of the day.

This has led to some problems when a parish priest with the support and urging of parishioners, is ready to take a stand against those above him whom he disagrees with over church policy that sacrifices children to save the clerical image.

Case in point – Springfield, Massachusetts.

For years, Church officials described the now retired Father James J. Scahill, former pastor of St. Michael's Parish in East Longmeadow, Massachusetts in the Springfield, Massachusetts diocese, as "disobedient." That is a canonical term when a priest uses his conscience to do the right thing and refuses to succumb to clerical autocracy.

Father Scahill's parish was expected to contribute nine percent of its monies to Archbishop Thomas Dupre's Springfield, Massachusetts' diocese, where Scahill's parish was located. For years, Father Scahill sent the monies to Dupre's diocesan office.

But, in 1992, the situation changed.

Of that nine percent, three percent was assigned to designated catholic charities. Father Scahill continued to transfer the three percent, but he refused to forward the remaining six percent to Archbishop Thomas Dupre.

Why?

Because the Bishop Dupre refused to laicize Father Richard Lavigne, who was a convicted sex offender as of 1992. Dupre removed Lavigne from the ministry in 1992, but he refused to laicize him. It took until 2003 for the Vatican's Holy See to laicize Lavigne.

When Lavigne was arrested in 1991, five boys had accused him of abuse although he was convicted for abusing only two boys. His sentence of four to six years was suspended, and he was given a sentence of ten years' probation.

Lavigne was registered as a Tier 3 sex offender in 1992. That means he was recognized as the equivalent of a repeat offender as much as the notorious late registered sex offender Jeffrey Epstein. Tier 3 means that authorities believe the offender will commit sex crimes in the future.

Lavigne was sent to St. Luke's Institute for rehabilitation. The day after he was released, 11 new accusers came forward. In 1994, a settlement was reached for $1.4 million with those survivors.

Even more victims were included in a later settlement in 2004. There were about 48 known victims and law enforcement estimated that there may have been as many as 250 victims. By 2021, Lavigne's attorney admitted his client was connected to "43" victims.

But there was a lingering black cloud that hovered over Lavigne for decades. He had been the prime suspect in the long-unsolved 1972 murder of Danny Croteau, a 13-year-old altar boy.

Law enforcement and Croteau's family and some of us in the media who covered this case suspected Lavigne of being the murderer.

In 2003, Lavigne responded to a *Boston Globe* reporter when asked about the Croteau case.

"My silence has been my salvation," said Lavigne.

Nearly 50 years after Danny Croteau's death in 2021, when Lavigne, then 80 years of age, was in a hospital for covid, a Massachusetts state trooper decided to approach Lavigne one more time.

During April and May 2021 over five days, Trooper Michael T. McNally recorded his interviews with Lavigne while he was in the hospital. The former priest never admitted to killing Danny Croteau per se, but Lavigne did admit he shoved Danny by the Chicopee River the night of April 14, 1972. Danny Croteau's body was found floating in the Chicopee River the next day. He had been beaten to death with a blunt instrument.

"I just remember being heartbroken when I saw his body going down the river knowing I was responsible for giving him a good shove, you know? He was a nice little kid…I would sooner forget the whole thing, frankly," said Lavigne.

Law enforcement had enough information and prepared paperwork to arrest Lavigne, but the priest died before they could arrest him.

Lavigne had befriended the Croteau family and had taken the Croteau brothers on outings and overnight trips. Lavigne even officiated at Danny Croteau's funeral Mass.

By November 2023, the Springfield diocese announced that there were new "credible" findings against Lavigne.

Back in the 1990s when Father Scahill objected to Bishop Thomas Dupre's support of Lavigne, Bishop Dupre claimed that any action against Lavigne would be "cumbersome," and he arrogantly stated that if he were forced to laicize Lavigne, he would continue to financially support him.

Lavigne was a diocesan priest. He had a retirement fund unlike the Jesuits which Jesuit Tom Smolich used as justification for not kicking out perverted Jesuits from his order. So, why did Dupre not act against a Tier 3 registered sex offender?

There were rumors for years that the priests in Dupre's diocese gathered once a month for a private dinner where they would have group confessions. If the rumors were true, the question in my mind was who knew what sins or crimes their fellow diocesan priests had committed? And what a clever way to keep the lid on the sex crimes against children among the clergy although that notion would make this story even darker.

The threat of excommunication under canon law for violating confidentiality in confession is serious business in the Catholic Church. But there is another notion in canon law that is also serious business. If a cleric causes a scandal in the church, it can be argued that excommunication is justified.

On some level, that is ironic because clearly, it is the hierarchy who is involved in the coverup of the church sex abuse cases. Those coverups have been causing scandals. When the dots have been connected in some cases, the settlements are huge and in some cases, causing bankruptcies and the need to sell off properties to pay the settlements in civil cases.

But there have not been too many excommunications of bishops, archbishops, cardinals, or Vatican Curia involved in these coverups.

It has been centuries since Catholics officially have practiced group confessions, so this notion was intriguing to me. I started asking good priests about group confessions within the clergy. Some told me they knew nothing about it. Some seemed surprised I was asking about it.

But, to my utter astonishment, I learned that some of the Catholic clergy indeed practice group confessions. Some literally confess their sins in a group overseen by another priest. But I could never get anyone to go on the record, and this notion lingered in the back of my mind for years as well as why Dupre refused to laicize someone like Lavigne years ago, especially when he had retirement funds and was a Tier 3 registered sex offender. What more does the church need to justify getting rid of someone like this?

Not only did Father Scahill think that Bishop Dupre's 1992 decision to not laicize Lavigne was immoral, so did his parishioners and the local community. Two friends of mine from Georgetown University were congregants in Scahill's parish and they had nothing but good things to say about Scahill. They believed he was grounded in moral courage.

Although Father Scahill had been subjected to scorn and ostracization by Bishop Dupre and other priests in his own diocese for years for standing up, calling out Bishop Dupre, and withholding some parish monies to Dupre's diocese, the truth surfaced in the end.

Dupre's 2002 public statement would eventually come back to haunt him.

"As a newly ordained priest in my first parish, I learned that an older priest whom I respected a great deal have been accused of molesting a 13-year-old boy," wrote Dupre in the March 2002 issue of the Catholic Observer. "I could hardly believe it. I was confused and many emotions welled up in me, including disbelief, anger, disappointment, and a feeling of being let down."

Common sense had told me as a journalist there had to be something more to this statement Dupre's refusal to get rid of Lavigne, and, yes, there was.

Dupre was a child sex offender. He was part of the "old boys' network."

By early 2004, two altars boys who served Mass with Bishop Dupre came forward with credible accusations of sexual abuse against the bishop during the 1970s. In one case, the abuse continued into the 1980s.

The victims alleged that Dupre gave them alcohol, showed them pornography, and sexually abused them.

Local clergy accused Dupre of covering up for other perverted priests, including Lavigne. Bishop Dupre resigned abruptly in February 2004 at the age of 71. Pope John Paul II accepted his resignation four years earlier than the customary age of a bishop's resignation at 75 years of age.

By the fall of 2004, Dupre was indicted by a grand jury on two counts of child molestation. He became the first American Catholic bishop to be indicted during this wave of the Church's sex scandals.

The district attorney was forced to drop the charges though because the statute of limitations had expired.

Dupre followed those before him and entered a rehab program at St. Luke's Institute in Suitland, Maryland. That is the same institution that Father Michael Peterson ran back in the 1980s when Peterson worked with Father Tom Doyle and attorney Ray Mouton.

By 2010, a civil suit was filed against former priest Alfred F. Graves for abusing a victim. Graves had been supervised by retired Springfield Bishops Joseph F. Maguire and Thomas Dupre.

During Dupre's deposition, he stated his name and then repeatedly took the Fifth Amendment when asked questions. His lawyers tried to seal his videotaped deposition, but the presiding judge denied that motion. That case was settled for $500,000 in 2012. [50]

Eventually, Dupre was moved to a residential facility for retired priests in Washington, D.C. and died in 2016, five years before Lavigne died.

By May 2021, Bishop William Byrne of the Diocese of Springfield, Massachusetts released a report naming 60 priests and laity who worked in or visited his diocese over previous decades. They had engaged in sexual misconduct with minors. Some of these predators were born in 1897, 1898, 1900, 1907, and 1920.

Two of Bishop Dupre's victims claimed that he introduced them to gay porn when they were 12 and 13 years of age. Some of the allegations included trips to Canada and Connecticut where the abuse continued. For years, Dupre would send his victims birthday cards and holidays notes with some money.

By 2002, the Catholic laity, even if they had no victims in their families, was standing up and speaking out about the scandals in the Church. In response, the hierarchy's arrogance rose like a phoenix from the desert.

They did not want to hear from the laity who were gathering in their parishes in groups like Voice of the Faithful which sprung up in Boston and started chapters across America. The church did not like the media attention from the Boston

---

[50]   https://www.ncronline.org/news/accountability/settlement-reached-civil-trial-retired-mass-bishops

Globe, New York Times, local newspapers, and television coverage. There were more Father Scahills emerging as more evidence was being revealed.

Ground Zero – Boston – My Birthplace

In April 2002, Cardinal Bernard Law of Boston had returned home from a mandatory Vatican meeting with the cardinals from around the globe. Pope John Paul II had called for the meeting during the implosion of the Boston diocese's sex scandals and its domino effect in other dioceses. The church was bleeding, and the pope knew it. Sources inside the Vatican shared with me that the hierarchy leadership was fighting among themselves how to address the matter. Some wanted to hold their ground to protect the church. Others wanted to wipe out the evil.

Upon Cardinal Law's return to Boston, the cardinal announced that the Father Geoghan sex scandal settlement agreement with 86 victims was off the table. The Boston hierarchy knew of Geoghan's abuse for decades. One victim was only four years of age.

One 81-year-old man, who had referred to Cardinal Law as "the most notorious co-pedophile" in America was infuriated with Law because of his participation in the coverup. He was disgusted with the cardinal's obfuscation, his arrogance towards the victims and their families, and the cardinal's protracted deflection over the seriousness of the matter and decided to confront Cardinal Law following his Sunday Mass at Holy Cross Cathedral.

This man was none other than our beloved late father, Thomas J. Dolan. Our 81-year-old Father was morally outraged that the Church hierarchy was not standing up for survivors and not ridding the Church of perverts having attended daily Mass since he was seven years of age.

Buddy, as everyone in our family and extended family affectionately called our father, was on rampage to support the victims and convince Cardinal Law to resign. He was horrified of the corruption and evil that penetrated the Church, but more disgusted by the coverup and "massive arrogance and immaturity of the church's leadership."

After Mass, Cardinal Law stood in the vestibule and greeted the congregation as they stood in line. Buddy joined them.

Cardinal Law was flanked on both sides with bodyguards cloaked in vestments. The media was present. Cardinal Law was the poster boy of the scandal in America by this time. Every day, the *Boston Globe* was hammering him and the church in their coverage.

Not one to ever kiss a Cardinal's ring even though the late Boston Cardinal Richard Cushing was his Father's best friend, Buddy extended his hand to Cardinal Law. They shook hands, but Buddy did not let go.

"You must resign so that the healing process can begin," Buddy told the Cardinal calmly as he shook his hand and grasped his other hand around the cardinal's hand.

"I have to take in everyone's opinion, Tom" Cardinal Law responded.

"Then you must listen to the 75% of the Catholic Bostonians who want you to resign," my father pleaded.

"Pray for me," the Cardinal stated.

"I pray every day that you have the humility and courage to resign. You are a *stress* to the Pope," Buddy reminded him.

"I talk to the Pope *every day*," Cardinal flippantly stated.

Then one of the Cardinal's cloaked attendants put his hand on Buddy's forearm. To which, my father continued to intently look into Law's eyes.

"Tell him to take his hand off me!"

Law did not respond.

Silence engulfed the vestibule.

A second request to remove his hand was made firmly.

Law just stared back at Buddy.

The attendant removed his hand.

The interaction ended and Daddy turned to leave.

A reporter heard the exchange and photographed the interaction.

He approached my father as he was walking away and asked for his name. Buddy brushed off the reporter telling him it "did not matter." But the reporter persisted and approached him a second time.

"Sir, do you mind if I characterize you as "elderly?"

My father laughed, "Just as long as you do not call me senile."

Buddy and the reporter both laughed.

These types of evasive dialogues that Law had with my father are typical and condoned by church officials all the time. [51]

Two days later, my oldest brother, Thomy, called me. He was reading the *St. Louis Post-Dispatch* and saw Daddy's picture in the paper.

"When's the last time you spoke with Daddy?"

"Sunday night," I said.

"This is really turning into a family crusade taking on the church – I am looking at Daddy's picture in the paper confronting Cardinal Law, and you are traveling the world confronting church perverts," exclaimed my brother, who was due to go sailing with my father for several weeks later that summer.

My next call was to Buddy.

"So, tell me what happened at the cathedral on Sunday," I asked.

Buddy obviously knew I was investigating the church. It was becoming a collaborative effort also with my uncle in Los Angeles, who had been at one point the Treasurer of Cardinal Roger Mahony's diocese in Los Angeles. We had friends in Chicago, N.Y.C., St. Louis, and were cross-referencing information with others across America and beyond through the Knights of Columbus and Knights and Dames of Malta. Catholics were rocking with moral outrage and more so when the Catholic hierarchy tried to tell the laity – *this is none of your business.* It was our business. It was our tradition and heritage. And we were standing with the victims and their families.

One Boston Catholic pastor, who offered to have a Voice of the Faithful (VOTF) meeting in his church basement, was told by Reverend Chris Coyne, a member of Cardinal Law's inner circle in the Boston diocese, that his "pension was in jeopardy" if he allowed VOTF to meet in the basement of his parish church.

In 2002, The World Affairs Council in Boston (WAC) invited me to give a lecture on human trafficking. State Street Corporation sponsored it, and it was to

---

[51] Interview with the "Tom Dolan," Spring 2002.

be held at the State Street Corporation Building in the Downtown Club on March 21, 2002.

Shortly before this date, Maureen Bateman, the General Counsel of State Street Corporation, was named by Cardinal Law to head his "crises" committee dealing with the imploding sex scandal.

The day before the event, a State Street representative called me and told me that I could not mention "Cardinal Law" or the "Archdiocese of Boston" during my presentation because the Boston scandal was not an "international issue."

Knowing that the Catholic Church was only one piece of the global pie of human trafficking, I understood the political game in play. I laughed it off to myself making no explicit promises although I heard the message loud and clear.

Some colleagues I discussed this with, including Buddy, asked me how I was going to handle this.

"Just pray, take a seat, and watch the show. God is in charge. I am going to tell the truth. I am not afraid of these deranged people."

The presentation forged ahead although at the last minute, the head of the Boston branch of the WAC instructed her staff not to release the second press advisory to lower audience attendance. I did not care. I understood their game.

After the lecture during the Q & A, the same WAC woman asked, "What does human trafficking have to do with the Catholic Church?"

She opened the door, and I walked right through it.

"The Boston scandal, its implosion, the systemic cover-up by Cardinal Law, his auxiliary bishops under him, who had been fanned out to other dioceses in Connecticut, New York and New Hampshire where they continued to duplicate the cover-up model, was in fact, institutional human trafficking," and then I went into detail.

"Investigating the church model as a criminal enterprise was the beginning of an international coverup story with massive implications on the institutional structure of human trafficking within the Church and its intentional coverup going back centuries with documentation will blow the minds of not only Catholics, but the public eventually," I added.

I predicted that "this investigation will reverberate well beyond the walls of the Vatican and the Catholic Church."

"The historical secret archives within dioceses and orders they have sent to the Vatican through embassies across the globe to the Office of the Congregation of the Faith for decades need to be seized in every diocese and every order," I said.

"Thank you for asking," is how I concluded.

I never took my eyes off her while answering her question. I noticed she had turned ashen.

I believed then as I believe now she wanted to put me on the spot and expected me to say there was no connection to human trafficking because of what she had said to me before the lecture, or why else ask the question.

I concluded that night that not only are some laity complicit with the church, but they are not exactly giant intellects either.

If these people truly believed that Catholics and the public will not hold the Church accountable for raping children, knowing the extent of these insidious crimes, they were literally out of their minds.

Later, over dinner, I predicted these cases will end up bankrupting some dioceses and create shame the likes of which the Church has never experienced. Even the popes knew of these crimes. They created the internal system that created the documents and the model that contributed to hiding the documents, namely, Canon Law.

Clerical Blackmail

The Roman Catholic Church hierarchy and some of its clergy are fearful that their own sexual histories and proclivities will become public well beyond the Catholic Church's child sexual abuse scandals. I firmly believe that some of them have chosen to look the other way and not report on clergy, who rape children, for fear of being exposed. It is just too risky for them. The Lavigne Dupre situation comes to mind for starters.

In 1990, the late Dr. Richard Sipe, an American Benedictine monk-priest for 18 years, and with 25 years of counselling priests and sexually abused survivors, concluded in one of his studies among 1,500 Catholic priests between 1960 and 1985 the following:

1. 6% were sexually involved with minors.
2. 20 – 25% were engaged with adult women.
3. 15% were sexually engaged with adult men.

A deposition of a bishop in the case of the notorious Monsignor Robert Trupia from Tucson, Arizona makes direct reference that clerical blackmail keeps priests silent for years.

The Reverend Ted Oswald, a Catholic pastor in Lakeport, California, recalled telling supervisors as far back as 1976 that several boys at St. Francis of Assisi in Yuma, Arizona had said they had been fondled by Trupia. When Oswald inquired of the diocese in 1977 about the boys' statements the diocese denied they had any such complaints from the boys. Oswald sent a letter to then Bishop Green in 2000.

The Catholic Archdiocese settled 11 lawsuits with 16 plaintiffs involving four priests who had molested children in Yuma, Arizona. The settlement included apologies to victims and their families and a financial settlement by some estimates as high as $15 million.

In referencing the Trupia settlement, Bishop Moreno, called it "very painful consequences to our diocese and its finances."

The diocese did not begin an official investigation until 1992, 17 years after the diocese first heard that Trupia was abusing children. Trupia committed these sexual acts in his rectory office and sodomized altar boys after Mass on a weekly basis for more than two years. Yet despite the knowledge of these acts, Trupia was promoted to increasingly powerful positions.

Trupia's sexual appetite was also well known to priests at California's St. John's Seminary in Camarillo. He used to attend "Come and See" weekends at the seminary known as Los Angeles Cardinal Roger Mahony's pride and joy. Trupia was caught on more than one occasion having sex with male clergy. Despite these complaints getting back to Bishop Moreno, Trupia kept returning to St. John's for six years before he was finally banned in 1988. At that point in time, Trupia was caught having sex with a male drug addict in the school's bell tower.

In 1992, Trupia admitted to Bishop Moreno that he was an abuser and "a man unfit for public ministry." Moreno withheld the truth of Trupia's statement from families and legal authorities.

Court records validated that Bishop Moreno's own deposition proved that "diocese officials protected one another, lied to a victim's family, failed to counsel victims, destroyed statements, did not notify child protective authorities, and were uncooperative with police."

The reason behind this unwillingness to stop Trupia suggests possible threats of sexual blackmail for other embarrassing sexual behaviors.

Moreno said during his deposition that he could not explain why he waited until 1995 to execute another canonical affidavit alleging that Trupia threatened to reveal personal sexual relationships with "High Church Officials" (including the late Bishop Rausch of Phoenix), if he were not allowed to retire instead of being kicked out of the church.

By 2002, Trupia was still considered a priest. According to Bishop Moreno, Trupia was entitled to receive a $ 1,200 per month stipend and full medical insurance, under canon law guidelines. A process to defrock Trupia had been stalled at the Vatican.

Trupia arrogantly cited canon law as his basis to exercise his right to appeal to the Vatican to get rid of him. For years, he had been successful to thwart the Vatican's highest tribunal to protect himself even though his nickname was "Chicken Hawk" due to his reputation for raping very young children.

This notorious "serial sexual predator" was later moved to Maryland where he worked from a distance for the Monterey, California diocese. In 2001, he was arrested on charges of molesting children in Arizona in the 1970s. He spent one night in jail because the statute of limitations expired. Finally, in 2004, Trupia was laicized from the Church.

To better understand this world where dirty little secrets are used by those afraid of losing power, it is best to understand that the church hierarchy is not in this game alone.

The Roman Catholic Church Infrastructure

During the summer of 2000, an Eastern European girl said to me during an interview, "No one cares about us."

What she did not know was that there are those of us who do care. One of the major hurdles is educating the public of this girl's cries for help and many millions like her is addressing the public's shameless apathy and refusal to deal with reality about child sexual abuse. There is nothing more powerfully destructive in society than ignorance and indifference. We need to recognize the harm done to survivors of child sexual abuse and hold those individuals and institutions accountable no matter how powerful they believe themselves above the law.

I can attest to my own shamefulness as a seasoned journalist for not having seen the magnitude and horrific ramifications of child sexual abuse worldwide until 2000. I shiver when I realize how long victims have had to live with their own horrors while ignorance and apathy permeate our society. This issue is not confined to the rank and file of Catholics. The sexual exploitation of children affects the very landscape of society on the most rudimentary levels.

Michael Skinner, a non-Catholic, and a victim of incest by both parents and their friends, knows about apathy extremely well. Teachers, neighbors, nurses, doctors, and friends' parents knew something was going on in his household in Cambridge, Massachusetts, when he was under ten years of age, but no one did anything. The abuse continued for years. Today, Michael is in his sixties, a musician, and speaks out in support of victims, and against apathy because his life as a child was a living hell. No one did anything to protect him and his siblings.

"Until the reality of such horror is finally acknowledged by society we will not start to see an end to childhood abuse and its severe consequences" Michael Skinner stated in 2002. 52

As a journalist, I am a huge supporter of law enforcement who investigates these perverted maggots. Law enforcement is the frontline of defense when it comes to protecting children who are caught up in this horror. So often, they are even overwhelmed with legal and investigative hurdles.

Hank Adema, a former Chicago police officer, and later, a Chicago private investigator was involved in Catholic scandals beginning in the 1980s.

"I became involved in the priest-pedophilia scandal because of the abuse of a seven-year-old son of a mutual friend of mine and another policeman. This was in about 1988 or 1989 and was the Lutz-Northbrook case here in the Chicago diocese. While investigating Father Robert Lutz and former nun Alice Halpin, I came across many more similar cases," remembers Adema. "I investigated Halpin at the parish school where she had served as the grammar school principal. In so doing, I met a then-adult young black man who had related to me he had been abused by Halpin as a child. Due to poverty, this young man, David Nolan, was turned over to Pastor Father Victor Stewart to live in Stewart's rectory, where Stewart abused him over a long period of time. We interviewed Stewart who lied about the entire allegation."

After Nolan gave Adema his statement, the information was turned over to the Archdiocese, pursuant to their subpoena during discovery in the John Doe v. Robert Lutz civil lawsuit. The criminal case had been closed by the state's attorney. Later, Nolan changed his story and said his statement was a lie. But that turned out to be another lie.

Two years after recanting his first statement, Nolan called the father of the abused victim out of the blue and told him the following:

- He felt terribly guilty for lying and recanting his first abuse charges against Halpin and Lutz.
- He did so because Father Victor Stewart, whom he was still dependent upon for support, had forced him to do so.

---

52 Interviews with Michael Skinner, Summer 2002 and Email, October 21, 2002.

- Besides being coached by Stewart, he was coached how to recant by Father Raymond Goedert, the then-Vicar of Priests, whose job it was to cover-up pedophilia cases. Another "coach" was Bettina, an associate of James A. Serritella's at Mayer Brown & Platt, who was the diocesan attorney, known as the church's "Chicago pit-bull."

Adema and his colleagues taped Nolan's "confession" and took him to the Chicago Police and state's attorney. Adema and his colleagues were then threatened with prosecution for obstruction of justice by the Cook County state's attorney.

The father of the abused victim was charged with contempt of court in his son's civil lawsuit against the Catholic Church. He was accused of violating a court order forbidding him to contact Nolan. The attorneys at Mayer, Brown & Platt obtained that court order. Hence, the father of an abused child was fined.

Hank Adema and his colleague, Bill Callaghan, were then deposed by attorneys Bettina Getse and Patricia Bobb.

Adema later investigated Father Robert Mayer, who had molested children in one parish after another, and in one case molested a group of four teenage boys, including the son of Jeanne Miller, the Founder of Victims of Clergy Abuse Linkup.

Despite four boys being abused in the same place in the same way, in each other's presence, neither the Lake County nor Cook County State Attorney's Offices in Illinois would prosecute Mayer.

The stated excuse was "inconsistencies," like details about what color bathing suit Mayer was wearing at the time of the abuses. Father Mayer was then moved through several more parishes where he molested children repeatedly.

Finally, Mayer caught the media's attention when the late Cardinal Joseph Bernardin of Chicago suspended him from St. Odillo's parish in Cicero where he had been promoted to pastor.

The Archdiocese of Chicago called one of its usual "parish meetings" to mollify the parishioners and convince them nothing happened. It was presided over by Vicar of Priests Bishop Goedert. Adema sneaked into this meeting with Jeanne Miller and Bill Callaghan. They kept asking questions from the audience about Mayer's history.

An "Archdiocesan psychologist" asked the school children to raise their hands if Mayer had abused them. One courageous girl publicly raised her hand.

"Well, now we know he likes girls as well as boys" Goedert's sarcastically remarked.

The media pressure ensued and resulted in the first criminal prosecution of a priest in Cook County in 1992 for abusing a 13-year-old girl. Mayer got three years in prison. By the time, Mayer died in 2019, 51 victims had come forward.

Protectors of children need to be creative and tenacious like Hank Adema and his colleagues were.

Father Norbert Maday was part of a group of over 20 priests, who became the subject of media attention in 1990-1991, when Cardinal Joseph Bernardin was forced to suspend or remove them. Despite many complaints and a long history of past child sex abuse complaints and transfers to new parishes the state's attorney refused to prosecute Maday.

Adema and his colleagues finally successfully prosecuted Maday in Wisconsin because he molested several Chicago youths in that jurisdiction. Maday was sentenced to 28 years in prison.

Father William Cloutier had molested two 11–12-year-old boys from Oak Forest, Illinois. Cloutier took them to his summer home 90 miles away in Putnam County, Illinois. He threatened them with a gun. Some of the children told their parents. The families called Oak Forest Police Department. The responding officer made a full report.

The next day, Police Chief Lexlaw told the reporting officer to "destroy all his paperwork – the church is going to handle it," Adema told me in a 2002 interview.

The Church sent Cloutier to the House of Affirmation in Whitinsville, Massachusetts for mental health reasons. House of Affirmations was another church dumping ground for perverted priests. Cloutier was treated for six months and reshuffled through Chicago parishes.

But, after the reporting officer had been told to destroy Cloutier's documentation, he had seen two priests meeting with the chief in his office so the reporting officer decided to keep his paperwork.

When Adema found out about the *order to destroy*, he made a cold call to the victim's mother and got the facts. He turned those facts over to Attorney Jeff Anderson, who filed a suit on behalf of the victims.

"Anderson got $300,000 for one kid," said Adema.

In the intervening 10 years, Cloutier stayed in various parishes, and even was made chaplain at University of Illinois, Chicago Circle. He was finally removed in 1991. The Church had been fully aware that Cloutier had been molesting children since 1976, one year after his ordination.

While the Church hierarchy was getting publicity appointing lay members to their diocesan boards after the implosion of sex scandals in 2002, their record of accomplishment was poor. In most parishes, where the actual abuse was occurring, the laity had no power independent of the clergy.

"They are a farce. The board members have never sat down and interviewed one victim. The church plays the stall game with all the victims and all cases are handled by a church person who writes up a summary of the allegations and if forced might fax them to some of the board members for a response. It is a total farce and controlled completely by the church," said Adema in a 2002 interview. [53]

The abuse was never confined to just America.

"A 1,029-page report of the official inquiry into Mount Cashel Irish Christian Brothers in Canada concludes sexual abuse at the orphanage in the 1970s was covered up by a deputy justice minister and the police chief. Retired Ontario Judge Samuel Hughes cited collusion and disdain for sex offenders and advised that public funds not be wasted in treating "people animated by evil."

"The Justice Department interfered when an inquiry was made into abuse in 1975, although ample evidence was found to charge Christian Brothers. Abuse was occurring long before then."[54]

Statutes of limitations have played a huge role in terms of prosecutions. For example, in Indiana, child abuse cases that occurred before 1988 could not be

---

[53] Interview, Hank Adema, November 7; Email, November 9, 2002.

[54] http://report.ca/archive/report/20020513/p45i020513f.html.

prosecuted. Under the law in 2002, victims had five years to report the incidents. If incidents had occurred after 1988, charges could be filed against the predator only up to when the victim was 31 years old. [55]

U.S. Attorney Jeffrey Anderson, who has relentlessly helped victims/survivors described the topic of Statute of Limitations, as the "Eleventh Commandment," – the church's "shield and sword."

"The church and offenders have successfully hid behind the Statute of Limitations which has been the major barrier to prevention, healing, and justice. Victims of abuse by trusted authority figures suffer in secrecy, silence, and shame – overwhelmed with confusion and blaming themselves – rendered helpless to stop it, much less report it to others or even realize the acts are abusive! Moreover, the victimized child is convinced that no one would believe them anyway and would no doubt suffer grievous spiritual punishment for even suggesting the priest had offended! The clerical culture itself has created an atmosphere of emotional duress like no other which overlays the actual duress by the secretive and trusted offender…existing U.S. state laws remain the primary barrier to justice…," wrote Anderson over 20 years ago. [56]

Anderson had successfully argued against the statutes of limitations in three cases by 2002. One was in Los Angeles and two were in Minnesota, which resulted in jury verdicts for the victims up to $30 million, but Anderson had been blocked in New York courts by that time.

In 1991, Anderson tried to sue the late Reverend Bruce Ritter of Covenant House in New York City on allegations of sexual abuse. Courts rejected the suit. Anderson said it was "because we didn't have sufficient basis to prove the fraudulent concealment."[57] The New York Statute of Limitations required an individual who had claimed that he was abused to file a suit no later than the age of 21 years of age.

---

[55] O'Brien, Gwen, Tribune Staff Writer, *Experts: Traumatized Abuse Victims May Not Tell for Years,* September 30, 2002.

[56] Anderson, Ibid, pp. 8.

[57] DePalma, Anthony, New York Times, *Suit Says 42 Were Abused by Clergymen,* October 16, 2002.

In October 2002, Michael Dowd, a New York attorney, filed a suit challenging state law hoping that his "fraudulent concealment" case would succeed. Dowd represented 42 adults who claimed that 12 priests and one religious brother groped, raped, and abused them when they were children. Dowd sued the 12 priests, the brother, and the Diocese of Brooklyn, which was overseen by Bishop Thomas V. Daily, a priest formerly under the auspices of Cardinal Bernard Law in Boston.

Because these alleged crimes had happened almost 50 years earlier, Dowd had hoped to circumvent the statute of limitation at the time of filing in October 2002. Dowd argued that church officials had threatened the victims and their families, and made intentionally misleading statements to them, which had prevented the parties from filing until 2002.

Dowd said that the Church's actions of suppressing information was equal to having "no legal right to avail themselves of the Statute of Limitations to avoid responsibility for the acts of the people they let run loose as sexual predators in the Diocese of Brooklyn for 40 to 50 years." [58]

"The men who have done this – not only the abusers but the facilitators – are outlaws who have attempted to hijack the Catholic Church," said Dowd in 2003.

By that time, Dowd had discovered a secret bank account called the Good Shepherd Fund, which bought victims' silence.

Dowd is one of the most formidable attorneys who has successfully helped victims and survivors. He is legally strategic. In one deposition, he listened to a bishop who was part of several dioceses' coverups claim that bishops were "independent contractors."

---

[58] DePalma, Anthony, New York Times, *Suit Says 42 Were Abused by Clergymen,* October 16, 2002, Of the 42 plaintiffs, 26 claim to have been abused by James T. Smith, 71, either at Holy Trinity Parish in Queens or in one of his other parishes from 1960 to 1977. Although most were boys, four women say they were abused by Smith – some as young as seven years of age. Dowd will try to prove that Daily and his predecessors knew for 20 years that Smith was a child molester and continued to move him from parish to parish and did not report him to the Queen's District Attorney's office, where Smith worked in the domestic violence unit until April 2002 when he was put on administrative leave.

As Dowd said one time in an interview with Ronnie Elridge, "No Catholic on earth believes that."

The bishop who asserted that argument was Cardinal Edward Egan, who had presided over the Bridgeport, Connecticut, and New York dioceses.

But even when the victims' attorneys were able to legally pass the test of the Statute of Limitations, the legal hurdles continued.

There was "the delicate interplay of the First Amendment with the imposition of civil liability," victims' lawyer Jeff Anderson claimed.

"Church defendants routinely asserted the First Amendment (Free Exercise and Establishment Clause) as an absolute barrier to discovery and liability. Rarely have such broad and bold assertions been well received by the courts. Fortunately, most courts have concluded churches do not enjoy anomalous immunity for the sins of the fathers in causing secular harm to children and vulnerable adults – nor should they! Many courts including the Supreme Court have held that secular misconduct can be regulated if subject to neutral principles in application. Only two courts have quite shockingly stretched the First Amendment to insulate churches against civil liability altogether." [59]

Anderson elaborated further on the "Free Exercise Clause."

"Churches often argue that claims for negligent supervision and retention are prohibited because such an inquiry violates the Free Exercise Clause of the First Amendment. By so claiming, the Churches corporations are claiming that they have an absolute right under the free exercise clause of the First Amendment to employ anyone it wants as a minister, regardless of whether this employment and lack of supervision causes foreseeable harm to third parties. That is simply not the law.

"The free exercise clause of the First Amendment of the United States Constitution does not bar claims of negligent supervision and retention. As the Supreme Court has more recently said:

"We have never held that an individual's religious beliefs excuse him from compliance with an otherwise valid law prohibiting conduct that the State is free

---

[59] See Gibson v. Brewer, 952 S.W.2d 239 (mo. 1997); *Pritzlaff v. Archdiocese of Milwaukee*, 533 N.W.2d 780 (Wis. 1995).

to regulate. On the contrary, the record of more than a century of our free exercise jurisprudence contradicts that proposition...Can a man excuse his practices to the contrary because of his religious belief? To permit this would be to make the professed doctrines of religious belief superior to the law of the land, and in effect to permit every citizen to become a law unto himself. [60]

"Generally, religious organizations are liable for their torts.[61] Therefore, it is well established that the First Amendment "right of free exercise does not relieve an individual or religious organization of the obligation to comply with a 'valid and neutral law of general applicability on the ground that the law proscribes (or prescribes) conduct that his religion prescribes (or proscribes)." Smith, 494 U.S. at 879. Negligent employment tort law is "valid and neutral law of general applicability" to all employers. A plaintiff simply seeks application of this law to a church in the same manner it is applied to all employers."

But even if one were to successfully apply all the laws, both civil and criminal, it does not mean that children are going to be protected in the future. The one case in point, which proves that even the secular laws need a drastic overall is the infamous Father Gilbert Gauthe case of 1984, which landed on Father Tom Doyle's doorstep in the 1980s.[62]

Gauthe pled guilty and was imprisoned. He was supposed to receive counseling for his so-called sexual addiction. He was supposed to be an incarcerated criminal, but because the presiding judge's relative knew Gauthe's relative, Gauthe was often granted furloughs to see his mother.

---

[60] *Employment Div. Dept. of Human Resources of Or.*, 494 U.S.872, 878, 100 S. Crt. 1595, 1600, 188 L. Ed. 2d 876 (1990).

[61] *Strock v. Pressnell*, 38 Ohio St.3d 207, 527 N.E.2d 1245, 1237-38 (Ohio 1988); *Rayburn v. Gen. Conference of Seventh Day Adventists*, 772 F.2d 1164, 1171 (4th Cir. 1985); *Moses v. Diocese of Colorado*, 863 P.2d 310 (Colo. 1993); Erickson v. Christenson, 781 P.2d 383 (Or. Ct. App. 1989).

[62] Gauthe first pled guilty in 1985 to 33 charges of child sexual abuse with 11 boys, but admitted that he molested dozens more. In exchange for pleading guilty, prosecutors gave him a free ride for any other charges involving children molested before 1985. In 1995, he was released after serving 10 years in prison of a 20 year sentence. Two years later he was charged for raping a 12-year-old girl in 1982. In 1996, he received seven years' probation for fondling a 3-year-old boy. He pled no contest to the child injury charge.

Then when Gauthe was freed from prison, he moved near Houston, Texas, where he did not have to register on the county sex registry even though he was a convicted sex offender in Louisiana.

Later, Gauthe was arrested for fondling a three-year-old boy. He pled guilty to a lesser crime, which did not require registering in Texas, and none of his Louisiana paperwork had been sent to the Texas authorities.

So, even though Gauthe was arrested, even after serving a decade in jail, and re-arrested, he never had to register on the Texas county sex registry.

That legal loophole was harmful. It made as much sense as an American convicted for raping a minor overseas and not requiring that person to register in the United States upon return.

To take this further to what is happening in the U.S. today with over 10 million illegals coming across the southern border since Joe Biden has been president - it makes no sense to allow those millions of immigrants into the U.S. not knowing who they are and if they have committed crimes against children overseas. It makes no sense that there is a movement in America in 2024 to get rid of sex registries or give a mild reprimand to pedophiles in states like Colorado and California even outside the Church. Matter of fact, Catholic priests who are not reported and hence, not tried or convicted, but evaluated at sex institutes do not have to register. Our policies to protect children are an abysmal failure and they have been for decades.

Benedictine Brother Richard Eckroth at St. John's Abbey in Collegeville, Minnesota was evaluated as a serial pedophile decades ago. His records were sent to his superior at the time he was released from St. Luke's Institute, where he was evaluated.

In 2002, I tracked down Eckroth in Minneapolis, and asked him directly, "Do you think God will forgive you for what you have done to children?"

"I pray every day that God will forgive me," he snapped at me.

Eckroth never had to register although his medical records could easily be interpreted as having been diagnosed as a serial pedophile.

Eckroth also had been under suspicion for the murder of two young girls who had been stabbed to death in 1974. Susanne Reker, 12-years-old, and her sister, Mary, then 15-years of age, were found in a remote quarry.

Eckroth received cover for decades. It has been estimated that the number of victims he abused exceeded 100. Eckroth's records at St. Luke's Institute nailed his lack of character as did his St. John's Abbey records.

Benedictine Brother Richard Eckroth at St. John's Abbey in Collegeville, Minnesota was a "danger" to children for decades. He died in 2015.

The day that I was at St. John's Abbey in 2002 and worked my way into the retirement/infirmary where Eckroth was housed, I was told that he would be brought to a sitting room late that morning after breakfast.

From a distance I saw him. He was about to take a sip of water as I approached him. He looked frail and his hands were shaking as he lifted the glass to his lips.

When I asked him if he thought God would forgive him is when he looked me dead in my eyes, and his hand stopped shaking. He looked absolutely frightened by the question. He had not lost his memory, but perhaps, he may have wished he had.

As we concluded this short interview because I was not supposed to be in that room, he said to me, "Please pray for my soul."

That said it all.

I was in the presence of evil.

Meet the 21st Century Monsters

THE INTERNET CHILD PORNOGRAPHERS

Sexual predators come in all sizes, ages, and ethnic groups. Some prey on infants, toddlers, and very young children. Others prefer adolescent teens or adults. They are heterosexual and homosexual. What makes sexual predator monsters of children so terrifying is that there are so many places and so many ways that he or she can hide in plain sight. And even more disturbing is that these predators are eager to share their vile passion with other like-minded perverted fiends. It cannot be overemphasized that sexual monsters cloaked in religious garments may be even more vile because they are wrapped "In the Name of God" vestments and nun habits.

One of the most disturbing tools of sexual predators is the consistent use of pornography to groom their young victims. Yes, grooming is real. Law enforcement, prosecutors, investigative journalists in this arena, as well as victims, know this to be factual no matter how many crazy political ideologues denounce the term.

Over the last two decades, the internet has become the Wild West where perverts discover like-minded perverts. They validate and empower each other to continue their perversions. The internet has become a fertile ground for abusing children. It is a cesspool and a clear and present danger to children worldwide as it has evolved into a sexual den of iniquity.

It will get worse in the future with the application of artificial intelligence, the movement to decriminalize and normalize pedophilia all wrapped up in the terminology of "minor attracted persons." Society has morphed even from denouncing and criminalizing female genital mutilation (FGM) to now legitimizing and pushing transgenderism operations onto children at a rapid speed of lightning that should shock the conscience of humanity. And it is happening over the internet.

The push to mutilate children based upon transgenderism ideology that results in life-changing decisions without parental consent is as harmful as the sexual trafficking and medical trafficking of perverted medical theories that abused billions as global medical guinea pigs for the COVID-19 mRNA shots. Those shots have been proven to be linked to cardio, neurological, and vascular injuries, and sudden deaths.

The U.S. Food and Drug Administration (FDA), National Institute of Health (NIH), National Institute of Allergy and Infectious Diseases (NIAID) and Centers for Disease Control and Prevention (CDC) have known about these COVID-19 injuries during the 2020 PHARMA clinical trials and since the rollouts of the COVID-19 shots.

COVID-19 vaccinated-injured reached out to these agencies. Some were asked to send their blood to the NIH, and some of the injured were even flown to the Washington, D.C. area and cared for on site.

I have interviewed COVID-19 vaccinated injured since early 2021. Many of them were employed by the health industry. They knew from their own professional experiences they had multiple injuries - cardio, vascular and neurological – although their colleagues studiously and intentionally refused to acknowledge the link between the shots and the injuries.

To date, as this book goes to print, none of those agencies have officially recognized the vascular and neurological injuries like they should even though Dr. Peter Marks, M.D. Ph.D. the director of the Center for Biologics Evaluation and Research (CBER) at the Food and Drug Administration, told one COVID-19 vaccination injured surgeon that he personally did recognize those injuries. But he told this same doctor that he "could not officially" recognize the vascular and neurological injuries.

The lack of ethics surrounding all these trafficking faces is massive on a scale that redefines the level of evil in this world.

When I first began investigating human trafficking in 2000, the elephant in the room was the internet. It is still today. With the growing onslaught and ever expansive nature of technology, evil has grown exponentially. Children cannot get away from the smut on the internet where the predators hang out.

In the spring of 2024, the Childlight Global Safety Institute at the University of Edinburgh released a global study, and according to Interpol, its findings amount to "a clear and present danger to the world's children." [63]

The Edinburgh researchers found that one in eight of the world's children has been victims of non-consensual talking, sharing and exposure to sexual images and videos during 2023-2024. That equals about 302 million children globally.

About 12.5% of children globally have been subject to online solicitation – unwanted sexual talk including, but not limited to non-consensual sexting, sexual questions, and sexual act requests by adults and other youths.

These acts include sextortion where predators demand money to keep images private, including those created by Artificial Intelligence (AI) deepfake technology.

The Edinburgh study concluded that American children are at a particular elevated risk.

Edinburgh University's Childlight Initiative, which has aimed to understand the prevalence of child abuse, includes a new global index, Into The Light, which has found that one in nine men in the U.S. (almost 14 million) admitted online offenses against children.

But these horrible statistics are not limited just to American men. Surveys found that 7% of British men, or 1.8 million, admitted to the same, as did 7.5% of Australian men.

The study found that many of these men have admitted they would commit physical sexual offenses against children if they thought their acts would never be exposed.

"This is a staggering scale that in the U.K. alone equates to forming a line of male offenders that could stretch all the way from Glasglow to London – or fill Wembley Stadium 20 times over. Child abuse material is so prevalent that files are on average reported to watchdogs and policing organizations once every second. This is a global health pandemic that has remained hidden for far too long. It

---

[63] https://www.edu.ac.uk/news/2024/scale-of-online-harm-to-children-revealed-in-globa

occurs in every country; it is growing exponentially, and it requires a global response. We need to act urgently. Children cannot wait," responded Paul Stanfield, CEO of Childlight.

The issue affects children "in every classroom, in every school, in every country," said Professor Deborah Fry of the international child protection at Edinburgh University. "These are not harmless images, they are deeply damaging, and the abuse continues with every view and the failure of taking down this abusive content."

"Online exploitation and abuse are a clear and present danger to the world's children, and traditional law enforcement approaches are struggling to keep up," said Stephen Kavanagh, Interpol's Executive Director. "We must do much more together at a global level, including specialist investigator training, better data sharing and equipment to effectively fight this pandemic and the harm it inflicts on millions of young lives around the world."

Equally horrifying are Google and META spearheading a push to kill New York legislation aimed at protecting children online with a lobbying effort poised to spend $1 million.

A group of BIG TECH firms, advocacy groups and companies from other sectors have, at the time of this book's publication, spent over $800,000 lobbying New York lawmakers to kill the two high-profile bills – The Stop Addictive Feeds Exploitation (SAFE) for Kids Act and the New York Child Data Protection Act.

The intention of the SAFE Act is to crack down on addictive recommendation algorithms used by social media apps by requiring them to provide default chronological feeds for users 18 years of age or younger unless they receive parental consent. It would also allow parents to impose time limits on social media use and in-app notifications.

META has claimed it supports U.S. federal and age requirements rather than a state-by-state legislative measures.

The Child Data Protection Act in New York would block apps from collecting or selling the users' personal or location data of those under 18 years of age unless they consented. Children under 13 years of age would need a parent's consent.

Mothers Against Media Addiction and the New York United Teachers Union are supporting the bills.

The irony of this lobbying fight has revealed the relentless hypocrisy of the TECH firms. On the one hand, while BIG TECH has profited off their relationship with PHARMA during COVID-19 era while receiving PHARMA advertising money, they have been partners with PHARMA and governments in the acts of censoring anyone who challenged their COVID-19 narratives.

Now, with these two New York bills, tech firms are citing fears that this legislation would stifle freedom of speech, online privacy for teens, limit internet access for migrants and other underserved communities, and essentially disable algorithms intended to crack down on hate speech.

What a hypocritical position after witnessing their COVID-19 censorship campaigns!

The New York financial disclosures show that META, Facebook, and Instagram's parent company, which already faces a massive federal lawsuit over allegations it has profited from apps that fuel teenagers' mental health crises, has spent the most money on lobbying efforts to derail these New York tech bills and other related matters.

META's response to why they do not want state-by-state laws is almost hilarious it is such a transparently ignorant statement.

"Teens move interchangeably between many websites and apps, and different laws in different states will mean teens and their parents have inconsistent experiences online," a META spokesperson wrote in a statement.

Like the public is to believe that Mark Zuckerberg cares about the world's children?

Nearly 15 years ago, I realized who Mark Zuckerberg was when Jim Gamble, the then CEO of the UK's Child Exploitation and Online Protection (CEOP), met with Facebook executives. This meeting took place several years before Facebook had reached its first billion users in 2012.

For over two decades, law enforcement agencies focused on child protection online have known about the connection between the internet and human trafficking and child abuse.

Gamble, who was the wind behind the sail that launched the Virtual Global Task Force (VGT) circa 2003, was a force to be reckoned with then and still is today. Gamble and four other international heads of these child protection agencies created VGT because BIG TECH lawyers in the U.S. operated much like the Catholic Church diocesan lawyers. They refused to turn over evidence to law enforcement.

On an overly concerning level, BIG TECH lawyers cited a lack of jurisdiction to the foreign law enforcement investigators. It was a nightmare for law enforcement whose only goals were to save children online and prosecute the perverts who rape and prey upon children, and to ultimately dismantle these perverted criminal syndicates.

So, five international law enforcement officials created VGT. It was the first international law enforcement task force created without an Act of Congress or an Act of Parliament. The five agencies represented were from the U.K., U.S., Australia, Canada, and New Zealand. VGT created an icon that looked like the old CBS network's "eye" icon.

VGT today is an international alliance of 15 "dedicated law enforcement agencies working alongside Affiliate members from private industry and non-governmental organizations to tackle the threat of child sexual abuse (CSA)," reads their website page.

The purpose of Gamble's meeting with Facebook employees around 2009 was to ask Facebook to place the VGT icon on every Facebook page so children – whether bullied or solicited sexually could turn to law enforcement, especially if they feared getting into trouble with their parents.

I have known Gamble and these law enforcement officials for over 20 years. They are committed to the protection of children.

When Gamble shared with me Facebook's response after that meeting, my jaw dropped.

"This is expensive real estate," Gamble reported.

In other words, Facebook refused Gamble's suggestion to put the VGT icon on every page to alert children there was a place to protect them online. Under Zuckerberg's leadership, either Facebook did not care, or the company intentionally refused to understand how the internet was harming children. The evidence was overwhelming at that point in time well before Facebook landed on the scene in 2004. Online crimes against children were found in the late 1990s when Craigslist was created.

Suffice it to state – in my honest opinion – Mark Zuckerberg was either too stupid to grasp the added value of child protection built into his business model, or he put greed above the protection of children and did not care.

So, what does this internet landscape have to do with the Roman Catholic Church?

A lot.

Since 2002, the Church has pretended to handle its sex scandals. The global domino effects across Catholic dioceses and religious orders have been devastating. The revelations have proven the institution has failed miserably. It has cost the Catholic Church billions of dollars and even bankrupt some dioceses. The depth and breadth of its institutional depravity has seeped out over the last twenty plus years and revealed what the institution has known for centuries. Their coverup has caused their own scandals.

The Church has pulled out the stops even partnering with some of BIG TECH and hosted conferences at the direction of the Vatican while knowing that among its perverted were cases connected to online sexual solicitation and possession of child pornography.

As recent as 2023, the Vatican hosted a conference on online child sexual abuse. Lurking in the background were Catholic cases connected to internet solicitations and what the civilized world calls "possessions of child pornography."

Bishopsaccountability.com, a U.S. based watchdog is relentless in their collection of information on the Church's perverts and those who have covered up the Church's crimes.

Although the Catholic Church priests' cases have involved the use of pornography in the past, their cases of priests using the internet has grown over the years.

One of the more scandalous cases involved a seasoned Vatican diplomat named Monsignor Carlo Alberto Capella. At the time he was caught in 2017, he had been assigned to the papal nunciature in the U.S. In short, the Vatican embassy in Washington, D.C. across the street from the vice-president's residence, which is next door to the British embassy on what is called embassy row in the nation's capital. Capella had been posted there for about a year.

He had previously served at the papal nunciatures in India and Hong Kong. Following those assignments, he became a Monsignor under the Chaplain of His Holiness and in 2011 served in the Vatican's Secretariat of State.

The U.S. Department of State informed the Vatican in 2017 that Capella was under investigation for possession and sharing child pornography. Canadian officials had issued a warrant for his arrest. Those investigators alleged that while visiting Canada in December 2016 Capella was in possession of child pornography and shared it. Because he held a diplomatic passport, he was immune from prosecution in the U.S. Pope Francis recalled Capella, 50, to the Vatican.

In 2018, the Vatican court successfully prosecuted Capella and sentenced him to five years in the Vatican prison and fined him US $5,833. He was found guilty of possession and distributing "a large quantity of child pornography."

During his sentencing, he referred to his possession and distribution of this smut as "a bump in the road in my priestly life."

Simultaneous to Capella's initial investigation in 2017, the Vatican was hosting its own "Child Dignity in the Digital World" conference that October in Rome. His case was a glaring embarrassment for the Vatican's Gregorian University's Center for Child Protection, which was hosting it in partnership with WePRO-TECT Alliance.

By 2021, Capella was allowed to leave the Vatican prison during the day to work in an office selling papal blessings.

Some of WePROTECT's alliance members include TikTok, Yahoo, META, Microsoft, Google, Grindr, and other internet companies, the very companies that want to self-police and create algorithms that have introduced the world to the new platforms normalizing porn.

It is important for the public to understand conceptually as gross as it is what today's internet pornography is compared to over twenty years ago according to law enforcement. In 2000, most of the internet pornography was 75% erotica and 25% horrible smut.

Today, erotica is around 20% per law enforcement officials who cover this beat.

In 2000, Homayra Sellier, the Founder of Innocence in Danger, nailed it when she raised her voice and said the term "child pornography" is an intentional mislabeling. These are crime scenes, and we need to call it "pedo-criminality."

In 2000, cybercrime law enforcement officials were adamant that there was a growing higher demand for younger victims of child abuse.

Nearly 25 years later, unfortunately their statements have been proven prophetic.

The International Centre for Missing and Exploited Children (ICMEC) released figures in 2022 that should be a massive wakeup call.

More than 800 million children globally are actively using social media alone. Children represent one-third of all internet users.

When I initially investigated the ties between human trafficking in 2000, there were on average 39,000 annual reports to the National Center for Missing & Exploited Children (NCMEC) based out of the U.S., which is the grandfather group to ICMEC.

According to ICMEC's 2022 report there were 32 million reports to NCMEC of "suspected online child sexual exploitation." They included "88 million child sexual abuse material (CSAM) images and videos."

INHOPE is a global network of internet hotlines combatting online child sexual abuse material. In 2022, ICMEC reported that INHOPE's members reported that 84% of the 587,852 suspected CSAM reports by INHOPE members were "never-before-seen material of child abusive images." Within those reports, nine in 10 victims depicted in these sexual abuse images were victims three years of age to twelve years of age. One percent of the 587,852 images reported by INHOPE members were infants, "0 – 2 years of age."

This level of perversion needs to be categorially recognized as not only criminal, but unacceptable and abhorrent human behavior in civilized society.

As a journalist, in 2000, I was brought into the Hague Porn Unit and educated about what the situation was then. I was shell-shocked and have been speaking out about the internet for almost a quarter of a century.

It is time the elders and adults in the room stand up and speak out against those in the TECH world. If not, we are raising generations of perverts and pedophiles.

Allow me to be clear – "child pornography" should never even be an acceptable term. That term dilutes the very nature of reality of what these images are.

As Homayra Sellier said years ago, we need to call this "pedo-criminality images."

For anyone to conclude these pedo-criminality images – real or virtual – are victimless crimes is ignorant and intellectually dishonest.

"Recent Catholic Church abuse cases have been documented for decades. While child abuse is not unique to the Catholic Church, the prevalence and handling of such cases within the Church has drawn significant attention and criticism. As more survivors came forward within the Catholic Church, their institutional abuse was not limited to one country and regions," states Homayra Sellier. "We have witnessed severe and long-lasting psychological effects on children, who have suffered sexual abuse by a person of faith. Common impacts include PTSD, depression, anxiety, guilt, shame, trust issues, sexual and emotional difficulties, and behavioral problems."

In 1997, Peter Jackson, an Australian rugby star, at the age of 33, died from a heroin overdose. He was a football star turned media celebrity. What the public did not realize was that he sought help repeatedly for drug addiction, manic depression, and shared with his doctors the sexual abuse he endured as a schoolboy at the Southport School in 1979 and 1980 at the hands of his teacher, Catholic Marist Brother Ossie McNamara.

Just weeks before Jackson died, he gave his attorney a synopsis of the abuse at the time he was 16 years of age. Jackson was tormented by his memories of abuse. No matter how much fame and happiness he had in his life, he could not block out the pain. Following his death, the private school settled with his widow, Siobhan.[64]

"The government is committed to tackling child abuse in any form – pedophiles and child pornographers must not be able to use new technologies with impunity. What is illegal off-line is also illegal online. However, if changes in the law prove necessary to prosecute and deter specific forms of online child abuse, the

---

[64] Eros Foundation, *Hyprocrites,* April 2000.

government will act," said British Home Office Secretary Jack Straw in March 2001 when announcing a task force to fight pedophiles' use of the internet. 65

The late Judith A. Reisman, President of The Institute for Media Education, wrote in 2002,

Eroticized violence by and to children and juveniles continues to explode as more and more youngsters obtain on-line access. In fact, The National Coalition for the Protection of Children & Families, in its brochure "Tips and Talking Points: An Age-Appropriate Guidebook for Discussing The Harms of Pornography With Your Family" states, "The San Diego Police department in California reports that solicitation of minors for sex online is growing at a rate of 1000% per month."

This increase in child sexual solicitation should be seen in concert with the fact that "stealth" sites seduce children into viewing pornography and that "80% of [children's] first-time hits on pornography sites are accidental." That is, the internet serves as a seduction device for trapping children into sexual conduct via pornography, and then sends the "pimps" from the street to recruit them into deviant conversation and too often later, into injurious, even fatal sexual conduct.[66]

---

[65] Veysey, Wayne, PA News, *Taskforce Launched to Combat Internet Paedophiles*, March 28, 2001.

[66] Reisman, Judith A., Ph.D., *How the FBI and DOJ Minimize Child Sexual Abuse Reporting – An Examination of Relevant Child Abuse Data Suggesting That Reported Decreased Violence to Adults May be a Function of Unreported Increased Violence to Children – Interim Report for Review and Comment*, The Institute for Media Education, pp. 33. July 2002.

The Real Horrors:
Not for the Faint of Heart

Words are cheap if they do not expose the truth. Words and phrases such as, unlawful sexual intercourse, indecent assaults, child sex offenses, aggravated assault, and inappropriate touches and gross indecent acts do not even begin to describe the torture inflicted upon innocent children. Below are descriptions of torture. These are testimonies of child torture in Australia.

In **Australia, Albury residents** locked children in cellars and cattle yards. One young girl was held by other children over an ant's nest while ants stirred up and the child was belted. Another girl, 10, was tied to a tree by a nun.

Neerkol Sisters of Mercy – an 11-year-old boy was raped at least once a week by Father John B. Anderson until he left the home at age 14.

At notorious **St. Alipius, Christian Brothers** massaged the buttocks of an 11-year-old boy while making him recite Catholic catechism in class.

At St. Joseph's Christian Brothers children's home, the Christian Brothers were known as "Christian Buggers." There the children were often made to work barefoot and used as slave laborers. If even the slightest infraction of the rules occurred, the children were brutally beaten and flogged and starved or forced to scavenge food from pig bins. There were 40 brothers who allegedly raped boys aged 7 or 8 years of age. One priest had intercourse with 8 to 10 years old boys in the shower, bedroom, and car. The priests possessed child pornography. In 1994, Catholic historian Brother Barry Coldrey claimed that there was evidence of sex rings at Castledare in early 1960s. Children were molested in confessional boxes.

The **Christian Brothers** were so barbaric that they demanded that the boys insert their penises in electric shock machine to control bedwetting. There were accusations of false imprisonment. Assaults were disguised as horseplay while the children's genitals and buttocks were fondled. Dirty language was used to entice them as well as alcohol, cigarettes, and pornographic videos before masturbating them and engaging in oral sex.

One young girl's genitals were fingered as the priest rubbed up against her until he ejaculated. One victim became pregnant, and the priest gave her $200 towards the cost of an abortion when she was a junior in high school. One priest took a boy for driving lessons before he masturbated him in the car. One priest warned a victim to "keep quiet [about the abuse] or you won't go to heaven."

One **Monsignor** had intercourse with 14 boys and two girls for 14 years. One priest who was the **Archbishop's secretary** sexually assaulted an emotionally impaired man. One priest persuaded a girl of 15 to have sex with him by telling him that he was terminally ill and gave her a copy of "Lolita." One priest beat, punched, kicked, and sexually abused boys. One priest digitally raped a boy on his 13th birthday and asked his victim to thank his mother for him.

The Chaplain at Neerkol Sisters of Mercy children's home raped a 14-year-old girl for 12 months. One priest at a boarding school would visit the dormitories late at night five times a week and masturbate sleeping boys. One priest asked a woman to supply him with menstrual blood. One priest who was a local celebrity on radio with a newspaper column pinned down one boy violently with his forearm as he fondled the boy. One victim described a predator as an "animal, criminal, pedophile...yet priests and bishops gathered at his funeral and said he was a great priest." The priest was called the "Groper." One boy was caned at 13 and his hand was permanently injured. One victim chose to leave school at the age of 13 to avoid abuse.

Sisters of Mercy victims were flogged, half starved, humiliated, and kept in solitary confinement. One priest gave his victim a penance of "three Hail Mary's" after his sexual assaults. One priest had sex with Asian boys in Thailand and bragged about it in front of 14 Sunday lunch guests, and then proceeded to threaten a guest who called him a "church-going pedophile." The witness was found dead two days later. One predator locked a victim in a classroom during lunch recesses before fondling his victim's genitals and anus for about 20 minutes on at least 40 occasions. One priest had sexually tortured over 100 children. One priest had oral sex in a school attic, on bus trips, and in his flat, and on retreats.

One priest forced a victim to fondle his genitals while he was swimming. One priest stood naked at the gate of his home while children walked to school. One priest used a girl's hand to rub his penis while the priest was talking to her parents in the front seat of the car. Other priests sodomized victims repeatedly. One priest who fondled and masturbated at least 10 altar boys – as young as 10 – not only admitted it but said that "they wanted it." One priest bribed victims with alcohol and cigarettes before engaging in groping, fondling, and touching boys during choir practice, swimming lessons, driving lessons, and on camping trips. The same priest inserted a thermometer into the anus of a boy during a first aid course and molested another boy while waiting for a church service.

A Catholic television priest made victims sodomize each other before sodomizing a younger boy and told that victim that he "would go to hell" and God would punish him if he complained about the assault to anyone. One predator raped a young girl after giving her parents expensive gifts and accompanying them on a trip. Other priests persuaded parents to let daughters spend the night in the rectory before abusing them sexually. On a camping trip, a priest stripped a boy and fondled him. Another boy was raped in his bedroom in front of the altar where he prayed.

St. Joseph's Sisters of Mercy children's home residents were repeatedly sodomized and fondled by priests, with the nuns' knowledge. Others were whipped until they bled. One nun thrust a hot poker on a child's back to "exorcise the devil." Others were locked in cellars. One victim had his leg thrust in a boiling pot by a nun. Children who ran away – when caught – were stripped naked in front of the entire assembly, and flogged. Others were forced to brush teeth with charcoal and to fight with each other on Sundays. Some were lent to pedophiles on Christmas with the nuns' permission because the pedophiles made donations to the home. Others lured victims with pocket money and the opportunity to watch television in exchange for sex. One used Vaseline on victims 'penises and then digitally raped them. Some priests silenced victims by telling them that "no one would believe them," or "no one would believe a ward of the state."

One of the most notorious pedophiles in Australia – **Father Gerald Francis Ridsdale** – who was finally sacked by the Pope in 1993 – targeted victims in toilets, showers, beds, and in confessional boxes. He carried a jar of Vaseline in his car and once rewarded a victim with a Eucharistic host after victimizing him while driving him home from Mass. Another of Ridsdale's victims underwent anal surgery after being sodomized by him. He even assaulted a girl of 10 after officiating at her father's funeral. One victim reached out to Ridsdale after being assaulted by another priest and then Ridsdale molested the victim again in a bike shed.

Another priest enticed victims with pornographic videos and magazines before orally and anally assaulting them. Another priest was finally removed from a parish after 50 people complained that the priest was taking children out of the school for a one-on-one sex education course. One priest even used his black cassock as a veil for sexual assault. One priest groped boys behind his desk during religion classes and threatened to whip one victim when he complained. One child abuse activist said that **Christian Brothers in Australia** should be "disbanded" in the interests of child protection.

Coldrey described the **Society of St. Gerard Majella**, which was eventually closed in 1994 as "something of a pedophile organization managing a male harem."

St. John of God – a Catholic Order – paid $3.64 million after allegations were made against 20 brothers for assaulting 24 intellectually disabled boys aged 10 and over from 1968 – 1994 at St. John of God training farms and homes.

Brother Gregory Joseph Sutton fled Australia and was arrested in U.S. where he was principal of a Catholic school. He is called "one of Australia's most serial sex offenders against children." The presiding judge called him "evil," and said that nowhere were children safe from him. Sutton attacked children in classrooms, playgrounds, cars, caravans, bush land, victims 'homes, and in his own bedroom.

One 10-year-old boy at St. Mary's Christian Brothers children's home was targeted because he had blue eyes. The Christian Brothers predators competed to see who could rape the boy 100 times first. The boy was so traumatized that he beat his eyes so that they would not be blue. Some of the boys at St. Mary's were forced to masturbate animals or be hung upside down above a well. One priest raped children on school camping trips. Father James Barry Whelan – who was known by the late George Pell and his predecessor, Frank Little, for abusing children for over 40 years, kissed, petted, and engaged in oral sex during his pastoral visits to Catholic schools, at his rectory and in his apartment.

Ritual Abuse Torture

To shift the paradigm on how we view this issue, it is imperative that we name these crimes – sexual torture - and ask who are these perverts among us? Seemingly, they are a group of individuals who gain pleasure from inflicting pain. In laymen's terms, we call this sadistic behavior - *Ritual Abuse Torture.*

When we asked the survivors for their opinions about the term ritual abuse torture, they all responded with a definite, "Yes, they had been tortured." [67]

Although Margaret Smith's research [68] was focused on "off the street" ritual abuse-torture and the involvement of clergy as perpetrators, the reality is this off-street form of exploitation has revealed itself to be the common technique used by pedophilic priests. The hunting patterns of these pedophilic priests were to invade the homes of trusting and/or vulnerable families looking for their child victims. Priests have been also engaged in the on-street exploitation of children.[69]

On July 18, 2002, two prominent New Jersey Catholic priests were arrested in Montreal, Canada in the heart of Montreal's gay village – a mere mile away from where the Roman Catholic Church's – Vatican-sponsored - World Youth Day activities were being held. Pope John Paul II was the guest of honor.

Reverend Eugene Heyndricks, 60, of Guttenberg, New Jersey was assigned to St. John Nepomucene Church. He was charged with soliciting sex from an under-age prostitute. Reverend William Giblin, 70, former headmaster of Seton Hall prep school, was charged with pimping, which carried up to 10 years in prison.

---

[67] Email to Author from Jeanne Sarson and Linda MacDonald, October 2, 2002.

[68] Smith, Margaret, *Ritual Abuse – What it is, Why it happens, How to help*, Harper, San Francisco, 1993.

[69] Email to Author from Jeanne Sarson and Linda MacDonald, October 2, 2002.

According to Montreal Police Constable Ian Lafreniere, "They were in street clothes. We did not know they were priests until one of them started panicking and told us about it."

According to Lafreniere, their arrests helped Montreal investigators uncover a "massive" sex-ring operating in Montreal that had catered to U.S. pedophiles.

"There were hundreds of young males being sold through the ring, some as young as 14," said Lafreniere.

Another 32 people were arrested in a series of raids where teens had been forced to perform sex for $15 to $150. Investigators claimed that the ring was especially established for the *American market.*

"We are very saddened and appalled at this news. They have removed themselves [from service] pending the results of the investigation," said the spokesman for the Archdiocese of Newark, New Jersey at the time. Giblin and Heyndricks were released on $1,000 bail.[70]

In 1993, the Canadian government commissioned a study. It concluded that Canada recognized a problem of ritual torture in five provinces. For the decades after the release of that report, Jeanne Sarson and Linda MacDonald, two nurses from Nova Scotia, who are experts on "Ritual Abuse Torture," successfully accomplished getting the United Nations to recognize ritual abuse torture based upon their interviews,

Here are some interview excerpts:

- *The family had many rules and customs. For instance, there was the routine of having children assessed...two major assessments at birth and at age seven...and others [ages] in between. I remember a man, the Assessor, who I think was my grandmother's brother from the States, doing an assessment on me as I stood naked and quiet on the chair while he checked me over...all body parts...mentioned men wanted children who were virgins – orally and anally.[71]*

---

[70] Massarella, Linda, New York Post, *Priests' Arrests Exposes Boy Ring,* July 29, 2002/

[71] Email to Author, October 2, 2002; Excerpt of an interview by Jeanne Sarson and Linda MacDonald of Hope, a victim, speaking of her experience of ritual abuse-torture.

- *Bungee cords, handcuffs, kiddie cuffs, ropes, whips that did not cut but left purple welts, all stuff Ken said he brought from Detroit.*

- *I went to the military base many times…my father worked on the base…they came to the store where my father rented me out to the military men.*

- *Extended family members would travel up from Florida and take part in the pedophilic family rituals.[72]*

- *Perpetrators inflict overwhelming physical pain on their victims – infants, toddlers, child, youth, or the "captive" adult – using brutally inhumane acts.*

- *I can still hear my father saying to the man who rented me; bring her back when you are done.[73]*

- *I enjoy seeing the terror in your eyes, bitch? That is why Ken seldom covered my eyes, he wanted the pleasure of seeing the terror his torturing created.[74]*

It is imperative that one understands that there is a co-culture living in the secular world – some dressed like civilians and others draped in clericalism who survive by inflicting pain upon others – even the most vulnerable of human beings – the youngest of children.

As difficult as it is to grasp that there are those among us who rape babies, infants, toddlers, and young children, it is even further unfathomable to comprehend there are those who consciously, and without a conscience, get pleasure from inflicting this pain.

---

[72] Email to Author, October 2, 2002; Excerpt of an interview by Jeanne Sarson and Linda MacDonald of Phoenix, who shared this information about her ritual abuse torture with a friend before her death.

[73] Sara commenting on her experience of off-street pedophilic exploitation, age approximate 18 months (excerpt from Pleasure and Pain, 2002.

[74] Dawn, in her mid-twenties, sharing her experiences of being held captive, of being tortured, enslaved, and exploited into the sex trade by her husband and gang, excerpt from Pleasure and Pain, 2002.

The Victims' Voices:
In Their Own Words

As the 2002 Roman Catholic Church scandal exploded in the United States, a man, who was working as a television repair man in the Midwest, found himself surrounded by the unfolding story while he worked. As a result, his childhood memory became a floodgate of his own horrific sexual torture by Catholic priests.

It was so vividly evil that he contacted three of his brothers and discovered they too had been abused by the same priest – the man who used to visit their family home on weekends and sometimes take the boys back to his rectory 80 miles away. How did this come to be?

Their step-grandmother was his housekeeper. This man contacted me and told me about one trip he took with this priest on a drive to the rectory. The boy was alone with the priest, who fed him some kind of "peppermint" drink which made him very tired. They stopped along the way in the woods.

There they met two other men dressed as priests. A blanket was laid on the ground. Then three German Shepard puppies were taken from a car. The priests slashed the throats of the puppies and poured their blood on the blanket, pulled down the pants of the seven-year-old boy, laid him on the blanket, and then each took turns anally raping the boy as they chanted something which the boy remembers as Latin.

As his memory unfolded, he was not able to cope and lost his job. Then he contacted a Bishop's office in the Midwest. The church agreed to compensate him with meager funds, i.e., paying his rent and paying for his therapy.

By April 2002, the victim had to be hospitalized. He was put on several SSRI drugs, which did not help his situation. He was overmedicated. After he was released, he was prescribed more SSRI drugs by an out-patient doctor who saw him for fifteen minutes. He then saw a second out-patient doctor, who got him off all the drugs and put him on a new drug – remeron. Again, this victim did not feel good. By the time he contacted me, his wife was very worried. Only after several consultations, did he get off all the drugs, and feel better. When he was on the drugs, he felt like he "was losing his mind."

He decided to contact the chancery for more help and was told that they were not going to do anything more and that if he had a problem with that decision, he should contact their attorney on the other side of the state, in St. Louis, Missouri.[75]

A Letter to Archbishop Roman Arrieta Villalobos from an American who was abused as a child in Costa Rica by Father Julio Cesar Lopez

May 21, 2002

Archbishop Roman Arrieta Villalobos

Archbishop of San Jose

San Jose, Costa Rica

Dear Archbishop Roman Arrieta:

It was a pleasure to receive your letter dated May 11, 2002…I accept the apologies of the Catholic Church from you. There are a few things that I would like to clarify. The reason for my letter to you was to try to start a dialogue of change within the Roman Catholic Church in Costa Rica, and to make sure that these sins and assaults against children are not repeated by anyone, especially Priests.

In your letter you write in very simple terms as if you were talking down to one of your lowly servants, and maybe you were misled because a copy of the   original letter went to the media. I wrote and copied the media because I needed to make sure that the letter I sent you would not get "LOST."

The reason that I cannot go to Church is much deeper than a simplistic approach of just going back, I am sure that in your schooling you have studied psychological behavior, so my attitude should not be a surprise to you, but I will explain.

When I go to Church the first thing that comes to mind is what the priest on the altar is thinking privately. Needless to say, these thoughts are not pretty. For me to

---

[75] Interviews with Tim Schroeder Summer of 2002.

remain sane I cannot expose myself to this type of thought process and I realize that I may never reach this particular goal of attending church regularly again.

I attend only when there are weddings or funerals because I have no other choice and I do not want to explain myself to the rest of the world, and I do it because my wife asks me, although I have to walk out sometimes before I start vomiting. God will not let down. He knows what type of life I lead, and I strive to be the best Catholic, in my thoughts, in my words and deeds, at work and at home. My Communion is my family, my children, and my grandchildren.

I have forgiven Father Julio Cesar Lopez. I know that he lived in his own hell, and he was repentant of what he did. And there is nothing else I can do, for my wellbeing. Nevertheless, the attitude of the Catholic Church is not only to forgive, but to hide these perpetrators, and that is totally wrong.

It is fine for the perpetrator to be forgiven by the church and by you, but you, as a human being and the trustee of thousands of souls, need to advise the authorities that this happened and let the law take over. If this person is innocent, so be it. If not, then even though he is forgiven by God, he should pay the price of the law just like any sinner.

This change of attitude will give the Catholic Church more credibility and will attract more to the priesthood and add to the flock that are getting disenchanted with the Catholic Church. I am sure that you have seen a decline in revenue from the Sunday masses already.

There are thousands of people on my email list from the Survivors Network that are victims of priests all over the world. These people are living their own hell, with no one to listen to them, with no one to take back the intrusions of a trusted individual that used that position of trust to perpetrate a heinous crime. Luckily, I have been able to make sacrifices for me to pay my therapist bills and to get better. Others have not and gone on to commit crimes or worse yet, commit suicide.

This is not a casual happenstance in the world. The Catholic Church has a MAJOR problem that needs to be addressed and would be great if a person such as you would take the lead and convince the prelates that this is the correct course of action.

Here in Los Angeles, Cardinal Mahony is under tremendous scrutiny and every other Cardinal and Archbishop is in that position because they placed themselves in that position. They did not behave ethically as far as I am concerned.

Your policy should be to hand over any priest that conducts himself in an unlawful manner, and let the courts decide his fate. Just because they are priests, this does not make them unaccountable for their sins, unless you advocate that any pedophile if he is repentant be free in society. Priests do not live in a vacuum.

One victim is TOO MANY. And the tolerance you propose is ONE VICTIM IS OK, the second one will get the priest thrown out of the protection of the Church.

I sincerely hope you READ this letter for what it is, a letter from a victim that needs to know that the Roman Catholic Church is actually interested in the people they serve and not their clergy.

This letter is a pledge to you that I will continue with my quest to make sure the priests or any person of authority over children is TOTALLY accountable for their indiscretions, and Zero Tolerance is applied, not just that an act of contrition will totally forgive the lasting damage to a person such as myself.

We must remember the victims of these pedophiles. We suffer from the rest of our lives and the "forgiven" continue their life and go on to molest again. I can tell you, as many psychiatrists will, that there are NO ex-pedophiles in this world, just like there are no ex-alcoholics, and no ex-drug addicts.

In my letter, I never said that the Church was at fault for the sins of the other priests. You seem to have thought that. The fault of the church is with humans that commit human acts and does not want [them] to be accountable for it, and that is not an ethical way of living.

I am not the only victim in my family. My sisters are victims of Father Julio. My parents are victims. They all trusted Father Julio with all their secrets. In the case of my Mother, he was her confidant. He was the one that helped her with her marital problems, and I can tell you there were many between my parents.

I would be glad to continue this exchange of ideas, and I hope that we do.

Thanks for writing back, for taking the time off your busy day to read these letters.

Sincerely,

Ernest Aguilar

Walnut, California

Parents of Victims

Fred Reker, a Catholic Deacon, and father of six children,

It was not until this past spring (2002) when the priest sex abuse scandal began to unfold nationally that we learned the full measure of what had happened in our area, St. Cloud, Minnesota, years ago.

Four of our children had gone with Benedictine Monk, Fr. Richard Eckroth from St. John's Abbey, to a cabin in Northern Minnesota owned by the monks on two occasions in 1972. Three of our children were among the group on each occasion. It tears my heart now to think that we were so trusting and naïve to send what was most precious to us with this man for an overnight stay at a cabin far from home.

On each occasion Mass was said, and meals were shared…but our kids were also lured into a sauna and were told that they had to go into the sauna naked. Our oldest daughter at 13 refused to go in at all. The other three kept their bathing suits on and towels wrapped around themselves. Our children only began to tell the details of this a few years ago.

This spring we learned that Fr. Richard had taken 100's of kids up to this cabin over a period of six or seven years. These kids were between the ages of 7 and 13 years of age…both boys and girls. As the details began to open we clearly saw the pattern of pedophilia.

Two of our children were later murdered in 1974. Their murders are still unsolved. Our surviving children say they were not molested, but that the atmosphere was sexually charged and weird. Other kids reported being molested. Some kids reported having a good time. When our kids came back after the second trip they were so quiet, and seemed to be so relieved to be home, I decided "never again" would I let them go.

Rita, my wife, has covered everything we wanted to say about this whole scandal at St. John's. I would like to add, though, that after working at St. John's for 39 years and having been in the seminary there for 3 years, I am deeply hurt by all of this. I knew Fr. Eckroth personally very well. We were in class together for one year more than

50 years ago. I considered him to be a friend. As Rita wrote, we thought he was only taking a few children to the cabin, children of some of the St. John's employees. Some of these employees talked to me about how much fun their children had on these outings to the cabin. Because of what they said when Fr. Eckroth asked if our children would like to go, I agreed to ask them. Because I trusted Fr. Eckroth, they thought it would be an enjoyable few days for them as well. I was betrayed by Fr. Eckroth. He also betrayed his brother monks. He not only took advantage of our children, but also of my confidence and trust in him. Never in my wildest imaginations would I have ever thought he would do what so many of those he took to the cabin said he did.

We know many of these children. We know they come from good families, families who were loyal and strong supporters of the monks of St. John's. I firmly believe these children are telling the truth. It hurt very much when our daughter and son started to tell us some of what happened on these trips to the cabin with him. Unfortunately, two of our children are no longer alive and cannot tell us what they saw. We know now how naïve we were, but 30 years ago, we never would have expected this kind of action from a priest. Now that it is too late, we know better.[76]

Fred Reker died on December 31, 2012.

Benedictine Monk Father Richard Eckroth was the man I tracked down and confronted in 2002, and asked if he thought God would forgive him for what he did to children. Eckroth died in 2015. He was identified by several victims, both boys and girls. He was listed on several lists as a predator in 2013, 2014 and named in two more lawsuits in 2014.

---

[76] Interviews with Fred and Rita Reker and family and families of St. John's Abbey, Spring/Summer, 2002; Email, October 29, 2002.

The Holy See's Institution of Arrogant Hypocrisy

On October 23, 2001, Archbishop Renato R. Martino, the Holy See's Permanent Observer to United Nations, wrote a letter before the Third Committee of the 56th Session of the U.N. General Assembly on Item 115 *The Promotion and Protection of the Rights of Children*. His letter reads:

The Holy See welcomes this opportunity to participate in the discussion on the promotion and protection of the rights of the child and looks forward to continue to share in those discussions which will lead to the adoption of the Declaration and Plan of Action "Creating a World Fit for Children," during the Twenty-seventh Special Session of the General Assembly on Children.

For many people, the scenes on television and in the print media of the World Trade Center disaster and the armed response against Afghanistan have had a lasting and profound impact. Fortunately, television will be the closest that many of the world's people will ever come to experience war and armed conflict.

Unfortunately, too many of the world's children are affected by war and conflict every day of their lives. They all bear the physical and psychological scars which might be the result of direct involvement as combatants and child soldiers or through abduction, abuse, separation from family, malnutrition, and lost educational opportunities.

That same might be said for those children who are victims of exploitation or abuse. For these children, unimaginable horrors are an everyday occurrence. These also suffer physical and psychological trauma which leaves scars that may never be healed.

With its almost universal ratification, the Convention on the Rights of the Child continues to guide governments in their actions regarding the well-being of children through the recognition of their dignity and the acknowledgment that the "the children, by reason of his physical and mental immaturity, needs special safeguards and care, including legal protection, before as well as after birth."

Having been the fourth State to ratify the Convention on the Rights of the Child and responding to the call by the Secretary General as well as the appeal of the Special Representative for Children and Armed Conflict, tomorrow, on behalf of the Holy See, I will deposit the instruments of ratification of the two Optional Protocols to the Convention on the involvement of children in armed conflict and on the sale of children, child prostitution and child pornography.

The Holy See does this not only because it is the next step after the signing but because the Holy See has always recognized the fundamental importance of protecting the human rights of children and promoting their well-being. This is most evident through the thousands of schools, hospitals, and care centers under the auspices of the Catholic Church, as well as in the work of the Church among children who are refugees and displaced, those living in poverty or who are separated from parents or their family. Another of the ways this recognition is carried out is certainly realized in protecting children from the atrocities of armed conflict and exploitation.

The Holy See is pleased to note that the number of ratifications required for the Optional Protocol on the Sale of children, child prostitution and child pornography to enter into force, has been reached and that the Holy See will now join with those States in what my Delegation hopes will also be a universal ratification of such an important instrument.

My Delegation is also pleased to note that with its ratification only three more states must ratify the Protocol on Child Soldiers before it can enter into force.

In depositing its instruments of ratification, the Holy See encourages all other States to join in furthering the legal protection of children by ratifying or acceding to the protocols.

At the same time, however, the Holy See acknowledges the fact that while codification is a legal guarantee, it does not give certainty of protection. True protection comes from the genuine love, care, and concern that each person is called to give in recognizing all children as a precious gift from God.

As my Delegation has read "We the Children", the Report of the Secretary General, much progress has been made but at the same time, action still needs to be taken to achieve the goals set during and since the World Summit for Children, especially those regarding immunization, nutrition, safe sanitation and drinking water, maternal and under-five mortality, adequate shelter, access to education and health.

There are many challenges in the world. Each and every action that the United Nations system can take helps to chip away at the problems that continue to hamper the realization of the rights and assurance of the well-being of children.

Parents and the family must be strengthened and helped in their role of providing the best for their children. Continuing to create a world fit for children can only be possible with real commitment and solidarity in our actions.

The Holy See has always recognized the human dignity of children which in turn has empowered its centuries-old tradition for their protection and care and affirms its determination to join with all others who do the same.

While Archbishop Martino wrote those *noble* statements in 2001, the late Cardinal Bernard Law of the Archdiocese of Boston was admittedly aware of priests, like Father Paul Shanley, who openly professed sex with young boys under the guise of North America Man Boy Love Association (NAMBLA).

It should be noted that every diocesan head – whether bishop, archbishop, or cardinal – has been aware of these predator-priests. Canon law had required documentation of their records in their historical secret archives in every diocese in the world. Much of which was housed in the Vatican.

On November 15, 2000, the General Assembly of the United Nations adopted by resolution the United Nation's Convention against Transnational Organized Crime.[77] The Convention consists of three distinct sections, each subjected to separate signature and ratification.[78]

The first section comprised Articles 1 through 41 which dealt with technical issues of definition, jurisdiction, and the obligations of signatory states in terms of criminalizing proscripted acts, mutual cooperation, and so forth. The second section was entitled the "Protocol to Prevent, Suppress and Punish Trafficking in Persons, Especially Women and Children, supplementing the United Nations

---

[77] Resolution **A/RES/55/25.**

[78] The period during which states could sign the Convention was specified as December 12, 2000, through December 12, 2002. As of the date of this Report, 143 States have signed the convention, 24 of which have ratified it.

Convention against Transnational Organized Crime."[79] The third section addressed the "Protocol against the Smuggling of Migrants by Land, Sea and Air, supplementing the United Nations Convention against Transnational Organized Crime."[80]

Article 3 of the Protocol:

(a) *"Trafficking in persons" shall mean the recruitment, transportation, transfer, harboring or receipt of persons, by means of the threat or use of force or other forms of coercion, of abduction, of fraud, of deception, of the abuse of power or of a position of vulnerability or of the giving or receiving of payments or benefits to achieve the consent of a person having control over another person, for the purpose of exploitation. Exploitation shall include, at a minimum, the exploitation of prostitution or others or other forms of sexual exploitation, forced labor or serviced, slavery or practices similar to slavery, servitude, or the removal of organs.*

(b) *The consent of a victim of trafficking in persons to the intended exploitation set forth in subparagraph (a) of this article shall be irrelevant where any of the means set forth in subparagraph (a) have been used.*

(c) *The recruitment, transportation, transfer, harbouring, or receipt of a child for the purpose of exploitation shall be considered "trafficking in persons" even if this does not involve any of the means set forth in subparagraph (a) of this article.*

(d) *"Child" shall mean any person under eighteen years of age.*[81]

Tested under these Protocol definitions, the actions by members of the Roman Catholic clergy, religious, and hierarchy, could constitute institutional human trafficking.

---

[79] To date, 109 States have signed the anti-trafficking protocol, of which 18 also have ratified it.

[80] [get numbers]

[81] Protocol to Prevent, Suppress and Punish Trafficking in Persons, Especially Women and Children, supplementing the United Nations Convention against Transnational Organized Crime, A/55/383, Article 3.

In October 2000, President William J. Clinton signed the U.S. Anti-Trafficking bill. This Congressional bill mandated that the trafficking in persons office be housed at U.S. State Department even though American officials recommended that foreign governments house their trafficking offices in their judicial departments.

The U.S. State Department's trafficking office annually grades foreign countries in tiers for their efforts to fight human trafficking. In simple terms, the first tier designates those nations addressing the trafficking issue; the second tier for those that make efforts, but incomplete; the third tier for those ignoring the trafficking issue. [82] Later, Tier 2 Watch was added.

Under this law, the U.S. is required to cease aid to nations by the end of the third year if a nation is on Tier 3, except for humanitarian aid.

In June 2001, the U.S. State Department released its first annual report, and every year since. Nowhere in the US Anti-Trafficking annual report was the U.S. listed until Hillary Clinton was appointed Secretary of State during the Obama administration. She claimed she was unaware that the U.S. was not listed in the annual report even though her husband signed the federal bill in 2000.

The Holy See has never been listed in the anti-trafficking report. It is time for it to be included for fostering institutional sex trafficking of children by its clerical predators.

Australian Catholic priest Father Morrie Crocker reflected upon Catholic perverted priests,

"If the young, vulnerable, and innocent are not protected by the laws then all of us become potential victims and we are all vulnerable. There is one universal trait associated with sex abusers and that is their arrogance. They act as if they are immune to retribution and, tragically, too often they are. That these men are still in positions of trust and responsibility is of real concern."

Conclusion

"Due to the severe sexual, physical, and emotional abuse I endured as a child, my life has been affected in so many ways. But I never could have imagined the mistreatment and abuse I experienced later in life as an adult, when I was given a diagnosis several years ago of Post Traumatic Stress Disorder and Major Depression. The subsequent loss of family, friends, and business associates was crippling in and of itself. Due to the prejudice, the fears, and the stigma of mental illness, you find your life being changed dramatically. You are treated as a second-class citizen by so many. I can now understand what others experience due to the color of their skin, their race, their religion, their creed. It is more than just an unpleasant experience."

— Michael Skinner – Survivor of sexual exploitation

By late October 2002, there was glimmer of hope when Irish government officials called for an ever-expanding investigation of clerical sex-abuse charges because of the public's reaction to the airing of a documentary throughout Ireland.

Cardinal Desmond Connell of Dublin pledged that Church officials would "cooperate fully."

"Canon law carries no more significance than the laws of a golf club," said Michael McDowell, Irish Justice Minister of Health and Children in 2002. [83]

"As far as the criminal law of the state is concerned, canon law per se has no particular status. We simply could not have a situation where a group of people, in the interest of the church which they loyally served effectively undertook as of

---

[83] Irish News, *Irish Cardinal Promises Cooperation with Government Probe*, October 25, 2002.

right, activities which involved contact by their members with children. They cannot simply set them aside or apply a different standard to them from that which is generally needed to protect children," McDowell emphasized. [84]

The head of the Catholic Church in England and Wales, Cardinal Cormac Murphy-O'Connor, explicitly stated in 2002 that it is "imperative" that the Church address the charges of sex abuse and offer formal apologies.

"I do want to stress the importance of honestly addressing the issues. We have a duty to ensure that children are protected," Murphy-O'Connor emphasized. [85]

In the U.S., Massachusetts Attorney General Tom Reilly, one of the leading law enforcement officials who fought to protect victims in 2002, expressed his frustration.

"For years, senior [Church] management had an elaborate system in place to keep the [molestations] secret and away from law enforcement. The Church had direct knowledge of the abuse. Although they knew of the abuse, they refused to report them to law enforcement and engaged in a pattern of serial cover-ups. Not just in Boston but throughout the Church. They used tools of confidentiality agreements to silence the victims and keep the abuse secret, and then repeatedly trafficked the priests from parish to parish, diocese to diocese, and even from country to country to hide the predators and the crimes. Whereas in New Hampshire, where there is a child-endangerment law, there is no such law in Massachusetts," said Reilly. [86]

Some still believe and accept that the Church hierarchy does not "get" the magnitude of the issue and does not "get" their complicity in these crimes and the seriousness of their intentional criminal coverups akin to a mafia omerta, an institutional code of silence.

Not for one nanosecond does this author believe that the Church hierarchy should get away with this coverup. It is so systemic.

---

[84] Black, Fergus, Irish Independent, *Canon Law has Same Status as Gold Rules,* October 24, 2002

[85] Irish News, *British Cardinal Calls for Church 'Honestly Addressing',* October 25, 2002.

[86] Keane, Jr., Thomas, Boston Herald, *Church Stonewalling Frustrates Reilly,* October 25, 2002.

The Church hierarchy knows its own history, its historical secret archives, and its canon law history. They are terrified of the consequences if prosecutors really comprehended the extent of their knowledge and the intent of their actions, and the purpose of this book is to lay it out for prosecutors to creatively ponder prosecuting the church institutionally for sexual trafficking.

As someone raised in the Catholic Church, whose religious heritage goes back generations and whose families on both sides grew up in the Catholic Church, I do not say this lightly – hold the Vatican accountable.

The Vatican created the Code of Canon Law. They created their internal secrecy machinations. They created their own omerta with the threat of excommunication.

What was more important to the hierarchy was the image of the Church. If the magnitude of the truth were ever to see the light of day, the Church's image would be even further tarnished and there would be even more anger towards the Church hierarchy. The hierarchy has only themselves to blame. Their institutional arrogance today is as profound as it was in 2002 when the Boston dioceses sex scandals first imploded and lit a fire globally.

In June 2002, I listened to two witnesses speak at a Voice of the Faithful (VOTF) meeting in Boston. This organization was started by the Catholic laity in response to the church scandals. VOTF members were standing with the survivors and wanted the church hierarchy to be held accountable. The hierarchy was furious that VOTF chapters were forming not just across Boston parishes, but in parishes in other dioceses across America.

During this meeting, the survivors said that they were hoping and waiting to meet with Cardinal Bernard Law. It took Cardinal Law four months to make the decision that a meeting with survivors was the right thing to do. His first meeting with these survivors was on October 29, 2002.

These men were the victims of Father Joseph Birmingham.

Birmingham raped children from 1962 to 1989 in Sudbury, Salem, Lowell, Brighton, Gloucester, and Lexington, Massachusetts. Birmingham died in 1989.

The Archdiocese first learned of Birmingham's abuse in 1964 after he admitted that he abused two boys. The church transferred him. He reoffended and again, the church officials transferred him. Basically, Birmingham raped children throughout his priesthood. He was ordained in 1964.

Survivors filed a suit for his offenses in 1995 and it was settled in 1996 for $50,000. By late 2002, 53 plaintiffs had joined a suit against the diocese, and Cardinal Law and his former colleagues. That was settled in 2003. [87]

Even Cardinal Law's auxiliary bishops duplicated his arrogant behavior.

Bishop Walter James Edyvean, otherwise referred to by some VOTF members as Cardinal Law's hatchet man, made some alarming statements in 2002.

"First we are going to talk about the authority of the bishop over all Catholics in this diocese, and ONLY AFTER that is established, will we talk about victims and the poor affected by the decline in donations," exclaimed Edyvean to three VOTF members in a private meeting. [88]

As if Catholic laity were serfs ran across my brain when I heard this.

The Catholic laity was emptying the pews in disgust by 2002, and when they were in the pews, they were not donating to the church's coffers. Church officials were feeling it in their financial coffers as they should have. That was a brilliant outcome that mirrored the Catholic laity's disgust with the Church officials' complicities in crimes and coverups. And it was organic as the media reported the abuses daily. The Boston Globe and New York Times and the local papers stepped up to the plate and took the Fourth Estate to a new level. They feared not!

Nevertheless, the same warped mindset of Edyvean was repeated by Cardinal Law when he met with the Boston – VOTF in late November 2002 when he stipulated that he "had problems with VOTF," and wanted to know what their agenda and their intentions were.

It took until December 13, 2002, after 58 Boston diocesan priests signed a letter telling Cardinal Law that he was no longer worthy of him being their "spiritual leader" that he finally resigned.

"The priests and people of Boston have lost confidence in you as their spiritual leader," they wrote in the letter.

---

[88] Interview with a VOTF member and survivor, October 25, 2002.

I knew what Buddy, our beloved father, was up to for months. He was committed to those courageous priests. At one point, he told me – God willing 90 priests may come forward. I called my father when Cardinal Law announced his resignation.

"Well done, Buddy!"

Little did we know that Cardinal Law was going to Rome and Pope John Paul II was going to elevate him as Archpriest of the Basilica di Santa Maria Maggiore in Rome in 2004.

Talk about the old boys' network!

Since that era, more information has come to light in every country. There have been statewide investigations in several states in the U.S., like Pennsylvania, Maryland, and Illinois. Prosecutors seized historical secret archives. They have done extensive reports elsewhere. Countries have held extensive inquires in Europe, Australia, U.K., Ireland, and Canada. The plethora of evidence has been overwhelming and heartbreaking to read.

But, as I have always said, "I do not care if you are a pope or a president, wealthy or powerful – if you abuse children or coverup for perverts, you need to be held accountable."

In 2023, what surfaced in Poland was profound, but I believed well before that someday the truth was going to surface about the popes well beyond what we knew over 20 years ago.

A documentary entitled "Franciszkanska 3" was released on TVN that shocked that nation. It focused on Pope John Paul II, who had died in 2005, and his alleged knowledge of pedophilia and sexual assault within the Catholic Church in Poland. It detailed his involvement in the coverup of priests' sexual crimes when he was the Archbishop of Krakow in the 1960s and 1970s before he became Pope John Paul II in 1978.

Karol Jozef Wojtyla, otherwise known as the "Polish Pope," was the single most popular figure in that country's 20th century for inspiring the country's transition away from communism in the 1990s.

Pope John Paul II headed the Catholic Church from 1978 until he died in 2005 as the 263rd successor to St. Peter. He was the first Slavic pope and the youngest ever elected at the age of 58. He was beatified in May 2011 by Pope Benedict XVI and canonized in April 2014 by Pope Francis.

Before he was ordained Archbishop of Krakow in 1964, he attended the Second Vatican Council and in 1965, he made three trips to Rome to work on the redraft of the Vatican II documents. He was elevated to Cardinal in 1967.

On January 25, 1983, Pope John Paul II published Sacrae Disciplinae Leges related to the Code of Canon Law. This document is very important because it was written by Pope John Paul II.

"Finally, the canonical laws by their very nature must be observed," he wrote. This document illustrated the binding norms issued by the highest-ranking member of the Roman Catholic Church.

Pope John Paul II headed the Church during the implosion in Boston in 2002, and for the next three years as the sex scandals erupted in dioceses and orders all over the world.

Pope Francis had the audacity to state that in those earlier decades secrecy was the norm.

Poland Ministry of Foreign Affairs not only issued a condemnation of the documentary on Pope John Paul II when he was Archbishop of Krakow but summoned the U.S. Ambassador to Poland Mark Brzezinski for a meeting because TVN is a subsidiary of Warner Brothers Discovery.

That film released followed what happened in Germany in 2022. The German law firm of Westphal Spilker Wastl (WSW) released a report and found that Pope Benedict XVI failed to prevent abuse of minors during his tenure as Archbishop of Munich and Freising from 1977 to 1982. The Church had commissioned this inquiry.

"I can only, as you know, acknowledge it [church sex scandals] with profound consternation," said Pope Benedict XVI in 2013. "But I never tried to cover up these things," he proffered.

The 2022 WSW report found otherwise in a remarkable rebuke to Pope Benedict's 2013 statement.

"During his time in office there were abuse cases happening," Martin Pusch said in 2022. "In those cases, those priests continued their work without sanctions. The church did not do anything. He [Pope Benedict XVI] claims that he did not know about certain facts, although we believe that this is not so, according to what we know."

"In a total of four cases, we reached a consensus there was a failure to act," said Pusch.

Two cases involved priests who were legally charged with child abuse and were allowed to continue as pastors. No care was given to victims and no official church discipline was taken against the priests.

Another case involved a notorious child molester who was transferred from Essen in West Germany to the Archdiocese of Munich and Freising in 1980, while Pope Benedict XVI led the archdiocese.

The law firm found at least 497 cases of abuse at the Archdiocese of Munich between 1945 and 2019. This 2022 report followed a 2018 report that found more than 37,000 cases of clerical abuse in Germany that spanned over 68 years.

In Ireland, 9,000 children died in uncertain circumstance in Catholic homes for mothers and babies. In Canada, 6,000 children died in Catholic residential school. A French inquiry released in 2021 found that at least 216,000 children were abused by Catholic clerics in France alone since the 1950s, according to the Independent Commission on Sexual Abuse in the Catholic Church (CIASE). That document is about 2,500 pages. Within that alone, 200 pages were devoted to survivors' witness testimonies. This panel was mandated in 2018 by the French Bishops' Council and the Conference of Monks and Nuns of France, known as CORREF.

It took the Catholic Church until December 2021 under Pope Francis to update Book VI of the 1983 Code of Canon Law. That book addresses the church's rules on many offenses, including sexual ones. Pope Francis stated that bishops had been too lenient for penalizing sexual predators and offenders in the past. That was 20 years after I first began this investigation.

For anyone to assume that the hierarchy was unaware of the 1922 and 1962 secret church documents that laid the groundwork for the internal coverup of clerical abuse secrets that even the popes knew is pure insanity because all those involved were sworn to secrecy with the threat of excommunication as severe as violating the confidentiality of confession.

One has only to review who the men are who have managed the Congregation of the Faith (CDF), where the sex abuse complaints are housed in the most recent decades to understand how important this office is within the Vatican.

Cardinal Joseph Ratzinger, later Pope Benedict XVI, ran CDF from 1981-2005 under Pope John Paul II. When Cardinal Ratzinger became pope, American Cardinal William Joseph Levada of San Francisco headed CDF from 2005-2012.

Pope Benedict XVI then chose German Cardinal Gerhard Ludwig Muller, a man from his homeland. After Pope Benedict XVI stepped aside in February 2013 and Cardinal Jorge Mario Bergoglio of Argentina was elected Pope Francis, Cardinal Muller remained head of CDF until 2017.

Then Pope Francis, the first Jesuit pope, chose Spanish Jesuit Francisco Ladaria Ferrer to run CDF until 2023. Today, Prelate Victor Manuel Fernandez runs the CDF, who, like Pope Francis is from Argentina.

It is imperative that the Roman Catholic Church hierarchy from the top down, and bottom up, and within every heart and soul of its laity, examine not only what their faith is, but ask themselves the question, what is the measurement of your faith if you sit on the sidelines on this issue?

We will all meet the face of God some day and there will be no surprise to me if His Almighty asks, "You knew what when, and what did you do about those who harmed children?"

There is no grey area on this issue.

The first time I heard the word, Holocaust" I was a nine-year-old innocent girl. That topic was mentioned at a seder at Bernie Fischlowitz's home. Bernie was my father's mentor and friend. I was the only child at the dinner table.

Inquisitively, I asked, "What's the holocaust, Mumy?"

The room fell silent.

My mother trusted Bernie.

"You tell Christine, Bernie," nodded my mother.

So, Bernie and I meandered into his living room. I remember Bernie telling me that there are good people and bad people, and sometimes bad people do mean things to good people.

I understood that.

Then he reminded me that he was Jewish, and I was Catholic. Then he said that some people do not like him because he is Jewish.

"Why, Uncle Bernie?" I asked.

"Just because I am Jewish, and a long time ago, some very bad people did some very bad things to people who were Jewish and some very good people did not stop them soon enough."

"Why did good people not stop the bad people?" I remember asking.

"They were scared, and they did not know how," said Uncle Bernie.

"Well, I love you, Uncle Bernie," and gave him a hug.

I have often thought about Uncle Bernie's words over the last decades.

So, what should be done now?

In The Name of God...

Get Off The Bench, Get In The Fight And

Protect All Children

And Hold Predators And Institutions Accountable!

Addendum

The following is a sample of but a few of the hundreds of Catholic clergy sex abuse cases and the Church hierarchy cover up attempts of these cases by 2002 across the globe. As you will see, the crimes had occurred in every corner of the United States and on every continent by 2002. The Vatican was fully aware but denied their cumulative seriousness.

UNITED STATES

Anchorage, Alaska

Priest accused of sex abuse kept his job in Alaska. Father Timothy Crowley was allowed to keep his job with the Archdiocese of Anchorage despite accusations that he sexually abused a 15-year-old boy.

"We want very much to keep him," says retired Archbishop Francis T. Hurley, who approved Crowley's transfer to Anchorage in 1995. "We are talking about someone who has rehabilitated his life."

Crowley had been removed from his parish duties in 1993 after what then Bishop Kenneth Povish called Crowley "Guilty of Grievous Sexual Misconduct." Crowley underwent a two-year rehabilitation program. Crowley had to undergo psychiatric evaluation, and the Bishop consulted the archdiocese Sexual Abuse Oversight committee and outside experts.

Crowley was allowed to live in a parish with a mentor and a lay person would check on him periodically.

Archbishop Francis T. Hurley admitted that he never once inquired about the victims of Father Crowley, when making his decision to accept the priest.

A Los Angeles grand jury issued subpoenas for personal files of three clerics accused of abuse. While Cardinal Mahoney was willing have the files turned over, the lawyers for the individual priests said that turning over the documents, which included psychological profiles, should not be turned over because they violated privacy laws. [89]

Tuscon, Arizona

Sexual Blackmail kept Bishop silent as serial sexual molester continued to rise in the ranks and attack children.

The names of 15 priests who had "credible" accusations of child sexual abuse against them were released Friday by the Catholic Diocese of Tuscan. The decision to dismiss came after the diocese came under harsh criticism of cover-up and secrecy following the settlement of civil actions in January.

The oldest accusation of sexual abuse in the list dated to the late 1950s, the most recent was in 1999. This suspension meant that the priests could: say Mass publicly but could wear clerical garb or present themselves as priests publicly. The priests could continue to receive retirement pay of $1,000 per month from the diocese and officials would not try to defrock them. Among the offending priests was 53-year-old Father Robert Trupia who the diocese had classified as a "Notorious and Serial Abuser."

California

Benicia, California

During a daytime patrol of a rundown cemetery, a police officer was shocked to see his parish priest, Father Jerome Hensen, kneeling in front of a boy the officer once coached. The officer just drove away, but according to his report, filed hours later, the priest was committing "Lewd acts with the 13-year-old." Even though another priest told police he "suspected Father Hensen from past incidents" police never investigated them, and no arrest was made. The church quickly transferred Hensen to a parish in Reno, Nevada.

Hensen later returned to California, where he became a parish priest and where he ran a youth ministry. Because of the allegations, in November 2001, Hensen was removed. No new allegations against him had surfaced. According to Nancy Sloan, a victim of sexual abuse by another priest, Fr. Oliver O'Grady, when she

---

[89] Associated Press, June 18, 2002.

was 11 years old, "No child should have to remember her first kiss coming from an adult priest." Sloan contended that high ranking clergy in Stockton, California protected the priest.

"They lied. They guilted. They stonewalled. They told the police in Stockton that they would take care of it. They promoted him. They moved him. They gave him new feeding grounds."

The Bishop who transferred the child molester priest around was Roger Mahoney- now Cardinal of the Archdiocese of Los Angeles. [90]

Carson, California

Woman Seeks to Find Priest She Says Fathered Her Child- Alleging She Was Impregnated By One Of Seven Clerics - She Asks For Cardinal's Help.

A woman who alleges that she was made pregnant at the age of 16 by one of seven Catholic priests who had sex with her 20 years ago said Monday that she wants Cardinal Roger M. Mahony to help her daughter identify which man is her father.

Rita Milla said she was sexually abused by Father Santiago Tamayo when she was attending St. Philomena Church in Carson. He allegedly introduced her to six other priests who she said also seduced her. When she became pregnant, she said, Tamayo sent her to the Philippines, telling her parents she was studying there. Instead, she secretly had the baby at Tamayo's brother's clinic.

Mahony, who was released from the hospital Sunday after being treated for blood clots in his lung, would not comment. But his spokesman, Tod Tamberg, said the cardinal would be very open to helping Milla identify the father of her daughter, who is 19. Tamberg said the archdiocese provided an annuity for the child when she was born but does not know how much was paid to the family. Milla's parents learned of the child upon her return from the Philippines.

Tamberg said Mahony did not know where the accused priests are located, nor does he know whether they are still in the priesthood. Milla said she believes at least two of the men are dead.

---

[90] CBS News.com. April 22, 2002.

In 1984, Milla filed a lawsuit against the Los Angeles archdiocese alleging fraud, clergy malpractice and conspiracy. Her attorney, Gloria Allred, said the day the lawsuit was filed that "all seven priests seemed to disappear from their parish offices." Allred said she lost the lawsuit in the state Court of Appeal because the statute of limitations had expired.

In March 1991, Tamayo apologized face-to-face to Milla, telling a news conference that he "had to go public and tell the whole truth. I knew that cheap absolution would not undo the evil of the past. I had her full trust and confidence, yet I got sexually involved with Rita."

"Weakened by the sense of my own sins, I failed as a pastor to rescue her from getting involved with the other priests." [91]

Los Angeles, California

The Los Angeles diocese is the largest in America with a current budget deficit of $4.3 million. The latest addition to the assets of the diocese is the $189 million cathedral in downtown Los Angeles, which has caused sufficient questions about Cardinal Roger Mahony, who insists that current cutbacks – in some departments as much as 50% as in the juvenile detention center – are not linked with the costs of the cathedral. As in many dioceses which are claiming budget cuts – Boston, Chicago, and Milwaukee, church leaders are blaming the cutbacks on the downturn in the market, a drop-off in contributions due to the sex scandals, continued rising operating costs, and the prospect of scandal settlements. As of early October 2002, the Los Angeles diocese paid out $3.6 million in settlements to victims.

In May 2002, eight men, including two police officers, in the Los Angeles diocese sued Father Fidencio Silva, his Order – the Missionaries of the Holy Spirit - and the Archdiocese of Los Angeles for battery, negligent supervision, and sexual abuse. The plaintiffs claim that from 1979 to about 1985 Silva abused them at Oxnard's Our Lady of Guadalupe Church, where he was pastor, and on trips. Silva is now working in Mexico.

---

[91] *Los Angeles Times*, July 29, 2002.

One seventh grader was told to disrobe because Silva was painting a picture of Christ rising for Easter Sunday. Silva took photographs of the seventh grader. In a television interview with a local reporter, Silva denied the accusations. An accusation was lodged against Silva in 1995 and out of the appearance of propriety, Silva was removed from his church although he then also denied the allegations. The Archdiocese ordered the Missionaries to investigate, and it was determined that a crime was not committed although Silva took a sabbatical for therapy and was then reassigned back to San Luis Potosi, Mexico where he today says Mass and hears confessions. Silva is not the only California priest to leave the country.

Father John Santillan allegedly molested Lorenzo Najera during the 1970s when Najera was 12 to 17 years of age. Santillan allegedly abused Najera at Santa Tereista Church, at retreats in San Bernandino County, and on a European trip. Najera sued civilly in 1998, and the case was dismissed. Santillan was assigned to a parish in Cochabamba, Bolivia in 1998.[92]

In late September 2002, two former priests, Carlos Rene Rodriquez, 46, and Michael Stephen Baker, 54, were arrested on sex abuse charges. Baker resigned in 2000 before the archdiocese agreed to pay two individuals $1.3 million in a civil suit. He is presently charged with 13 counts of committing a lewd act upon a child under 14, and 16 counts of oral copulation with a minor. One victim was a 9-year-old boy, and his abuse often took place in the rectory between 1976 and September 1985. In 1986, Baker told Cardinal Mahoney that he was having sex with young boys. Mahoney then chose to send Baker for treatment and then reassigned him to another parish, and there was no disclosure about Baker's situation to the new parish. Rodriquez left the priesthood in 1993. He was charged with eight counts of abuse against a child under 14 from 1984 to 1986 at St. Vincent Church in Los Angeles. [93]

---

[92] Shuster, Beth, and Richard Winton, The Los Angeles Times, 8 Men Claim Former Oxnard Priest Sexually Abused Them as Children, Investigation: Police are Pursuing allegations against a Pastor now working in Mexico. Suits have been filed against him, his Order and the LA diocese, May 3, 2002.

[93] Whitaker, Barbara, The New York Times, 2 Ex-Priests Are Charged in Los Angeles, September 27, 2002.

Oakland, California

In April 2000, the then Bishop Cummins stated in an apology to a group of 130 people, which included victims and their families, "For our lack of facing the truth regarding abuse by clergy and others, for our tendency to retreat into denial and self-protection in the face of such abuse, for our response of fear and avoidance rather than of care for the survivors of clergy sexual abuse, we ask pardon and forgiveness."[94]

San Francisco, California

Brother Sal's Victim Committed Suicide.

Seven years after being sexually molested at a church camp and on a trip to Disneyland by Catholic Salesian Brother Salvatore Dominic Billante, an unnamed 17-year-old boy committed suicide in November. Billante, a youth ministry advisor at Corpus Christi Church in San Francisco for 25 years, was convicted and sentenced to prison for eight years for the molestation of another child. After four years he was released from San Quentin on parole. Billante is known to have molested 24 children. The suicide victim had severe emotional trouble after the abuse, yet the church refused to pay for his institutionalization. The Archdiocese of San Francisco did pay $6,855 for counselling fees over a two-year period for the boy. Sgt. Bruce Frediani, who knew the boy, said the suicide "speaks volumes of what happens to children who are molested. It is not something kids get over." The archdiocese denies knowing Billante is a pedophile. [95]

Santa Rosa, California

In the nineties, scandals rocked the Santa Rosa diocese – sexual wrongdoings, hush money, financial improprieties, child molestation charges, and extortion and embezzlement. Even Bishop G. Patrick Ziemann's, who was brought into the diocese to clean it up in 1992 resigned after Reverend Jorge Hume Salas filed a lawsuit accusing the bishop of sexual abuse and battery, forced oral copulation, and abuse

---

[94] American Press, Inc. in association with The Gale Group and Looksmart, *Oakland Diocesan Service Offers Apology for Clergy Sex Abuse,* April 15, 2000.

[95] *San Francisco Examiner* April 24, 1994; *San Francisco Chronicle* April 28, 1994.

of authority. In Santa Rosa, one priest was jailed. Another committed suicide and a third fled to Mexico. One Sonoma priest was accused of sexually assaulting a female parishioner. A Santa Rosa clergyman was accused of molesting children at a parish and parochial high school. After Bishop Ziemann resigned, Archbishop William Levada tried to rebuild trust in the diocese. According to Mike Meadows, a Walnut Creek attorney, Santa Rosa diocese paid out $5 million just to his clients who were sexual abuse victims of Reverend Gary Timmons, who is in prison and Reverend Vincent O'Neill, who died of cancer. [96]

Although the Catholic Church has shelled out $1 billion in lawsuits and settlements since 1985, and 187 dioceses have been sued over the sexual abuse of children, Santa Rosa diocese alone has paid out $6 million. Five priests, who were accused of sexual misconduct involving children and teenagers, including Father Don Kimball, left the diocese. One priest was sentenced to eight years in prison for molesting two altar boys during a camping trip. The diocese spent at least $6 million on lawsuits and counselling fees for victims. Kimball was accused by four plaintiffs of sexual molestation in a lawsuit. Although not a party to this case, Mary Holden Agbayani told the story of how Kimball raped her on the floor of Resurrection Chapel when she was 14, and later held her hand as she had an abortion.[97]

Stockton, California

In 1998, a Stockton, California jury awarded $24 million in punitive damages and $6 million in compensatory damages to two brothers, aged 19 and 23. They accused the diocese of Stockton of concealing Reverend Oliver Francis O'Grady's history of abusing children. In 1976, O'Grady and his immediate supervisor signed an apologetic letter to the parents of an 11-year-old girl after O'Grady allegedly touched her inappropriately. O'Grady was sentenced in 1994 for molesting two brothers and is serving a 14-year prison term. The ruling came one week after

---

[96] Lattin, Don, San Francisco Chronicle, *Sex Scandals Bare Church's Sordid Secrets, Santa Rosa Cases Reveal Code of Collusion,* August 14, 1999.

[97] Glionna, John, M., Los Angeles Times, *Parishioners Find Strength as Scandals Rock Diocese Faith: Amid Allegations of Sexual, Monetary Misdeeds by Northern California Priests, Congregants Turn to Activism,* February 2, 2000.

the Catholic Diocese of Dallas agreed to pay $23.4 million to nine former altar boys who claimed that they were sexually molested by a priest.[98]

San Jose, California

An 80-year-old Roman Catholic priest was sentenced Friday to two years in state prison for molesting an intellectually disabled man at a Jesuit retreat for a period of several years.

Father Edward Thomas Burke sat motionless in Santa Clara County Superior Court as Judge Kevin J. Murphy told a hushed courtroom that the former high school teacher deserved to be punished for "inflicting severe, emotional injury" on his victim.

"This was not simply abuse by a caregiver. This was abuse by a friend," Murphy said. "A parent figure and a spiritual counselor."

The victim's sister, Debra Sullivan, said she was relieved and happy that Burke would have to spend time in a prison cell. She had asked Murphy to send the retired Jesuit to jail for three years.

"This is right. This is fair," Sullivan said. "I am so happy that I can go to my brother and tell him that there is a true consequence for what Father Burke did. That will be my happiest moment."

Burke becomes the fifth Jesuit in Northern California ordered to register as a lifetime sex offender. All five in recent years of the Catholic priests have lived at Sacred Heart Jesuit Center in Los Gatos, a picturesque retreat nestled in the foothills above Santa Clara Valley. Burke pleaded guilty on May 23 to committing a felony sex crime on a 50-year-old former kitchen worker at Sacred Heart. The case came to the attention of law enforcement authorities in March after the Los Angeles Times reported that top Jesuit officials quietly relocated Burke in April 2000 after he admitted engaging in sexual misconduct. Instead of notifying authorities, the Jesuit leaders moved Burke to a residence on the campus of Santa Clara University.

With credit for time served, Burke is expected to spend one year in prison. Burke received a much harsher term than Charles Leonard Connor, also 80, a

---

[98] Newsday, *Diocese Ordered to Pay $30 million,* July 17, 1998.

Jesuit brother who was sentenced to six months of home detention in January of last year for molesting another intellectually disabled man at Sacred Heart. Unlike Burke, Connor's case received no publicity and was tried a year before the sexual abuse scandal made headlines around the country.

Connor and Burke are among four Jesuits named in a lawsuit filed by attorneys on behalf of the two intellectually disabled men who worked as dishwashers at the Sacred Heart facility. The suit alleges that the two men were subjected to repeated acts of sodomy, molestation, and false imprisonment for as long as 15 years.

Denver, Colorado

A former seminarian recalls his 1980s days at St. Thomas Seminary, which was formerly known as St. John of Vianney Seminary. He was 22 years old at the time. "…most of the other guys were in their 30's and 40's and even 50's…" As part of his initial visit to the seminary, Dr. Walter Limbacher, one of the seminary psychologists, asked him "how many times a day I masturbated, and whether I had any homosexual experiences. This was standard procedure back then…they make you take an AIDS test too."

While studying at St. Thomas, this seminarian ran across Joe Lessard, who was also studying to become a priest. "I was told to watch out for him he 'liked the boys.'" "In 1985, he [Lessard] was arrested and accused of sexual misconduct with a minor in Phoenix, Arizona. Years later in 1989 I remember reading an article in a Phoenix, Arizona newspaper while I was down there resting, about his arrest on charges of indecency with a minor."

According to Perry Harper, a former diocesan administrator, "He [Lessard] had ten- to fourteen-year-olds in his room with him, only wore his underwear, that sort of stuff." Then Harper received a phone call from some parents whom he knew who told Harper that Lessard had molested their son. Lessard first denied the charges of oral sex on this boy and later admitted it.

Bishop Thomas O'Brien admitted that he knew of the incident but would not speak about it because the details had been presented in a 'confessional situation.' Bishop O'Brien sent him to a home in Jemez Springs, New Mexico. There, psychologist Jay Feierman "diagnosed Father Joe [Lessard] as the type of pedophile who on occasion will get involved with children, but who is also attracted to adults."

Feierman went on to claim, "the prognosis was good for Lessard not ever getting involved with children again." Lessard's probation officer disagreed. "It is the opinion of this officer that the defendant has exhibited the characteristics of a classic pedophile. His social background is virtually male-oriented and that he has progressively focused his activities and association on your children, especially adolescent boys. This officer is of the opinion that the defendant used his position as a priest to gain the confidence and trust of adolescent boys with the intent to seduce them and involve them in sexual acts which eventually resulted in the completion of the instant offense."

The local Catholic hierarchy – Monsignor James McFadden pleaded for leniency. Maricopa County Superior Court Judge Michael Ryan "allowed him to plead guilty to a lesser charge of aggravated assault, which is a misdemeanor." Lessard never served any time and received three-year probation. The lesser charge enabled Lessard to have his record wiped clean upon a successful completion of his probation. He completed his counselling and was transferred to the Midwest and assigned to a hospital.[99]

Bridgeport, Connecticut

Roman Catholic Bishop William E. Lori Saturday announced sanctions against two pastors who failed to tell the Bridgeport diocese that they knew a notorious pedophile priest was living secretly for a decade on a Caribbean island.

The Rev. David W. Howell, of St. Joseph Parish in South Norwalk, and the Rev. Gerald T. Devore, of St. Maurice Parish in Stamford, were temporarily stripped of their duties and ordered confined to religious houses outside the diocese. There, for a period yet to be determined, they are to follow strict regimens of reflection, prayer, and penance - a punishment considered the harshest possible under church law, a diocesan spokesman said.

"I am gravely disappointed," said Lori, who has publicly claimed several times that he hoped the missing priest, the Rev. Laurence F.X. Brett, would be found and brought to justice. The pastors' actions violated diocese policy, he said, and

---

[99] http://www.doitnow.com/~azweb/seminary.htm, A First Hand Account of Life Inside the Former St. Thomas Seminary in Denver, Colorado.

threatened to undermine "the trust of the faithful in their pastors and in the church itself."

The sanctions followed a *Courant* report last week that Brett, accused of molesting more than two dozen children and young men in four states, has been living on St. Maarten. While in hiding, Brett kept in contact with a handful of friends from his days as a clergyman - including Howell, but not Devore.

In an interview last week, Howell denied knowing Brett's whereabouts. Devore was not available for comment.

But during later interviews with diocesan officials, Howell and Devore admitted that they knew Brett's whereabouts and expressed remorse. Under church law, not divulging that information constitutes disloyalty to the bishop and is considered a "moral failing," diocesan spokesman Joseph McAleer said.

He said the diocese will tell authorities in New Mexico, California, and St. Maarten that Brett has been found. Earlier in the week, the diocese notified prosecutors in Maryland and Connecticut, where at least a dozen men have accused Brett of assaulting them as children. [100]

Coral Gables, Florida

Parents revisit late son's sex case-Two clerics are accused

A Coral Gables couple has revived a 25-year-old sex-abuse allegation against a Roman Catholic priest and leveled a new claim against another local cleric, saying their son, now deceased, was molested by the priests as a teen.

In a lawsuit to be filed today, the couple says Miguel Chinchilla, a former altar boy at Church of the Little Flower, was abused between 1975 and 1977 by the Reverends Ricardo Castellanos and Alvaro Guichard.

Rita and Miguel Chinchilla Sr. said their son was pressured to recant the allegation against Castellanos in an affidavit, on videotape, when he confronted the Archdiocese of Miami in 1988.

---

[100] *Hartford Courant* September 1, 2002.

The archdiocese and Castellanos vehemently deny the family's claim that their son was molested between the ages of 14 and 16.

The negligence lawsuit, to be filed in Miami-Dade Circuit Court, claims senior church leaders did not supervise the two priests.

"When Miguel was the approximate age of 14-15, Father Guichard and Father Castellanos each would sexually molest Miguel on a frequent and regular basis with the knowledge and consent of the other," according to the draft of the lawsuit.

The family said Castellanos soon began dining out with Chinchilla and taking him on overnight trips to Key West, Disney World and Europe, including stops in Paris and the Vatican for the youth's 16th birthday.

After Chinchilla returned from Europe in June 1977, the family said he entered drug treatment and later told his parents and counselor about Castellanos' alleged abuse.

"I was in shock, I was hysterical, I was devastated," said Rita Chinchilla, who added that she and her husband had trusted Castellanos because he was a priest.

That fall, the family said, they complained to then-Monsignor Agustin Roman but were asked to keep quiet, she said.

"Monsignor Roman accused Miguel of lying and said that we would ruin this priest's life if we talked about it," Rita Chinchilla said. "He ordered my husband to secrecy under penalty of sin." [101]

Palm Beach, Florida

Florida bishop steps down over sex abuse.

It took former priest Christopher Dixon almost 25 years to talk publicly about the sexual abuse he suffered as a teen-ager from his former rector at St. Thomas Aquinas Seminary in Hannibal, Mo. Less than 24 hours later, that rector, now Bishop Anthony J. O'Connell, resigned.

O'Connell, Bishop of the Diocese of Palm Beach, Fla., stepped down Friday, asking people to pray that he be forgiven. He is the highest-ranking clergyman in

---

[101] Miami Herald November 2002.

the Roman Catholic Church to be affected in a series of sex scandals that started in the Boston Archdiocese.

"I am truly deeply sorry for the pain, hurt, anger and confusion I have caused," said O'Connell. "I've been loved since I entered this diocese, far more than anyone should be loved."

In an interview published in the Post-Dispatch on Friday, O'Connell admitted sexually abusing Dixon more than 25 years ago when Dixon told him about being abused by another priest as a child. O'Connell said it was an "ill-advised" way of trying to treat the boy.

"My heart bleeds for Chris Dixon," O'Connell said. He described Dixon as a great friend. "I deeply regret anything that has happened to him."

In his news conference Friday, O'Connell said another abuse victim may come forward.

"For those who will be angry, I certainly ask, when the time is right that they pray for my forgiveness," O'Connell said.

Dixon, who lives in St. Louis and is no longer a priest, said the resignation is bittersweet. In 1996, the Jefferson City Diocese gave Dixon $125,000 in a confidential settlement, with the promise that he did not pursue any further claims against the diocese and the priests.

O'Connell's confirmation to the Post-Dispatch on Thursday of the abuse came only hours after 10 Florida bishops issued a four-paragraph statement calling sexual abuse "both criminal and sinful." O'Connell was one of them.

Dixon said that when he was a freshman at St. Thomas, he approached O'Connell and told him about being abused by Fischer.

Instead of reporting the abuse, O'Connell persuaded Dixon to undress and then touched him inappropriately in bed. Dixon said the encounters continued from ninth through 12th grade.

O'Connell described the encounters as an "approach" to helping Dixon deal with his own issues.

But an expert on sexual abuse questioned O'Connell's explanation.

Miami, Florida

Seven Florida priests have been suspended and four others have retired since 1998 because of sex-abuse allegations. In addition, two former priests – Ernesto Garcia-Rubio, a Cuban by birth, and Ronald John Luka, along with the Archdiocese of Miami have also been sued for abuse allegedly during the 1970s and 1980s.

A Salvadoran refugee claimed that he was abused by Rubio when he was 16 and lived in a church shelter for refugees at Our Lady of Divine Providence. He claims that he reported it then and was threatened with deportation if he was not silent about it. Four years later, there was a second allegation made against Rubio and he was then transferred to Honduras in 1989.

Before he arrived in Honduras, Rubio spent 10 months in Colombia for counselling at a Catholic psychological center. Rubio was laicized by the Vatican within the last decade. Luka was sued by two former altar boys, and a third victim, Thomas Murphy. Luka allegedly abused Murphy two or three times between 1976 to 1978 when Murphy was in the sixth and seventh grades.

In 1999, more allegations surfaced reaching back to his assignment in New York twenty years earlier. At that time, the archdiocese sent Luka to St. Luke's Institute in Maryland for evaluation and treatment. Luka is now at Wounded Brothers Project in Robertsville, Missouri – a halfway house for pedophile priests.[102]

Miami, Florida

In May 2002, Jose Albino Currais, 45, filed a lawsuit against Father Richardo Castellanos and Father Alvaro Guichard, as well as the Vatican. Currais claims that between 1971 and 1974, he and other teenage boys participated in a prostitution ring with the two defendants and other visiting seminarians from the Vatican.

Currais met Castellanos at a parish in Miami. Currais claims that Castellanos took him on a trip to Disneyland, where the abuse began. Currais claims that both defendants organized orgies and passed the victims around to other predators. This is the second suit against Castellanos and Guichard. The first suit was filed by Mr.

---

[102] Driscoll, Amy, and Jay Weaver, Miami Herald, *2 South Florida Ex-Priests Sued, Allegations of Sex Abuse in '70s, '80s,* May 29, 2002.

and Mrs. Chinchilla. They claim that their deceased son, Miguel, was molested by the priests between 1975 and 1977 at Church of the Little Flower in Miami.

The parents claim that the Miami archdiocese tried to cover the scandal and threatened them into silence.[103]

Chicago, Illinois

The Chicago diocese listed a $38 million deficit in its operating fund for fiscal year 2001.

In 1999, Reverend Walter DeRoeck, pastor of St. Celestine Catholic Church in Elmwood Park and one of the rotating hosts of "Sanctuary," a religious talk show co-produced by an area religious organization and WLS-TV was placed on administrative leave by the Chicago diocese after two men came forward with allegations of inappropriate sexual behavior 13 years earlier in Chicago.

The allegations occurred in 1986 when DeRoeck was pastor of St. John Berchman's Church in Logan Square. The two men were minors at the time. The diocese at the time forwarded the allegations to the Cook County state attorney's office, and the Francis Cardinal George's office stated that the allegations were to be reviewed by a committee of nine members who consisted of three priests, a psychologist, a lawyer, and laypeople.[104]

In late September 2002, Bill Cloutier, 53, an ex-priest, and former Chaplain at the University of Illinois at Chicago, did the unusual when confronted by an email from Matthew Dalton, 29, accusing him of abusing him. Cloutier does not know if he abused Dalton per se but does admit that he abused three teenagers while he was at St. Damian's in Oak Forest in 1979 while he was part of the archdiocese of Chicago. Furthermore, Cloutier claims that the archdiocese knew about the incidents.

Cloutier was sent to a treatment center for six months and received therapy for years. Cloutier claims, "I got away with murder." He resigned from the priesthood

---

[104] Kloehn, Steve, *Chicago Tribune*, "Archdiocese Probing Sex Charges Against Priest," March 31, 1999.

in 1993. After his resignation, he remembered that he had been abused by a priest when he was younger and now claims that he may have joined the priesthood to repeat the pattern he experienced. He is now married with two children and runs a computer consulting business. Dalton plans to sue the archdiocese of Chicago and Cloutier.

Dalton plans to file a civil lawsuit against the archdiocese and Cloutier in the next few weeks. Cloutier claims that he was assigned to Dalton's parish and told the late Cardinal Joseph Bernadin that he did not think that he should do parish work. Cloutier's wishes were ignored. [105]

On May 4, Father Sleeva Raju Policetti, 43, a native of India, was wanted for questioning after an allegation of sexual misconduct with a minor was lodged in the Chicago Diocese. Two days later, before the police were able to question Policetti, he was gone. He left a note, saying he was heading for India and left Chicago. By the end of the month, the Indian Embassy in Washington, the Archdiocese in Chicago, and the Bishop in India were called, and the FBI issued an arrest warrant charging Policetti for criminal assault accusing him of unlawful flight to avoid prosecution.

Policetti came to Chicago in 1996 from Hyderabad and was assigned to St. Tarcissus. This is the first time that a priest has been charged with sexual misconduct involving a child in the Archdiocese of Chicago since 1993. A dozen priests have been reported to the authorities since 1992 when the diocese implemented a new policy. The most recent case in which charges were filed was against Father Ralph Strand. He pled guilty to sexually assaulting a 15-year-old and was sentenced in 1995 to jail for four years.

In March, Father Robert Kealy was accused of sexually abusing a teenager at St. Germaine Church in Oak Lawn. The abuse allegedly occurred over 25 years ago.

In April 2002, a letter was filed with the Chicago Archdiocese claiming that the retired Father Richard Fassbinder molested a minor in the 1970s.[106]

---

[105] Grossman, Kate N., *Chicago Sun Times*, Ex-Priest: 'I got away with Murder' October 4, 2002.

[106] *Hanschel, Alison, Chicago Tribune,* Accused priest leaves country: Is facing allegations he abused a girl while in Chicago, *Saturday, May 11, 2002.*

Victims Slam Chicago Archdiocese

Advocates demand swifter action on sex abuse allegations against pastor.

Demanding to know why a priest accused of abusing two young girls still is a pastor at a north suburban church and school, clergy abuse victims gathered at Holy Name Cathedral Thursday afternoon and sharply criticized the Chicago Catholic church.

"We want to make sure that children are safe in this archdiocese, and we believe that the women who brought these charges did so in good faith," said Barbara Blaine, founder of the Survivors Network of those Abused by Priests. "It has now been 89 days for one of the victims and 30 days for the other victim. We are here to ask that the archdiocese follow its own policies."

In April, a woman accused the Rev. Raymond Skriba, pastor of St. Joseph Church in Round Lake, of molesting her 40 years ago when Skriba served at St. Gertrude in Franklin Park. More than a month passed before the Archdiocese of Chicago's independent review board, which investigates priest abuse claims, notified the woman its investigation had not begun, Blaine said.

In the next two months, the woman provided the board numerous statements of corroboration from family. Board members continued to ask for more information. Last month, because of newspaper reports about Skriba, a second woman came forward making similar accusations against the priest, Blaine said. In a letter the first victim sent to attorney Jeffrey Anderson asking him to represent her, she described in detail Skriba's abuse, which began when she was in her early teens.

"He told me I was a 'dirty' girl, and that he was 'helping' me," she wrote. "He also told me that if my mother ever found out about it, she would kill me." Skriba, who was ordained in 1957, also served at two South Side parishes: Queen of the Universe, 7114 S. Hamlin Ave., from 1957 to 1962; and St. Walter, 11722 S. Oakley Ave., from 1967 to 1970.

The Archdiocese of Chicago's policy on clergy sexual misconduct mandates removing any priest against whom a credible allegation is made. However, church officials said, the review board did not have enough information about Skriba to determine whether he should be removed. "There wasn't enough information just in interviewing the victim and the priest," spokeswoman Diane Dunagan said. "The review board needed more information and that took time."

Officials did tell Skriba not to be alone with minors and to report to a monitor at St. Joseph. Since receiving the second allegation and more information about the first, the review board is ready to make its recommendation, which must be approved by Cardinal Francis George. Blaine said other Chicago-area victims also were disappointed with the pace of the archdiocese's abuse investigations. "This clearly violates the long-standing archdiocesan policy on sexual abuse. This clearly violates the Dallas charter, recently enacted by America's bishops," she said, adding that Skriba should resign, and George should explain the review board's delay.

"Both of those documents promise quick action to remove perpetrators. Both of those documents remain promises only. Broken promises, at least here in Chicago." [107]

Cardinal discusses effects of abuse

Victims of sexual abuse by priests lose their hearts, souls and, in a way, their sense of time. "It could have been 30 years ago, but it's as if it happened yesterday," Cardinal Francis George said Monday. "It stays with them for life."

The cardinal spoke at a daylong seminar sponsored by DePaul University's Center for Church/State Studies and the Cook County state's attorney's office. George announced on Sunday that eight priests accused of sexual misconduct will be withdrawn from the ministry. Two have resigned and a third has retired.

Asked how he would look back on this period in years to come, George said, "Hopefully as a moment of purification. Sex abuse is continuous over a long period of time," said assistant state's attorney Al Thomas. "It slowly and continuously steals the heart and soul of these children."

His boss, state's attorney Richard Devine, said archdioceses and their leaders are unlikely to be prosecuted, even when they knowingly transfer abusing priests from one parish to another. "In obstruction of justice, it could be part of our overall analysis," he said. "But it's not the element we are looking for." [108]

---

[107] *SouthTown* Friday, July 12, 2002.

[108] *Chicago Sun Times* June 25, 2002.

Joliet, Illinois

Grace under Fire-Court records: Bishop showed little regard for sex abuse claims

Concealed in court papers, some hidden for a decade is a tale of secrecy and shame in the Diocese of Joliet, which local church leaders have worked relentlessly to guard from public view. Bishop Joseph Imesch transferred at least three priests accused of sexual abuse to new ministries where they again had the opportunity to molest children. Imesch shook off complaints about sexually aggressive priests from worried parents, writing one concerned family that he knew of several instances where sexual abuse did no permanent damage to the victims. He and his diocese have faced at least nine lawsuits in the past decade from churchgoing parents and children. Trusted priests violated the families' innocence, they claim, and Imesch knew and covered it up.

In depositions for some of those lawsuits, Imesch declared that he did not investigate allegations of abuse against the priests; he did not ask the priests if they molested minors, and he often could not remember if he had been told about the priests' conduct. With criticism mounting, Imesch says he did not always believe it was his role to investigate abuse claims, a statement that echoes the descriptions of some priests who view him as reluctant to micromanage the day-to-day affairs of the diocese. Imesch said he now has a strong policy to explore every allegation of sexual abuse. "If it's an anonymous phone call, we investigate," he said. "If we get a letter, we investigate, even if there is no name on the letter. If it is a rumor, we investigate." But that has not always been so.

His words today are contradicted by his own statements in depositions taken during the past decade. Victims of his priests and the lawyers who have sued the diocese say the bishop disregarded their words and their pain. "Imesch told me he knew nothing` about what was going on, and I found that very hard to believe." said Detroit lawyer Vlark Bello, who questioned Imesch in a lawsuit in 1984. "His attitude about this was sarcastic and nasty. When I asked him what the penalty was for breaking the vow of celibacy He said, 'Eternal hellfire,' and laughed.

Peoria, Illinois

In October 1997, after 35 years at Holy Family Church, Monsignor Norman Goodman abruptly left his parish. In December 1997, four former altar boys accused Goodman of sexual abuse. Three of them accused Goodman of striking them with a Bible for sexual gratification. Then the number climbed to 12 accusers. The alleged abuse occurred between 1970 and 1991. A suit was later filed.

In 1999, the Peoria diocese agreed to a settlement agreement with 12 former altar boys and another boy. The initial suit sought $650,000 in compensatory damages and $1 million in punitive damages. Monsignor denied the allegations and was not party to the confidential settlement agreement.

Kansas City, Kansas

Females – forgotten victims of clergy sex abuse

The cases of female abuse victims suggest that the issue of sexual abuse in the church extends beyond gay priests and pedophiles. Half of the members of the Survivors Network of those Abused by Priests are women

"People who say fundamentally it's homosexuality are almost as much off-base as those who say it's about our litigious society or our salacious media," said David Clohessy, national director of the Survivors Network. "It's a simple solution to a complex issue."

Cardinal Adam Maida of Detroit told CNN that, according to experts, "It's not truly a pedophilia-type problem, but a homosexual-type problem." Maida said the church needed to "look at this homosexual element as it exists, to what extent it is operative in our seminaries and our priesthood, and how to address it."

To be sure, homosexual priests do present a problem when those men ignore their vows of celibacy and prey on teen-agers and boys. But some experts think that focusing on homosexuals may backfire on the church. "If they weed out the homosexuals, they'd lose a third of all the bishops and priests," said A.W. Richard Sipe, a therapist who has studied clergy sexuality for decades. "And that's a conservative estimate."

Fred Berlin, a psychiatrist at John Hopkins University Hospital, said, "There is no evidence that a homosexual man is any more a risk to a boy than is a heterosexual man to girl."

And the number of female victims believes the notion that the church's problem can be solved simply by purging the priesthood and seminaries of homosexuals, or that the issue is relegated to "man-boy sex," said Sue Archibald, an advocate for abuse victims who said she was sexually abused by a priest when she was a teenager.

"When you look at this scandal as a whole, there's one common factor," Archibald said. "All of them involve an abuse of power. Victims can have the same vulnerabilities whether they are 8 or 18 or 48. And the traumatic suffering that comes from the abuse extends beyond any age or gender barrier." [109]

Cumberland County, Maine

In 1991, the State legislature voted to eliminate the statute of limitations for sexual abuse against victims who were less than 16 years old at the time of the abuse. It was not eliminated retroactively. And, since it was not eliminated retroactively, the lawmakers voted to have the cutoff date for prosecution for rape and gross sexual assault as of October 9, 1985, with a possible exception. If the defendant left the state, the time lapse increased by five years.

This past year the Attorney General's office and the Cumberland County District Attorney's office received church records containing allegations against priests going back 75 years. As of September 16, 2002, most of Maine's 16 counties do not expect to bring sexual assault charges against any Catholic priests. Although a disappointment, not all the prosecutorial evaluations are complete. Law enforcement is not suggesting that sexual assaults did not happen. What they are suggesting is that they cannot file indictments for two primary reasons: the accused are dead, or the statute of limitations has run out.

Maryland

Archdiocese lists names of abusive priests who abused Seminary Students

The Catholic Archdiocese of Baltimore released the names of six suspended and former priests accused of abusing minors while seminary students in the 1970s and 1980s.

---

[109] *Kansas City Star*, July 12, 2002.

The charges against five of the men date from the 1970s, and a sixth is accused of abuse in the 1980s, while all were students at St. Mary's Seminary and University.

The six are accused of molesting additional youths while serving in other cities. Archdiocesan officials said they were releasing the names to encourage any additional victims to come forward.

"We want to let victims know we believe them. We hope they come forward so we can apologize and offer help," spokesman Stephen Kearney said.

Monsignor Richard Woy, the chancellor and the director of the Office of Child and Youth Protection, said the system of seminary internships was much more informal three decades ago, when the abuses occurred. A seminarian would often make his own arrangements for a summer internship in a parish or other ministry and there is often no record of it

"We were concerned with this particular group in that they may have served in locations that are unknown to us," Monsignor Woy said. The Rev. Robert Leavitt, president and rector of St. Mary's Seminary and University, said the school had "no knowledge of any incidents involving its students prior to recent disclosure."

"A review of these cases disclosed no indications or allegations of sexual abuse in seminary records," he said. [110]

Boston, Massachusetts

The Boston diocese must cut this year's budget by 40%. At one point, church leaders were suggesting that they may file for bankruptcy as a last resort because of the over 400 sex abuse claims filed against the diocese.

John J. Geoghan, the now defrocked priest, has had 141 child abuse claims brought against him since 1994. Most of them have now been settled. The church paid out an estimated $15 million to 40 Geoghan victims.

In September 2002, Mitchell Garabedian, plaintiffs' attorney, reached a $10 million settlement with the Archdiocese of Boston in another 86 cases. On October 3, 2002, 17 new civil lawsuits were filed against John J. Geoghan by plaintiffs

[110] *The Washington Times* August 22, 2002.

who claim that Geoghan groped, molested, and raped them as children from 1964 to 1996 when they were between the ages of 7 to 15 years of age. That brings a total of 19 cases still pending against Geoghan.

In this latest case, one plaintiff is 17 years old. In addition to Geoghan, 20 other clergy were implicated in this suit. They include Cardinal Bernard F. Law, Bishop William Murphy, and retired Bishop Joseph Maguire of Springfield, Massachusetts. All three are named in two lawsuits. Bishop Thomas V. Daily, now of Brooklyn, NY is named in six lawsuits. These recent claims assert that Geoghan while on sick leave from St. Joseph's parish in Hyde Park, he was being considered for work at another parish while undergoing pedophilia treatment.[111]

Falls River, Massachusetts

In 1993, ex-priest James Porter admitted to molesting as many as 100 children in three states and was charged with 46 counts of sodomy and indecent assault committed against 32 people 30 years earlier. In 1993, he pled guilty to 46 charges of sexual misconduct. In 1992, Porter was convicted in Minnesota for molesting his own children's babysitter in 1987. For that, he was sentenced to six months in jail. While a priest, Porter was confronted by his superiors for sexual abuse claims on at least five occasions in 1963 and 1964. The claims were backed up with substantial evidence, but he was returned to parish work after receiving treatment.[112]

Worcester, Massachusetts

Father Thomas A. Kane, who administered the House of Affirmation for troubled priests in Whitinsville, and now runs a language school in Guadalajara, Mexico, sold off properties in Florida and the Bay Back to a longtime companion and monsignor just before he was sued in two molestation suits in 1993 and filed bankruptcy.

The Worcester diocese acknowledged that they had been sending payments to Kane and now state that they will suspend such payments. According to court documents, Kane sold his Florida condominium valued at about $30,000 to Monsignor Brendan Riordan of Long Island, New York for $18,000 and sold his Back

---

[111] New York Times, *17 Suits Name Former Priest in Sex Abuse*, October 4, 2002.

[112] Reuter, September 23, 1992; Rolling Stone Magazine, 1994.

Bay condominium to his roommate, Babk Bagheral for $70,000 in January 1994. Both sales were six months before Kane initiated bankruptcy proceedings. Riordan is pastor of St. Aloysius in Great Neck, New York and Bagheral runs the Boston branch of Kane's Worldwide Teachers Development Institute.[113]

In 1993, Kane was accused of sexual abuse in a lawsuit filed by Mark Barry of Uxbridge. It was settled out of court with a gag order. Barry alleged that during the summer of 1968 that Kane – then a visiting priest in Uxbridge – provided Barry with alcohol, took him to a cabin in Upton, and raped him at the age of nine. That was the first of dozens of encounters with Kane and other men. Abuse allegedly occurred at House of Affirmation, at St. Mary's Church and other locations. Barry was bribed with expensive gifts and money to not only have sex with Kane but to have sex with other priests at rural retreats – all arranged by Kane, and in some incidents, Kane would watch and take photographs.[114]

Detroit, Michigan

Priest's accusers scared silent removal was 40 years to late

In the late 1960s, Bishop Foley High School in Madison Heights was abuzz with so many stories about the principal abusing boys that church officials were forced to act. But not against the Rev. Robert Haener, the accused principal.

Instead, several priests the students had never seen before swept into the school, pulled 30 boys out of class, and put the fear of God into them for questioning Haener's behavior.

"These guys were ticked, very ticked at us," said Ray Cunningham, who now lives in Florida but was one of the stunned boys sitting in the room that day. "They scared the hell out of me, to be honest. They told us what we were doing was spreading rumors about Father Haener and that was a mortal sin and could lead to eternal damnation.

---

[113] Washington, *Robin, Priest in Abuse Suit Sold Condos Before Claiming Bankruptcy*, February 22, 2002.

[114]*Shaw, Kathleen, and Richard Nangle, Telegram & Gazette,* Accused Priest in Mexico, *February 7, 2002.*

"They said, 'Do not tell your parents, because that is further spreading the rumors.' And they said, 'Let us stop it all right now. Father Haener's a very nice man. You are defaming him.'"

Now, more than 30 years later, Detroit Cardinal Adam Maida finally has removed Haener and other priests accused of abusing minors from church-related jobs. In most cases, including Haener's, Maida's staff is discreetly saying the men are being put on leave or forced into retirement for "a credible allegation of sexual misconduct with minors."

If church leaders had listened to kids 40 years ago, Haener's career would have been cut short, said Sgt. Kenneth Zalenski, an Allen Park police officer who was an altar boy in the early 1960s when Haener was associate pastor at St. Frances Cabrini in Allen Park. [115]

Omaha, Nebraska

Omaha officials accept responsibility- Catholic archdiocese *admits negligent oversight* of priest who abused boy

In 1998 Father Daniel Herek was convicted for manufacturing child pornography and fondling a former altar boy. He was sentenced to 20 months to five years in prison and five years' probation after his release. In 1999, the plaintiff in this case sued the Omaha Catholic Archdiocese claiming that diocese was negligent in supervising Herek. The diocesan attorneys argued that the suit should be thrown out because Herek's actions were outside the scope of his church duties. The court ruled that plaintiff could sue the diocese.[116]

In 1999, Reverend Richard Whiteing, 52, was arrested for soliciting sex from an uncovered police office in a city park. Whiteing informed his superiors of the arrest and asked to be removed as the parish priest of Holy Ghost Catholic Church.[117]

---

[115] *Detroit Free Press* August 8, 2002.

[116] Associated Press, Omaha, Nebraska, March 30, 1999.

[117] Eiserer, Tanya, Omaha World Herald, *Priest Accused of Soliciting Officer in City Park Resigns,* April 4, 1999.

The chancellor of the archdiocese, the Rev. Michael Gutgsell, said Herek's conviction played a part in the decision to admit negligence.

"Father Herek was convicted of a criminal charge with this specific individual," Gutgsell said. "As that point, basic liability has been admitted."

Herek was ordained in 1971 and served in parishes in the archdiocese until his removal from St. Richard's in 1997.

Other former altar boys have filed lawsuits against the archdiocese regarding Herek. Two suits have been settled out of court; four others are scheduled for trial later this year.

Nashua, New Hampshire

Father James A. Seamus MacCormack sued Bishop John B. McCormack and other church officials for fraud and wrongful termination. Father MacCormack alleges that Bishop McCormack put him under house arrest and attempted to discredit him by sending him for a psychiatric evaluation to keep him from talking and being believed if he talked about the largess of homosexual pornography, he witnessed that was removed from St. Pius X rectory in Manchester, New Hampshire after a priest was discovered dead with a leather sexual device strapped around his genitals.

After the American Catholic Church scandal began to implode during early 2002, Father MacCormack began to wonder if the Church was a subculture of sexual deviants. He alleges that the Bishop suggested to people that he was mentally disturbed and threatened to remove him from his parish. The diocese filed a Motion to Dismiss which was denied. The trial is set for 2003. The genesis of Father MacCormack's concern began in November 1999 when he was called by police to identify a body of a priest in a rectory.

Once there, Monsignor John Quinn arrived with a wrecking crew to dismantle the place. They peeled back carpets, removed drawers, overturned mattresses and seat covers and searched pockets of clothes. They found hundreds of pornographic tapes and images depicting homosexual acts and child pornography, as well as Viagra and amyl nitrate. MacCormack asked the Bishop for a leave of absence from St. Patrick's parish. The Bishop granted him a three-month vacation and ordered him to reside at St. Joseph's Cathedral. McCormack then installed Father Roland

Cote to replace MacCormack at St. Patrick's even though he knew that Cote had a six-year homosexual relationship.[118]

Pedophile ex-priest lives in city

Man, who is on parole, admitted to molesting more than 40 males.

In a third-story Main Street apartment, upstairs from the boutiques and cafes and the State House lawn, a former pedophile priest lives quietly on parole. Robert M. Burns left New Hampshire's prison in 1999, three years after he pleaded guilty to molesting an 11-year-old boy in Salem.

Documents in his court files show that Burns has admitted molesting more than 40 males between the ages of 11 and 22, most while he was a priest in Ohio and Massachusetts. At least five civil lawsuits brought by victims have been settled quietly, the church's payments kept secret.

In those lawsuits, victims accuse church officials of responding to sexual assault allegations by moving Burns from parish to parish. At one point, they say, church officials even placed him in charge of altar boys. [119]

Atlantic City, New Jersey

Abuse suit against priests too late, judge rules

"At the time it was occurring, I understood it to be nothing more than an affectionate relationship with somebody that I absolutely revered," he testified. In his ruling, Himmelberger said he found that difficult to believe.

"They have not convinced me that they did not appreciate that what the priests did to them was wrong," the judge said. He said he believed both brothers understood the harm years before they filed the lawsuit and thus, should have come to court sooner.

A spokesman for the diocese today lauded the judge's ruling but added: "It will not wipe away the tremendous hurt the Depman family feels." Andrew J. Walton,

[118] Meersman, Nancy, *Manchester Union Leader*, "Church Lawyers Contesting MacCormack Suit," May 29, 2002.

[119] *Concord Monitor* May 31, 2002.

the diocesan spokesman, said the church had offered to pay for counseling for the Depmans.

The diocese clearly was expecting a win today. Walton appeared in court with a press release on the judge's favorable ruling already prepared for reporters.

Himmelberger's decision brings the number of plaintiffs to four in the case whose claims he has dismissed. In May, he tossed out a lawsuit brought by Robert and Philip Young, who said they were sexually abused by a priest when they were teenagers. That suit, too, was filed after the statute of limitations had expired, and Himmelberger declined to make an exception to the law and allow it to proceed. The Depmans said they would consider an appeal.

Mark Depman wept as the judge spoke of the abuse Depman had suffered as a teenager.

"It burns and sears through me every time I hear it," he said outside the courtroom. "It's almost like I'm watching a movie that I can't quite believe is my story."

Despite the legal setback, Depman said he believed he and his brother were helping other victims by highlighting how difficult it is to come to terms with the effects of childhood sexual abuse.

"The trauma inflicted by these priests damaged brains and souls, and there's no limit on how long it takes to put these pieces together," he said. "You do not want childhood sexual abuse to be a life sentence. You have to give people as long as it takes to figure it out, and our testimony spoke clearly and urgently to that issue." [120]

Brooklyn, New York

The Brooklyn diocese serves 1.6 million Catholics in the boroughs of both Brooklyn and Queens. Bishop Thomas Daily, who used to serve under Cardinal Law in Boston has served in Brooklyn since 1990. On October 15, 2002, a $300 million lawsuit was filed on behalf of 42 victims who are accusing 12 priests of sexual abuse. Daily is named as one of the co-defendants.

---

[120] *Philadelphia Inquirer* July 10, 2002.

The allegations go back more than 50 years. The complaint claims that top clergy paid off victims and their families for silence as they transferred the priests to new parishes. Earlier this year, Daily was singled out for his involvement in transferring (two priests) accused of abuse while he was with the archdiocese of Boston.[121]

Wilmington, North Carolina

Ex-Philadelphia Priest loses N.C. post

A priest who once taught at North Catholic High School has been removed as pastor of a church in Wilmington, N.C., after a former student accused him of committing acts of abuse in Philadelphia and in North Carolina more than 20 years ago.

The Rev. James J. Behan, 58, was relieved as pastor of Immaculate Conception Church in Wilmington, N.C., in April after a complaint was raised by the former student.

The former student, now 39 and a resident of Medford, Burlington County, said in an interview yesterday that Behan had had a sexual relationship with him over a five-year period beginning in 1977, when the student was 14 and a high school freshman.

Behan was transferred to North Carolina in 1980. The ex-student visited him there, and the relationship continued. The Inquirer, as is its policy in cases involving sexual abuse, is withholding the man's name at his request.

At the time the relationship began, Behan was a religion teacher at North Catholic High School and a friend of the boy's family. According to the former student, Behan invited him to take part in a peer-advocate group at the school. Eventually, Behan invited the student to visit him in his living quarters. There, the former student said, the priest first molested him.

The former student said Behan maintained a sexual relationship with him until 1981, when he told Behan he felt their interaction was "wrong." The man said he decided to come forward in April after he learned Behan was leading youth retreats in the Diocese of Raleigh.

---

[121] Reuters, *$300 Million Abuse Suit Filed Against 12 Priests,* October 15, 2002.

"I didn't want to see this happen to anyone else," he said.

The man first called the Archdiocese of Philadelphia to report Behan and then reached the Raleigh Diocese. Behan was removed from his duties the next day.

The Archdiocese of Philadelphia referred calls about Behan to his religious order, the Oblates of St. Francis De Sales. The Rev. Joseph G. Morrisey, the Provincial for the Oblates in this region, could not be reached for comment. [122]

Tulsa, Oklahoma

Six men accused Father Kenneth Lewis of making unwanted sexual advances while he was associate pastor at St. Mary in Tulsa in the early 1990's. He resigned from the priesthood. A 16-year-old girl accused Father John Jangam of fondling her and repeatedly kissing her three years ago. The diocese says that the priest was excommunicated and returned to his native India. [123]

Portland, Oregon

Father Maurice Grammond, 82, died of Alzheimer's. He was a priest for 52 years. He retired in 1988 and was suspended from the priesthood in 1991 after more than 40 boys accused him of molesting them.

Former altar described in court documents and in interviews how Grammond groped and violently attacked them on camping trips, in his car, in the rectory and even during fake confessions. He even abused two nephews. Grammond was never charged because the statute of limitations elapsed. The crimes occurred from the 1950s into the 1980s.

Grammond's first accuser went public in 1999. Since then, about 100 victims have come forward accusing some 30 priests of abuse since 1938. [124]

---

[122] *Philadelphia Inquirer* June 14, 2002.

[123] Bellamy, Clayton, The Associated Press, *Priest Sex Abuse Victims Groups Criticizes Tulsa Bishop,* September 16, 2002.

[124] Wilson, Michael, The New York Times, *Death of Disgraced Priest Brings Conflict Over Burial,* October 7, 2002.

Erie, Pennsylvania

In 1999, Reverend Robert Francis Bower brought his computer to Hometown Computers to be overhauled. Rick Miller, general manager of Hometown, found hundreds of pornographic pictures, including child pornography, in the computer. Some of the images had been on the computer since 1996. Miller called the police when he entered the recycle bin and discovered "Dad-baby" file. Miller called the Pennsylvania State Police, and Bower was arrested and charged with three counts of child pornography.[125]

Providence, Rhode Island

In 1997, Monsignor Louis Ward Dunn was found guilty of raping a female parishioner in her 1982 Providence apartment after the court found that they had engaged in consensual sex for four years before that. Dunn chose to have Judge Stephen J. Fortunato hear the case without a jury. Following the trial, Fortunato overturned his own verdict after receiving over 80 letters raising the issue that Dunn had ineffective counsel because he had little experience in felony cases.

Dunn never raised the question of "ineffective counsel" during the trial. (Dunn had been acquitted in an earlier rape trial where he was represented by the same attorney). The State Attorney General's Office requested that the Rhode Island Supreme Court review the decision, and the Court overturned Fortunato's decision to overturn his initial decision and ordered the reinstatement of the verdict against Dunn. Monsignor Dunn, then 78, was the first Rhode Island priest to be convicted of rape, or first-degree sexual assault, as it was defined in the Rhode Island statute. Dunn had been suspended from his priestly duties in 1994 when the woman first reported the rape claims.[126]

---

[125] Associated Press, Erie, Pennsylvania, *Store Technician Surprised to Find Child Porn on Priest's Computer*, March 29, 1999.

[126] Breton, Tracy, Providence Journal Company, *High Court Reinstates Priest's Rape Conviction*, March 23, 1999.

Rapid City, South Dakota

Pastor's History of Abuse Shocks a South Dakota City

Last week Mr. Forsythe, an openly gay Catholic priest told The Kansas City Star: "I love the ministry and loved the priesthood. I thought I made a good priest. But I am not called to be celibate. And for me to be in that environment was not healthy." He also said that while he had told officials of the local church about his past, he had not told the entire congregation.

His lawyer, Timothy J. Rensch, said Mr. Forsythe had been unaware until recently of the state requirement that he register with the local authorities as a sex offender. The disclosure of his past has caused Mr. Forsythe shame and worry, Mr. Rensch said, "I know that he's embarrassed," the lawyer added. "I think somebody in his position would naturally be worried about what might happen. He was labelled pedophile and failed to register. One always worries about the depth of backlash you can get by virtue of that label."

The sexual abuse that Mr. Forsythe admitted to a judge in December 1989 occurred while he was a priest at Holy Cross Church in Overland, Kansas, outside Kansas City. He pleaded guilty to one count of molestation and, said Tom Bath, the prosecutor who handled that case, agreed to 120 days in prison.

Later, in the early 1990s, Mr. Forsythe first became active at a Metropolitan Community Church, in Denver, and informed church officials there of his past, said Jim Birkitt, national spokesman for the denomination.

Mr. Birkitt said the Metropolitan Community Churches had a policy of "zero tolerance" for sexual abuse of children. But in addition to that early candor with church officials, Mr. Birkitt pointed out that Mr. Forsythe had served his time, undergone seven months of residential treatment after being released from prison, and committed no subsequent offenses.

The Rev. Charles McGlinn, vicar general of the Kansas City Archdiocese, was another associate pastor at the Overland Park church when Mr. Forsythe was charged with sexual abuse. He remembers him as "an enjoyable person with a very outgoing personality" and as "a very kind and compassionate person." [127]

Dallas, Texas

In 1998, the Catholic diocese of Dallas agreed to pay US $23.4 million to eight former altar boys and the family of a ninth boy who committed suicide at the age of 21, who were sexually abused by former priest, Rudolph "Rudy" Kos. The diocese paid three other Kos victims $7.5million. The settlement came after the jury initially awarded the 11 victims US$119.6 million in 1997.[128]

Burlington, Vermont

The state Attorney General William Sorrell has begun a sexual abuse investigation into 10 current and 30 former Vermont priests. Michael Bernier, 45, who is a San Jose, California resident, is suing the Vermont Catholic diocese and Father James McShane for sexually abusing, exploiting, and assaulting him as an elementary pupil while he attended St. Mary's Catholic Church and School in St. Albans, Vermont.

Bernier is a vice president of a San Jose investment company and sued in the Chittenden Superior Court in Burlington. McShane is on sabbatical. McShane took Bernier on parish-sponsored hiking, swimming, and overnight camping trips, as well as to saunas. The complaint states, "While plaintiff was a child, defendant McShane repeatedly committed unpermitted, harmful and offensive sexual conduct." Bernier further claims that the diocese is liable because McShane was under their supervision and placed him "in a situation where he had the opportunity to and did molest and otherwise sexually abuse a number of pre-teen and teenage boys."

Bernier claims that the diocese had "actual knowledge" of McShane's abuse "but took no action to remove him from the priesthood or to investigate his well-known proclivities." The suit was filed on July 2, 2002. McShane was served on

---

[127] *The New York Times*, June 9, 2002.

[128] *New York Times*, July 1998.

July 12, 2002. McShane's attorneys filed a Motion to Dismiss and one of the arguments was the fact that Vermont law at the time of the alleged assaults referred to rape victims as "female."

McShane's attorneys argued that "Since plaintiff is male, his alleged rape could not have violated the law." The judge denied McShane's Motion to Dismiss. The Motion to Dismiss, which allowed the case to be under seal at that point, was the same time that the diocese's annual summer Bishop's Fund drive was trying to raise $2.3 million.[129]

Milwaukee, Wisconsin

Pope John Paul II has accepted the resignation of the Roman Catholic Archbishop of Milwaukee who is alleged to have sexually abused a young priest. Four years ago, Paul Marcoux accepted $450,000 in 1997 in exchange for his silence about what he says was sexual misconduct by Archbishop Rembert G. Weakland of Milwaukee decades earlier.

The one-line announcement from the Vatican came hours after Archbishop Rembert Weakland, 75, asked to be dismissed.

In his statement, the cleric, who had resigned on 2 April, said he had asked Rome to accelerate his removal to allow the Church to "regain its credibility."

He also rejected Mr. Marcus's claims that he assaulted him.

It is the latest blow to the Roman Catholic Church, which has already been engulfed by scandal over sexual abuse of children by its priests. Some high-ranking US clerics - including Mr. Weakland - knew of pedophiles in holy orders, but allowed them to continue in active ministry, it has been claimed.

Mr. Marcoux told ABC television that the abuse began when he was a student in his thirties hoping to enter the priesthood.

Mr. Weakland - from whom he was seeking advice - "started to try and kiss me and continued to force himself on me, pull down my trousers and attempted to fondle me," said Mr. Marcoux.

---

[129] O'Connor, Kevin, Rutland Herald, *Lawsuit Claims Abuse by Vermont Priest*, October 1, 2002.

Mr. Marcoux also acknowledged that he went to Mr. Weakland twice in the following years to extract hush money from him.

He got one initial payment of at least $14,000 and a further $450,000 in 1997 after threatening to file a lawsuit, according to the ABC interview.

Legal experts say the archbishop should be entitled to get his money back, because Marcoux violated his non-disclosure agreement by revealing the terms of the agreement. Mr. Marcoux's interviews with ABC News and The Milwaukee Journal Sentinel would seem to be a plain breach of the confidentiality clause, which prohibits disclosures to "any newspaper, any electronic media, reporters, and any other individual."

If Marcoux had not made the agreement public, the public would never have known of the abuse and the Archbishop would still be in power today. [130]

CANADA

In 1992, the Canadian Conference of Catholic Bishops produced a document on child sexual abuse entitled, *From Pain to Hope*, in response to several high profiled child sexual abuse cases, including the Mount Cashel orphanage scandal in Newfoundland. It contained recommendations to dioceses although it was up to each diocese to implement policies. Each diocese was to have a committee, which would handle allegations, consisting of a social worker, psychologist, lawyer, and other lay people. A delegate was to be appointed to conduct the preliminary inquiry upon receipt of a complaint, and until the inquiry was completed, the alleged offender was to be put on administrative leave.

If the sexual abuse is of a child, the police and/or child aid offices are immediately contacted. All complaints were to be taken seriously – even those which sounded just too bizarre. [131]

On August 10, 2001, Justice Paul Williamson awarded four defendants of abuse a total of $800,000 in damages for the "sheer horror" they suffered from the hands of Derk Clarke, who was the Dormitory Supervisor of St. George's School

---

[130] BBC May 24, 2002.

[131] Stephan, Cheryl, St. Catherine's Standard, *A Matter of Trust: The Father of a Priest's Sexual Assault Victim Expected Compassion from his Church: Instead He Ended up in a Legal Fight*, April 9, 1999.

in Lytton (Anglican). Williamson cited, "the institutional defendants' failure over so many years to uncover the terrible crimes of Clarke, the failure to report the matter to the police demonstrated an award of punitive damages.

The defendants' conduct was both arrogant and high-handed. The well-being of these violated children was sacrificed." The Anglican diocese of Cariboo – although only responsible for 60% of the verdict – announced that it would declare bankruptcy on October 15, 2001. In 1988, Clarke was sentenced to 12 years in prison for sexually assaulting 17 boys in Lytton and Vancouver over a 23-year period.[132]

More than 1,800 lawsuits were filed by natives who alleged abuse while attending schools operated by the Catholic, Anglican, and United churches while under contract to the federal government.[133]

In 1996, Bishop Hubert O'Connor was sentenced to 30 months in jail for sex crimes against native Indian women at a boarding school he ran in the 1960s. At that point, O'Connor was the most senior Catholic clergyman in Canada to be convicted. [134]

The Cornwall area of Ontario may be a sleepy hollow of relatively poor citizens on the banks of the St. Lawrence River, but it is a time bomb waiting to happen in exposing a satanic ring of pedophiles which stretches from the St. Lawrence to Florida in the United States, and consists of bishop, priests, judges, policemen, probation officers, and businessmen. It involves unsolved murders and clandestine meetings with sordid and fatal goals.

The ring allegedly involves community leaders engaged in hebophilia (sexual abusing of male teens), and ritual abuse. The alleged victims are older than is typical in previous MVMO (Multiple-Victim, Multiple-Offenders) cases. Three of the alleged perpetrators have committed suicide. There are allegations that the Ro-

---

[132] Edmonton Journal, *Abuse Victims Awarded Damages; They were raped by Supervisor at School*, August 11, 2001.

[133] Sarick, Lila, The Globe and Mail, *Compensation Could Beggar Churches, Religious Leaders Warn*, April 16, 1999.

[134] Sunday Age, September 15, 1996.

man Catholic Church paid hush money to at least one victim. There are accusations of a cover-up, perpetrated by the local police, by the Ontario Provincial Police (OPP), and even by the office of the Attorney General of Ontario.

Every Friday night, for many decades, Roman Catholic priests and other leading professionals from the Cornwall community would meet with selected church altar boys. The boys would be subjected to ritual abuse.

According to a 1996 affidavit of Ron Leroux, a 54-year-old painting contractor now living in Maine. "I have witnessed a 'clan' of pedophiles. During this party, l observed a ceremonious ritual of candles in the altar boys' rectums with sheets over them. These altar boys were walking around with the candle in the rectum and the sheet over them with no clothes on, and during this ceremony, several members of the clergy were fondling these young boys and molesting them." The statement also says: "I have witnessed sexual improprieties -- molestation, fondling, oral sex, intercourse (anal) between the above-mentioned clan members and minors."

This sex-ring is believed to be multi-layered, highly organized, and intergenerational.

Since the perpetrators were in positions of power in the community, they were able to manipulate the system so that they were never arrested. When a victim complained to the police, a cover-up was organized so that the abuse could continue. The cover-up extended to the Cornwall police, the Ontario Provincial Police (OPP), and even the office of attorney general of the province.

This concealment has resulted in few criminal trials and no convictions. Police incompetence may also be a factor.

For seven years, Bishop Eugene LaRocque of the Diocese of Alexandria – Cornwall has been determined to keep his name out of lawsuits filed against diocesan priests even though depositions name him as a participant in satanic sex rituals. For example, Shelley McDonald testified that LaRocque forcibly raped her during a satanic ritual while Dr. Arthur Peachy, who has since committed suicide, assisted him.

McDonald also witnessed LaRocque and several others raping her brother, Robbie. With the continued exposure of LaRocque comes more attention to Diocese of London and other priests who were ordained at the same time as LaRocque, i.e., Bishop James Doyle of Peterborough, and a renewed interest in the death of the late Alexandria-Cornwall Bishop Adolphe Proulx of Hull, who was found fatally castrated in the water at his cottage.

What started this domino investigation?

Ron Leroux, who was molested as a boy, and later became a member of this pedophile ring signed an affidavit on May 13, 1996. Subsequent trials and investigations have added names of prominent members of the community to the list of pedophiles in this ring. Leroux filed charges and named 15 men in the Cornwall area who are part of this pedophile network. Other victims also made statements. Through the years, the list has grown and had reached into the Knight of Columbus, doctors and even members of the Mormon Church.

The original fifteen names included only 3 laymen: Claude Shaver is the former Chief of Police; Ken Seguin was a probation officer, who committed suicide in 1993; Malcolm MacDonald was former Roman Catholic attorney who committed suicide. The twelve original clergy named by Leroux include: Bishop Eugene LaRocque; Father Donald McDougald, Father Bernard Cameron, Father Gary Ostler, Father Kevin Maloney, Father David Ostler, Father Ronald (Rory) Mac-Donald, and Ron Wilson, a local priest. Four priests have since died: Monsignor RJ MacDonald, John McPahial, John Donihee, and Norman Loney. Except for LaRocque, all the clergy spent time at St. Columbana Church in Cornwall, either as pastor or associate pastor. McDougald, Cameron, Gary Ostler, and Maloney were all pastors.

According to Leroux, this pedophile ring met throughout Cornwall and in Fort Lauderdale, Florida. In Cornwall, they met and allegedly abused the minors at Camerona's Point, Ken Seguin'a home in Summerstown, Malcolm MacDonald's summer residence on Stanley Island, and St. Andrew's Parish house. In Fort Lauderdale, they gathered in places where young male prostitutes would spend time together such as Birch Avenue and the Marlin Beach Hotel. Leroux claims that he saw the "pedophile network members" from the late 1950s through 1993 engage in "sexual improprieties, molestations, fondling, oral sex, intercourse (anal) between the clan members and minors" at regular meeting spots and at Malcolm MacDonald's law office.

Leroux claims that MacDonald collected child pornography. In an affidavit, Leroux claims to have observed Bishop LaRocque fondling and molesting altar boys at a cottage at Camerona Point. He claimed that an adult dropped off him and his friend, Stan Legalais at the Point, where he observed a ceremonious ritual of candles in the altar boys' rectums with sheets over them. He claimed that he not only observed Cameron and McDougal molesting boys, but claimed that LaRocque, Cameron, and McDougal molested him as a minor.

These rituals were allegedly held on a weekly basis. Carmerona Point was the location of one priest's death. Leroux states that he observed LaRocque and Claude Shaver (Chief of Police in Cornwall) talking to male prostitutes who were minors in Fort Lauderdale. He claimed that he witnessed Malcolm MacDonald and minors engaging in sex in a Florida hotel, and that he saw Ken Sequin and Ron Wilson, a police officer, in Florida as well. Over the years, those named and charged in the dioceses have been highly active and some are still in the priesthood.[135]

On February 2, 1991, Archbishop Alphonsus Penney of St. John's, Newfoundland, resigned after a church commission criticized him for failing to prevent extensive abuse of boys living in Newfoundland orphanages. [136]

On September 13, 1996, Bishop Hubert O'Connor was sentenced to two years and six months for sexually assaulting to two teenage girls at a boarding school in central British Columbia in the 1960s when he was the principal. [137]

CARRIBEAN

HAITI

Father Jude Berthomieux Frederic, headmaster of Frere Paulin School and a philosophy teacher at Jeremie High School, was suspended by his local Bishop Willy Romelus of Jeremie. Frederic stated that several of his diocesan colleagues have violated the Code of Canon Law involving chastity and honesty. Bishop Hubert Constant of For-Liberte, President of the Haitian Bishop's Conference, supported the suspension. Frederic did not elaborate on his remarks. Bishop Romelus imposed a vow of silence upon Frederic and suspended his right to celebrate Mass.[138]

---

[135]Likoudis, Paul, *The Wanderer*, Pending Arrest of Pedophiles Expected to Implicate Bishop, Cornwall, Ontario.

[136] www.bishopaccountability.org

[137] www.bishopaccountability.org

[138] National Catholic Reporter, *Priest who Made Allegations of Abuse is Suspended*, May 24, 2002.

EUROPE

In 2001, The European Parliament passed a motion, "Responsibility of the Vatican in Regard to the Violation of Human Rights by Catholic Priests." It was passed by a vote of 65-49, with six abstentions. The Parliament requested the Vatican "to seriously examine every indication of sexual abuse committed in the heart of its organizations..."

The parliamentary motion had no executive character. Instead, it was intended to demonstrate a "moral judgment." It went on to state that the EU "condemns all the sexual violations against women, particularly against Catholic nuns." The EU requested that the "Vatican seriously examines every indication of sexual abuse committed in the heart of its organization...[And] to re-establish women in their posts in the religious hierarchy, who were removed from their responsibilities because they called the attention of their superiors to these abuses."

The Vatican released a press statement claiming that the superiors of the religious congregations and the bishops of the localities where the abuses took place have already taken precautions to make sure these situations do not happen again. This was in response to the comprehensive Report prepared by Sr. Marie O'Donohue on sexual abuse by priests against nuns.[139] It was presented to the Vatican Congregation for Institutes of Consecrated Life and Societies of Apostolic Life.[140]

On July 19, 2002, the European Union passed the Council Framework Decision on Combatting Trafficking in Human Beings.[141]

AUSTRIA

In 1995, Austrian Archbishop of Vienna, Hans Cardinal Hermann Groer was accused of molesting up to 2,000 pupils, monks, and seminarians. He resigned April

---

[139] O'Donohue, Sr. Maura, *Memo from Sr. Maura O'Donohue MMM: Urgent Concerns for the Church in the Context of HIV/AIDS*, February 1994.

[140] Zenit.org, *European Parliament Assails Vatican Over Abuse Cases, Measure Seen as Attempt to Impede Papal Visit*, Strasbourg, France, April 6. 2001.

[141] COUNCIL FRAMEWORK DECISION of 19 July 2002 on Combatting Trafficking in Human Beings, Official Journal of the European Communities.

1995 although he denied the allegations. [142] The Catholic Church in Austria released a statement stating that the allegations were "in essence true." The Vatican
lodged its own investigation and the top four bishops in Austria issued the statement. The sexual abuse took place at an all-male high school in Hollabrunn in the
1970s.

Most Austrians are Catholic although approximately 25% or 1.2 million regularly attend Mass.[143]

The Catholic Church has addressed the issue of pedophilia by appointing ombudsmen and establishing a hotline for victims.

BELGIUM

Child Focus, a Belgian child protection agency, published a study which found
that an alarming number of children who are immigrants in Belgian, have gone
missing. In 2001, approximately 1,500 "unaccompanied minors" were registered
as arriving in Belgian. In 2002, 400 of them are now missing. Child Focus suggested that 24% of them may be involved in prostitution or forced labor.[144]

The Catholic Church has addressed the issue of pedophilia by appointing ombudsmen and establishing a hotline for victims.

FRANCE

In September 2002, French and Romania officials agreed to exert a new level of
fighting the trafficking of Romanian children to France. Thousands of Romanian
children are involved in prostitution in France, as well as aggressive begging and
illegal immigration.

President Jacques Chirac's new Minister of Interior, Nicolas Sarkozy, plans to
introduce legislation, which would deport all prostitutes from France who are outside of the 15-country member European Union. Prostitution in France is legal
although solicitation is illegal. Approximately a decade ago, a new wave of Eastern
European and Balkan prostitutes started to show up in France.

---

[142] Profile Magazine, 1995.

[143] Erlanger, Steven, The New York Times, *Vienna Buries Child Victims of the Nazis,* April 29, 2002.

[144] Wheeler, Sharon, BBC Europe, *Belgiums' Missing Migrant Children,* June 18, 2002.

There are about 15,000 – 20,000 prostitutes in France. More than 50% of them operate in Paris. More than 50% of those in Paris are foreigners from Romania and Albania, Nigeria, Sierra Leone, Benin and Cameroon, and a recent influx of Chinese. The debate has escalated into a debate among women's groups and even to the point of discussing whether the famed Parisian brothels, which were closed after World War II, would once again open.

In September 2002, 10 men – nine French and one German – were tried and convicted of orchestrating a pedophile network in France. They recruited and raped children. The predators ranged in age from 34 to 59 and had previous records for sex crimes. Some had been incarcerated in Thailand and the Czech Republic.

The kingpin, Miquel Albenque, had already been convicted four times in France for sexual abuse. There were originally 19 victims in all who claimed that they were sexually violated between 1991 and 1996. On the day that the trial began, a 20th victim came forward because he recognized one of the defendants. The 20th victim claimed that he was raped when he was 13 years old. Albenque recruited the victims from poor families or single parent households in poor sections of Paris. He offered them money, vacations, and gifts in exchange for sex. The rest of the group then abused the young boys. Three of defendants admitted to being pedophiles.

Others claimed that they were not pedophiles but were homosexuals and asserted that was the reason that they were being persecuted. Albenque received 15 years. The professions ranged from dog handler, salesman, lab assistant, gardener to translator.

Abbot Rene Bissey was a parish priest in Monsignor Pierre Pican's diocese. Pican was Bishop of Bayeux and Lisieux in Normandy. Bissey confessed to Pican that he had molested children. Pican chose not to report the crime because he argued it was heard in "confession." Bissey was convicted and sentenced to 18 years in prison in October 2000 for his sexual crimes against children. The abuses occurred between 1987 and 1996. He repeatedly raped one boy and abused 10 others. The bishop knew of Bissey's crimes for two years before Bissey was arrested.

In 1996, Pican removed Bissey from his parish work and sent him to a home to rest for 6 months. Pican then reassigned Bissey to another parish.[145] French prosecutors indicted Pican for not going to French law enforcement. Pican maintained that since he heard the crimes in confession, he could not breach that confidentiality. Father Stanislas Lalanne, Spokesperson for the French Bishop's Conference, stated on Vatican Radio that when Bishop Pican first learned of Bissey's criminal acts, Bissey was on the verge of suicide and that is why Pican did not go to the police. He believed that Bishop Pican exercised "freedom of conscience."

When Pican took the stand during Bissey's trial, he refused to answer the question as to whether he knew of Bissey's criminal acts. At his own trial, it was acknowledged that Bishop Pican learned of Bissey's offenses from the Vicar General of Normandy in 1996. Pican claimed that he did not know of the extent of Bissey's acts. Bishop Pican was convicted for failing to blow the whistle on a pedophile priest in his parish and the Court sentenced him to a three-month suspended prison term and ordered to pay one franc to each of the four victims as a symbolic gesture. Pican's conviction was the first time in more than 150 years that a high-ranking clergyman in France was found guilty of a crime. [146]

In a similar case in Aix-en-Provence, a court sentenced Father Hubert Barral to five years in jail (three suspended) for failure to assist a person in danger and failure to denounce a crime. Barral, 67, turned a blind eye as Marc Ruther, 49, raped two young minor boys who were entrusted to the parish church, as well as a third boy who was not a minor but who was psychological impaired and under the care of the parish as well. Barral and Ruther used to be lovers. Ruther would take the boys to his bedroom which was adjoined to Barral's and sometime Barral would watch Ruther raping the boys.[147]

The Lourdes Bishops' Conference was held in 2001 after the Bissey trial. The conference's edict states that the church promises to report priests suspected of

---

[145] www.ireland.com, *Bishop to be Tried for not Denouncing Child Abuse, April 22, 2001.*

[146] Zenit.org – Paris, *Prosecutor Says Secrecy of Confession Is No Excuse – Wants Bishop Imprisoned for Failing to Denounce Pedophile,* June 17, 2001.

[147] http://sg.news.yahoo.com/010904/1/1e53e.html, Caen, France, *French Bishop, Priest, Found Guilty of Pedophilia,* September 4, 2001.

child abuse in the future. "Priests who are guilty of pedophile actions must answer for them in court. They must make good the ill they have done and bear the weight of the punishment imposed by the church and by society." Between 1998 and 2002, 30 French priests were tried or investigated. Today, 11 are currently serving prison sentences. There are currently an additional 19 under investigation for rape or sexual assault on minors. There are approximately 25, 000 Catholic priests in France.

In December 2000, former Bishop Jacques Gaillot admitted that he placed a Canadian priest in a French parish in the late 1980s despite knowing that the priest may have been a pedophile. In 1997, the Vatican removed Gaillot from his Normandy diocese and demoted him to another diocese but for unrelated reasons.

GERMANY

Some German priests have been convicted for abusing children in the last decade, but there has been no scandal in German akin to that in the United States. German Bishops agreed in April 2002 to study new guidelines on handling clergy's sex abuse of minors. Several Roman Catholic Church officials have been suspended and are under investigation. An investigation was launched against four clergymen. One is being investigated for sexually assaulting a 13-year-old boy in 1998.

There are three cases in the diocese of Essen. One 57-year-old priest was forced into retirement when he was accused of pedophilia 22 years ago. The other two cases are related to incidents which allegedly occurred in 1992 and 1999.

Another priest in Mainz diocese is accused of abusing a 14-year-old boy in the 1980s. Two priests in Paderborn district were suspended on pedophilia charges, and another two were suspended in the Bavarian district.

Bishop Franz Grave of Essen estimates that there may be 300 to 300 cases in Germany, where there are 18,000 Catholic priests and 27 million Catholics, which equals one-third of the national population although only a fraction of that regularly attends Church. German priests adopted a charter in June 2002 barring sexually abusive priests from their duties.

They submitted their charter to the Vatican for approval. Victims' groups in German consider the charter "too mild." Cardinal Karl Lehmann, the Archbishop of Mainz, stated, "Looking at this objectively, we probably should expect more revelations of this kind." While the Vatican seems to have taken the position that the pedophile priest scandal may be an American scandal, Lehmann disagrees.

"Sexual abuse is not just a problem of one country, and not merely of one professional group, like priests. The experiences of the Catholic Church in America have also greatly affected us."

This position was taken after Lehmann in the spring of 2002 stated that the German Catholic Church took the issue of pedophilia very seriously but felt that what was happening in America was not the same situation in Germany. A 62-year-ol priest, with a criminal record of involvement in a pedophilia network of abusing minors, is still on the payroll in the diocese of Aachen in western Germany. In June 2002, the German Church started a hotline for victims.[148]

Germany Auxiliary Bishop Franziskus Eisenbach of Mainz resigned on April 16, 2002, after a female university professor accused him of sexually assaulting her during an exorcism. He denied the allegation and the Vatican said his resignation was not an admission of guilt. [149]

HOLY SEE

See Miami, Florida notes on Vatican seminarians going to Miami's Our Lady of Little Flower Church for orgies.

In May 2002, a two-day conference "21st Century Slavery," was held in Rome. One of the principal organizers was Jim Nicholson, US Ambassador to Holy See's office.[150]

---

[148] Mouslon, Geir, The Independent, *German Priest Faces Abuse Charges*, July 16, 2002; Associated Press, *Two German Church Officials Suspected of Sexual Offences Against Minors*, August 22, 2002; Boston Herald, *German Church Leader Pledges Stronger Fight Against Pedophilia*, July 22, 2002; Xinhua News Agency, *Germans Lead Attack on Internet Pornography*, March 20, 20002; Coonan, Clifford, Reuters, *German Cardinal Sees More Priest Sex Abuse Charges*, July 22, 2002; abcnews.go.com, *German Priest Scandal Likely to Widen*, July 22, 2002; Agence France Presse, *Over 200 Cases of Pedophilia by German Priests*, July 22, 2002; Kim, Lucian, Boston Globe, *Catholic Hierarchy in Germany Rejects Criticism on Abuse*, August 4, 2002; Erlanger, Steven, The New York Times, *Catholic Church in Germany Learns from U.S. on Child Abuse*, July 25, 2002.

[149] www.bishopaccountability.org

[150] Darlington, Shasta, Reuters, *Rome Forum Aims to Battle Slavery*, May 16, 2002; Agence France-Presse, *US Urges Rich Countries to Fight Trafficking*, May 15, 2002.

IRELAND

Ireland was mentioned in Sr. Maura O'Donohue's 1994 report which found that young nuns were seen as targets for sex by Catholic priests, and in some cases, the priests impregnated the nuns and then encouraged them to have abortions.

There has been an emotional public outcry about abuse in the Church. The Irish Bishops have backed a wide-ranging investigation into child abuse over the past 60 years after more than 20 priests, brothers and nuns were convicted of molesting children. The Catholic Church agreed to pay $110 million in compensation to victims of abuse in church-run vocational schools.[151] In January 2002, the government established a compensation fund for victims, which was expected to pay out more than $500 million.

In 1997, Father Brendan Smyth, a 70-year-old priest, died of a heart attack when he began serving a 12-year prison term after pleading guilty to 74 counts of sexually abusing 20 boys and girls between 1958 and 1993. Irish Bishops apologized to their congregations for the Church's insufficient attention to pedophiles in the priesthood.

In a 1999 meeting with the Bishops of Ireland, Pope John Paul II said, "These scandals, and a sociological rather than theological concept of the Church, sometimes lead to calls for a change in the discipline of celibacy. The difficulties involved in preserving chastity are not sufficient reason for overturning the law of celibacy."[152]

In 1999, James Kelly, known as Brother Ambrose of the Brothers of Charity Order in Cork, pled guilty to sexual offenses going back 40 years against three boys, then between the ages of eight and 18 years. Kelly, 74, received two 18-year consecutive years for a total of 36 years.[153]

---

[151] Feminist Daily News Wire, *Priest Scandal Extends Worldwide; Catholic Heartland of Ireland Reels with Revelations,* August 13, 2002.

[152] Associate Press, *Pope & Sexual Abuse,* June 27, 1999; Catholic World News, *Pedophile Priest Dies in Irish Prison,* August 25, 1997; The Associated Press, *Pope Close in Prayer to Victims of Sexual Abuse, But No Change to Celibacy Rules for Priests,* June 27, 1999.

[153] *Electronic Telegraph,* "Priest of 74 is Jailed for 36 Years," November 24, 1999.

Father James Murphy pled guilty to 11 charges against seven boys as young as 10 years of age. Police believe that there may have been hundreds more offences. Murphy's actions remained secret for 20 years. One of his victims had a nervous breakdown and told the police about Murphy's abuse. Murphy received a 30-month jail sentence.[154]

In 1999, Nora Wall, a Roman Catholic nun, was found guilty of raping a ten-year-old girl in 1988. Wall pinned down a girl, who was entrusted to her care, while a homeless man raped her in at St. Michael's orphanage run by the Sisters of Mercy in Waterford. Wall was ordained in 1966 and was appointed director of St. Michael's in 1978. Wall was the first nun to be convicted of rape in Ireland and the 35th member of the Catholic clergy to be convicted of sexual child abuse.

The Sisters of Mercy have also been sued by hundreds of former residents at Goldengridge, another one of them orphanages in Dublin. The Sisters paid out monies to a couple whose 11-month-old infant died four days after arriving at the home in 1955. The baby's legs were burned. According to witnesses, they had holes "the size of a silver dollar." In another case, 230 complaints were made against 75 priests who were employed at Artane, a Christian Brothers school in Dublin.[155]

Father Sean Fortune, a notorious pedophile, was known in the church and in the community in a small Irish village of Fethard-on-Sea in County Wexford. As he had been abusing young boys for decades, he was blackmailing them into silence and pressuring their parents for money while stripping the elderly of their pensions. Even though parishioners organized a delegation to two Bishops and wrote to the Papal Nuncio in Ireland, nothing was done.

One victim even told his parents and the late Bishop Herlihey. After he died, the boy's father complained to Herlihey's successor, Bishop Comiskey, who was also informed not just about Fortune, but many priests as well. Fortune stayed in Wexford for six years until Comiskey sent him to London to study and receive treatment. Two years later, Comiskey brought Fortune back to Ireland, where he began once again his sexual prowess upon children.

---

[154] *The Mirror*, "2 ½ Years for Sex Priest," June 2001.

[155] *The Times* Foreign News, June 12, 1999.

In 1995, Colm O'Gorman, a former Fortune victim, told the police about Fortune which resulted in Fortune being charged with 66 counts for sexual, indecent assault and buggery against eight boys. The Catholic Church was forced to remove Fortune at this time – 18 years after the first complaint against Fortune. Bishop Comiskey then disappeared to the US for alcohol treatment. Fortune killed himself in 1999 during the first week of his criminal trial.

In 1995, Comiskey vanished after Irish newspapers reported that Comiskey made more than one solo trip to Thailand for holidays and stayed in a Bangkok hotel known for prostitution with underage boys. In April 2202, Comiskey, the Bishop of Fern, resigned following these heavy criticisms of his handling of sex abuse allegations.[156]

On April 1, 2002, Bishop Brendan Comiskey of Ferns was the first known member of the church hierarchy to resign voluntarily over his management of an abusive priest. He came under fire for his handling of Reverend Sean Fortune. In the end, Comiskey apologized, and the church launched a full-fledged probe into the scandal. [157]

In April 2002, Irish law enforcement officials announced that a former senior Department of Education official was involved in a pedophile network in which children were allegedly tortured and forced to have sex with animals at residential centres in Kilkenny City, Cappoquin, and Clonmel. Law enforcement claimed that some clerics were regular visitors to St. Michael's residential center in Cappoquin.[158]

On May 7, 1992, Bishop Eamonn Casey stepped down after admitting he had fathered a son with a woman in Connecticut in the U.S. back in 1973. Bishop Casey had used child funds to provide her thousands of dollars in child support.[159]

[156] Pogatchnik, Shawn, *Irish bishop Resigns Amid Scandal,* April 1, 2002.

[157] www.bishopaccountability.org.

[158] Hennessy, Mark, The Irish Times, *Retired Civil Servant was in Paedophile Ring, says TD,* April 30, 2002.

[159] www.bishopaccountability.org.

ITALY

Mentioned in Sr. Maura O'Donohue's 1994 report which found that young nuns were seen as targets for sex by Catholic priests, and in some cases, the priests impregnated the nuns and then encouraged them to have abortions.

A week after the Pope met with the US Cardinals in Rome in April 2002, Famiglia Cristiana (Christian Family) reported that at least seven priests in Italy were sentenced to prison for pedophilia. Two other priests were under investigation, one had to pay damages to his victim, and dozens of others were sent for treatment to Jesuit-run center for "troubled" priests in northern Italy over the years. Father Giannantonio Fincato told the magazine that he is watching six other priests. He was quoted, "It is hard. A pedophile priest is like any other pedophile, he hides it."[160]

In August 2002, Terres des Hommes, released a study, which stipulates that Italy is a "main gateway" into Europe for children sold into sex slavery. The non-governmental organization claims that some 6,000 children aged 12 to 16 are victims of child trafficking. Under Italian law, minors are guaranteed protection and the right to education. This exacerbates the problem since some impoverished parents believe that if their children get to Italy, they will be taken care of. The victims come from Albania, Romania, Moldova, and Nigeria. New Italian law calls for digitally fingerprinting new arrivals. Many of these victims are then moved onto Britain, France, Spain, Belgium, Holland, and Germany.[161]

In September 2002 in Mexico, Father Edgar Gaudencio Hidalgo, 46, was arrested for having had sex with minors, and in orgies at the San Casterest in Quarto Sacristy in Naples, Italy. The Italian officials swore out a warrant for this Mexican priest in November 1999 and the Mexican authorities collaborated with Interpol and responded to the Italian extradition request. A young girl reported to police that when she was 11 in 1997, Gaudencio Hildago forcefully raped her. The priest

---

[160] The Washington Post, *Catholic Magazine Reveals Pedophilia,* May 1, 2002; Associated Press, *Catholic Magazine Reveals Pedophilia* ,May 1, 2002.

[161] Reuters, *Italy gateway to Europe for Child Sex Slaves,* August 1, 2002.

was found at a parish in Santa Maria de Guadalupe in Iztapalapa in southeastern Mexico City.[162]

In October 2002, the Italian Carabinieri paramilitary force, in conjunction with Interpol and officials in Spain, Portugal, Germany, France, Austria, Poland, Russia, Ukraine and Belarus, orchestrated "Operation Sunflower" – an international bust of human traffickers. About 80 people were arrested – 63 of them in Italy. About 150 search warrants were served and over 120 people identified. At least five nightclubs were shut down and searched.

Of the 63 arrested in Italy, three of them were Russian women who are members of the Russian mafia and leaders of the trafficking ring. Many of the immigrants were sex slaves. Many of Ukraine travel agencies supplied the fake passports and visas. Many of the traffickers were routed to Italy through Poland, Germany, and Austria, from Belarus and Ukraine.[163]

THE NETHERLANDS

The Catholic Church addressed the issue of pedophilia by appointing ombudsmen and establishing a hotline for victims.

POLAND

Archbishop Juliusz Paetz of Pozna, who was a remarkably close associate of Pope John Paul II, resigned on March 28, 2002, when the allegations arose that he had made sexual overtures to young clerics. He denied the accusations. Nevertheless, he stated that he was resigning for the "good of the church." The Vatican investigated, but the outcome was inconclusive.

PORTUGAL

In 2001, Christian Albert Mullenders, a Dutch citizen, was found guilty of pedophilia and received a four-year sentence in prison and was ordered to pay $3,750 euros to each of his three minor victims. He used them in pornographic films. He

---

[162] TheNewsMexico.com, *Priest Wanted in Italy on Sex Charges Arrested in Mexico City,* September 19, 2002.

[163] Associated Press, *Alleged Human Traffickers Arrested,* October 3, 2002.

is a trained chef. Mullenders will serve his sentence in the Netherlands and is prohibited from entering Portugal for five years after his release.[164]

Police arrested a 55-year-old man for sexually molesting at least 19 minors. A dozen more allegations were still under investigation. Ten cases were proven through DNA samples. Nine more children identified him in a police lineup.[165]

At Fatima in 1991, Father Boniface de Rosario, a Malaysian posing as a bishop of the African Comboni missionary order, solicited funds from an unsuspecting pilgrim for a seminary that was never to be built on the outskirts of Fatima. He was also a notorious pedophile. In 1990, Boniface was arrested, convicted, and sentenced, but also received an amnesty for his crimes under an amnesty granted by President Mario Sares to mark the visit to Portugal of Pope John Paul II in 1991.[166]

SPAIN

A priest in rural Spain was arrested in early February 2002 as a suspect in an Internet child pornography ring that also served as a chat room for child abusers to exchange their experiences. That same month, a parish priest from Casares de Hurdes, an impoverished village of several hundred inhabitants in southwest Spain, was among nine people arrested by police in a three-country bust of online internet child pornography ring.

Four people were arrested in Argentina, a 15-year-old boy in Mexico, and three other adults in Spain. The ring circulated child pornography materials and swamped child abuse experiences online.[167]

---

[164] Portuguese News, *Dutch Pedophile Given 4-Year Jail Sentence,* April 7, 2001.

[165] Portuguese News, *Notorious Paedophile to Go Free?,* September 8, 2001.

[166] Interview with Carlos Evaristo, Fatima, Portugal, August 2002; Letter from James Louis Bair to The Honorable Niel Wicks at the British Embassy in Lisbon, February 28, 1991; Letter from Nigel Wicks, British Vice Consul to James L. Baird, March 11, 1991; Letter from David Glenday mccj, Combaoni Missionaries of the Heart of Jesus, May 13, 1990; Sevicos do Ministerio Publico Comarca de Ourem documents, November 13, 1991.

[167] Reuters, *Spanish Priest Arrested in Child Porn Ring Bust,* February 14, 2002.

In August 2002, Spain set up a radar and sensitive night-sight camera network along its southern coast to catch traffickers in dinghies and boats trafficking victims from Morocco to the shores of Spain. The primary route is across the hazardous Strait of Gibraltar, which is only nine miles wide at Tarifa. [168]

SWITZERLAND

The Catholic Church has addressed the issue of pedophilia by appointing ombudsmen and establishing a hotline for victims.

Bishop Hansjoerg Vogel of Basel resigned June 2, 1995, after admitting he had impregnated a woman following his appointment to the hierarchy the year before. [169]

In the Geneva Court of Assizes, the head of an Albanian mafia band which forced minors to sell heroin and abducted and sexually brutalized children was found guilty and sentenced to 10 years in prison. [170]

THE UNITED KINGDOM

Officials in the UK believe that there are 250,000 pedophiles in the UK alone. *The Hunt for Britain's Pedophile* is a book and BBC television series which aired in the UK in mid-2002. It was a two-year television project in which television cameras were allowed within Scotland Yard's pedophilia unit following investigations. During the initial investigation, "Operation Doorknock" unfolded. This initial investigation led to the uncovering of a sinister pedophile ring which had been operating for 30 years where thousands of children were abused.

In 1996, the Working Party of the Catholic Bishops' Conference of England and Wales produced "Healing the Wound," a document concerned with the victims of abuse and called upon people to appreciate the depth of pain in the lives of victims, to listen carefully to victims and survivors, to promote dialogue about abuse within the Church, and to activate pastoral resources. This was the second document on child abuse from the Bishops' Conference of England and Wales.

---

[168] Nash, Elizabeth, The Independent, *Spain Sets Radar on Refugees,* August 16, 2002.

[169] www.bishopaccountability.org.

[170] Le Temps, June 20, 2001.

In February 2002, the United Nations Office for Drug Control and Crime Prevention launched a global project in London using television to warn the public about the dangers of human trafficking. It aired in nine languages.

On October 1, 2002, six individuals were arrested across England – 10 addresses in Birmingham, London, and Bedford, and one in Dessau, Germany for their participation in an Indian mafia gang, whose members all have British nationality. They are allegedly involved with a significant group who has smuggled hundreds of human beings into UK.[171]

Between 1995 and 1999, 21 of 5,600 Catholic priests in England and Wales were convicted of offenses against children. One archbishop resigned over his handling of pedophile priests.

In 1999, Reverend John Gerard Stock, then 69, pled guilty to gross indecency on altar boys going back to the mid-70's. The victim was 10 to 12 years old at the time. He pled guilty to sexually assaulting another London altar boy 20 years ago. He was given in total a concurrent conditional sentence of two years less a day.

Earlier Stock pled guilty to 34 counts of gross indecency spanning 22 years from 1959 to 1981 involving 16 young males. Barb MacQuarrie of the Sexual Assault Centre of London, stated, "Stock seems to have received lenient treatment compared to how others might have fared. If this had been a nobody, a poor man, a man of color, he probably never would have gotten off so lightly." Stock is required to live and work at the Scarborough Foreign Mission where he will be supervised by members of that community, and he will have no contact with young people.[172]

Father James Murphy sexually assaulted altar boys and church attendees' sons from 1977-1983. His acts remained secret for 20 years. One of his victims had a nervous breakdown and Kelly's torment was revealed. One victim was assaulted

[171] BBC News, *Human Trafficking Ring Smashed,* October 1, 2002.

[172] Geigen-Miller, Peter, London Free Press, *Sentencing fails to Reflect Seriousness,* January 17, 1999.

after a funeral, another in Kelly's car on the way to football training and a third on a holiday. The boys were as young as 10. Murphy, 53, was jailed for 30 months.[173]

Although new guidelines were established by the Catholic Bishops of England and Wales in 1994, which state that clergy should pass on all allegations of abuse by clergy to the children's protection group, Father Joseph Jordan's allegations were not passed over to the protection group until after his arrest, which was four years after the warning was given in a 1995 letter by Bishop Budd of Plymouth to the Archbishop of Cardiff, the Most Reverend John Aloysius Ward.

In 2000, Father Joseph Jordan, 42, was sentenced to 8 years in jail after he pled guilty to six charges of indecent assaults against two boys aged nine and 10 between 1987 and 1989, obstructing justice, and possession of indecent computer pictures of children. Judge Peter Jacobs called the pornographic pictures" totally depraved." Five hundred pornographic images of boys were found on Jordan's computer. The Judge ordered Jordan to be placed on the Sex Offenders Register for 10 years.[174]

In 2000, Archbishop of Birmingham Vincent Nichols granted "administrative leave" to Father Gerard Flahive during the duration of the investigation into the 1980 alleged child sexual abuse allegations.[175]

In 2000, 69-year-old Father Robert Deadman – otherwise known as Father James – was sentenced to six years for indecent assaults on four women between 1983 and 1993. The trial outlined ten years of abuse silenced by brainwashing of the victims after going to a religious man for help. One victim was threatened with dire consequences if she did not continue to see him. He told another that she would die in six months and go to hell if she did not continue to see him.[176]

---

[173] The Mirror, *2 ½ Years for Sex Priest,* http://www.ic24.net/mgn/THE_MIRROR/NEWS/P10S3.html.

[174] BBC News Online, *Church Didn't Report Alleged Abuser,* October 23, 2000; BBC News Online, *Eight Years Jail for Welsh Priest, October* 20, 2000.

[175] BBC Online, *Priest Suspended In Abuse Probe: The Roman Catholic Church is Rocked by More Allegations,* October 29, 2000.

[176] Dowling, Nicola, Source Newspaper Unknown, *Supporters of Convicted Priest Vowing to Appeal,* October 30, 2000.

In 1996, Father Adrian McLeish, was jailed for six years after admitting to 12 charges of sexual abuse of boys under 14, eight possessing and distributing child pornography and two of importing illegal videos. McLeish abused the boys for five years. McLeish had an extensive child pornography collection   which could have filled 24 volumes of Encyclopedia Britannia 11 times over. His collection included 9,000 images.[177]

"She cost me 800 pounds and brought me in 250 pounds an hour," said Carlos, a trafficker of girls for prostitution in London. "Of course, I deal with under-age girls – it is safer for me. Even then, English girls can always bring you down by talking, but the foreign girls do not talk, they are gagas – like babies."

They come from a deprived area in black South Africa, say they are 14 but I have my doubts – they are younger. They are going home in a couple of months because they have made so much money. I have been sending between 500 and 700 pounds back to their families each week. It is a two-way deal: they help me, and I help them. They are not even property; they are commodities. You never use force on English girls, no matter how young she is, because she can run away or tell the police. But the foreign girls are yours: you have bought them, and they must do what you tell them."[178]

The Church in England and Wales set up an independent committee to advise how to stop sexual abuse after several pedophile cases surfaced. The Archbishop of Wales resigned after receiving criticism over his handling of pedophile cases.

In late September 2002, Shetland island local police announced that a new wave of human traffickers use a circuitous route to Shetland via the Faroes. Both islands are being used by traffickers moving victims from Scandinavia, Russia, and Europe. Many of the victims have been caught on the triangular route between Shetland, the Faroes, Scandinavia, Denmark, and Iceland. There are also Indians and Chinese being moved along this route.

There has also been a huge increase in trafficking in Dumfries and Galloway, where more than 400 people have been caught in the last year. Together with the Irish and Scottish criminals, the Russian mafia, Chinese Snakehead gangs, and

---

[177] *The Age*, November 14, 1996.

[178] www.guardian.co.uk, December 24, 2000.

Eastern European criminal syndicates are making headway into Ireland and Scotland with trafficked victims. [179]

Pope John Paul II forced Archbishop John Aloysius Ward of Cardiff, Wales, to resign on October 26, 2001. Ward had been accused of ignoring warnings about two priests, who were later convicted of child abuse. [180]

NORDIC COUTRIES

DENMARK

Denmark's Presidency of the Europe Union post began July 1, 2002. The 4th Asia-Europe (Asem) Summit was held in Copenhagen in September 2002. The EU was represented by 15 leaders while the heads of China, Japan, and South Korea joined seven other Asian leaders. One of the topics focused upon was "human trafficking and poverty."[181]

BALKANS

BULGARIA

In August 2002, the Bulgarian government approved a bill which provides for the formation of a "National Anti-Human Trafficking Committee. The committee is to collect information, analyze it, and provide suggestions for combating human trafficking. The bill calls for an overall state committee and several local committees.[182]

ROMANIA

The Organization for Security and Cooperation (OSCE) claims that trafficking victims from 13 – 18 are thrown into prostitution by traffickers. Helga Konrad of OSCE is quoted, "Women are sold like animals. Their teeth and bodies are inspected. A woman can be sold for US$1250 and then sold for US$350 or US$450

---

[179] Briggs, Billy, The Herald UK, *Shetland Gateway for Human Traffickers*, September 30, 2002.

[180] www.bishopaccountability.org

[181] Star Publications, *Denmark gets set for 4th Asem Summit*, September 15, 2002.

[182] BTA, *Bulgarian Government Passes Bill on Combatting Human Trafficking*, August 16, 2002.

an hour. Many of the women and girls in Balkans come from eastern European countries. Ninety percent of the prostitutes are trafficked. [183] In 2001, Romania passed a law prohibiting trafficking. Offenders may receive anywhere from 3 to 12 years. Up to date, 77 people have been prosecuted. [184] During Ceauşescu's reign of terror, thousands of orphans were abused in orphanages. Since his execution, even though there are still 100,000 orphans in homes, orphans and prisons, there are thousands more now on the street, which make them vulnerable to pedophiles. Bucharest has become a pedophile Mecca recently because of the 5,000 street children. In November 1997, Michael Taylor, a Church of England Vicar, was caught in bed with a 14-year-old boy near Bucharest's main railroad station. Many of the street children of Bucharest hang out at the station and sleep in the sewage systems close to warm pipes during the winter.[185]

EASTERN EUROPEAN COUNTRIES

CZECH

At the 2002 International Conference on human trafficking held in Brussels, Belgium in September 2002, the Czech Republic Justice Minister Pavel Rychetsky stated that his country was turning from a transit country of trafficking into a country of destination. He said that the victims "are coming from Ukraine, Russia, Moldova, Lithuania, Slovakia, Romania, Bulgaria, Vietnam, and China."[186]

POLAND

Approximately 90% of the people in Poland are Catholic. Archbishop Juliusz Paetz, 67, resigned as Archbishop of Poznan. "Rzeczpospolita" reported that the

---

[183] Mutler, Alison, Associated Press, *Up to 170,000 People, Mostly Women and Young Girls, are Trafficked in Southeast Europe Each Year,* June 3, 2002.

[184] Binder, David, MSNBC, *Country Report: Romania, A Trafficking Transit Point, Romania Also has its Victims,* 2002.

[185] BBC World: *British Vicar Charged,* November 13, 2002; SoRelle, Ruth, Houston Chronicle, *Children of the Streets,* 1996; Delaney, Bill, CNN WORLD, *Sewers Home to Romania's Forgotten Orphans,* July 23, 1997; Briley, Harold, BBC News, *Bitter Winter for Romania's Street Children,* January 2, 1998.

[186] Radio Free Europe/Radio Liberty, Crime and Corruption Watch, *Human Trafficking in the Czech Republic,* September 26, 2002.

Archbishop had been accused by numerous priests of making sexual advances and demands on them.

Before his resignation, Paetz was banned from a seminary because of his known homosexual proclivities. The Vatican commission sent to Poznan confirmed the allegations against Paetz. He worked at the Vatican from 1967 to 1976 in the Bishops Synod Secretariat. He was nominated bishop in 1982 and elevated to Archbishop by Pope John Paul II in 1996.[187]

GREECE

In October 1999, Terres des homes hired Mrs. Nathalie Heppell, a former Canadian police officer to investigate the trafficking of Albanian children into Greece. This was in response to the enormous disappearance of Albanian children in Elbasan, Korce, and Berat. I visited Berat and Korce in 2000.

In both of those villages, there was no presence of children. Over 1,000 children had disappeared in Berat alone. More than a thousand Albanian children were in Greece. The children worked 12 – 15 hours a day in Greece. One Albanian boy was sent back to Albania to have his arm amputated so that he would be more effective as a beggar in Greece. That is organ/medical trafficking.

There were also many Iraqi (Kurdish), Greek, Afghan, and Russian children on the streets. In addition, there were street children from Sierra Leone, Eritrea, Kashmir, Türkiye, Sri Lanka, and Romania. In Athens, 75% of the street children were Albanian and were between 2 – 12 years of age.[188]

In December 2001 at an Athens Conference on trafficking, it was announced that up to 20,000 foreign women – the majority from the Soviet bloc – were trafficked to Greece as sex slaves. Although prostitution is legal in Greece, the laws on trafficking stipulate longer sentences for those found guilty of trafficking underage children. The fines range between 50,000 and 100,000 Euros.[189]

---

[187] BBC Poland, *Polish Archbishop 'Molested' Students*, February 23, 2002; Associated Press, *Archbishop in Poland Denies Sex Harassment Allegations*, March 17, 2002.

[188] Terre de Hommes, *Stop Child Trafficking, Presentation files for Albania-Greece Programme*, October 2001.

[189] Howden, Daniel, BBC News, *Greek Sex Industry Uncovered*, December 24, 2001.

AFRICA

Twelve percent – 116.6 million - of the world's one billion Catholics lived in Africa. According to the 2001 Catholic Almanac, 561 were bishops and archbishops. There were approximately 26,000 priests and 51,000 nuns. Sexual abuse of nuns, including rape was a genuine problem in Africa. Some nuns had become impregnated and encouraged to seek abortions. Priests preyed upon nuns and young girls and used the AIDS prevention argument as an excuse – "engaging with a virgin would prevent AIDS," however insane and erroneous that argument was.

The clerics also exploited financial and spiritual authority to win sexual favors from the nuns. The convents and nuns were dependent upon the priests and the Bishops for money, transportation, and pastoral assignments. Reports about Africa Catholic clerics had been compiled, presented, and discussed at the highest levels in the Vatican.

The Vatican responded on March 20, 2002, "The Holy See is dealing with the question in collaboration with the bishops, with the Union of Superior General and with the International Union of Superiors General."

In April 2002, 79 religious leaders representing religious institutes and Orders from Botswana, Swaziland, and South Africa attended a conference in South Africa and committed to acting against clergy who were guilty of sexual abuse within the Church. Their released the Report from the Leadership Conference of Consecrated Life.

"Any incident of sexual misconduct and abuse is a cause of grave concern, calling for immediate action and redress," read the report.

They noted that the structures established by the Church within the last five years to handle sexual abuse have been "limited."[190]

In February 1994, Sr. Maura O'Donohue, who spent six years as AIDS coordinator for the Catholic Fund for Overseas Development, authored a scathing report on the Catholic religious sex scandals. **O'Donohue's comprehensive report**

---

[190] Schaeffer, Pamela, National Catholic Reporter, *Ex-Nun Tells of Rape by African Priest,* April 6, 2001; National Catholic Reporter, *South African Bishops Denounce Abuse,* May 4, 2001; National Catholic Reporter, *African Leaders Vow Action on Clergy Sex Abuse,* June 29, 2001, Farley, Margaret, National Catholic Reporter, *End Silence, Then Take Action,* April 6, 2001.

covered 23 countries: Botswana, Burundi, Brazil, Colombia, Ghana, India, Ireland, Italy, Kenya, Lesotho, Malawi, Nigeria, Papua Guinea, Philippines, South Africa, Sierra Leone, Tanzania, Tonga, Uganda, United States, Zambia, the Congo (DRC), Zimbabwe.

O'Donohue found that since the 1980's many nuns were refusing to travel alone with priests for fear of sexual harassment and rape.

In March 1994, Fr. Robert J. Vitillo, spoke to a theological study group at Boston College. His presentation was entitled, "Theological Challenges Posed by the Global Pandemic of HIV/AIDS."

"The last ethical issue which I find especially delicate but necessary to mention involves the need to denounce sexual abuse which has arisen as a specific result of HIV/AIDS. In many parts of the world, men have decreased their reliance on commercial sex workers because of their fear of contracting HIV. As a result of this widespread fear, many men (and some women) have turned to young (and therefore presumably uninfected) girls (and boys) for sexual favors. Religious women have also been targeted by such men, and especially by clergy who may have previously frequented prostitutes. I have heard the tragic stories of religious women who were forced to have sex with the local priest or with a spiritual counsellor who insisted that this activity was 'good 'for the both of them." Frequent attempts to raise these issues with local and international church authorities have met with deaf ears," claimed Vitillo.

On February 18, 1995, Cardinal Eduardo Martinex, prefect for the Vatican congregation for religious life, along with his staff, was briefed on the African problem by Medical Missionary Mary Sr. Maura O'Donohue, a physician.

In November 1998, Sr. Marie McDonald presented her Report, "The Problem of the Sexual Abuse of African Religious in Africa and Rome" to the Council of 16, which consisted of delegates from the Union of Superiors General, a community of men's religious communities based in Rome, the International Union of Superiors General, a community of women's religious communities based in Rome, and the Congregation for Institutes of Consecrated Life and Societies of Apostolic Life, the primary Vatican office which oversees religious life in the Catholic Church.

McDonald found eight primary factors which contribute to these cleric acts:

- Celibacy and chastity are not values in some countries.

- The inferior position of women in society and the Church. Nuns, who are taught to be subservient to priests, find it impossible to say NO to priests.

- The AIDS pandemic. Nuns are viewed as safe prey as are young boys and girls.

- Financial pressures since nuns are paid low stipends.

- An insufficient understanding of a consecrated life at all religious levels.

- Naivety by young African nuns who lack the social and educational skills to say NO.

- Cultural ignorance.

- Conspiracy of silence.

In September 2000, Benedictine Sr. Esther Fangman addressed 250 Benedictine abbots in Rome addressing the problems among the religious.[191]

BOTSWANA

Mentioned in Sr. Maura O'Donohue's 1994 report which found that young nuns were seen as targets for sex by Catholic priests, and in some cases, the priests impregnated the nuns and then encouraged them to have abortions.

BURUNDI

Mentioned in Sr. Maura O'Donohue's 1994 report which found that young nuns were seen as targets for sex by Catholic priests, and in some cases, the priests impregnated the nuns and then encouraged them to have abortions.

---

[191] National Catholic Reporter Cover Story, *Reports of abuse, AIDS exacerbates sexual exploitation of nuns, reports allege,* March 16, 2001.

COTE d'IVOIRE

Ben & Jerry's Ice Cream of Vermont, in conjunction with Population Media Center, UNICEF, Anti-Slavery Organisation, and the International Labour Organisation conducted a sweeping study into the child labor slavery conditions in the chocolate industry in the Republic of Côte d'Ivoire.

CONGO

Mentioned in Sr. Maura O'Donohue's 1994 report which found that young nuns were seen as targets for sex by Catholic priests, and in some cases, the priests impregnated the nuns and then encouraged them to have abortions.

GABON

Tens of thousands of children as young as five-years-old are trafficked each year in West and Central Africa. In 2001, 40 children were found on board of a Nigerian-registered ship; 23 children were between three and 14 years old; 17 were aged 15 to 24. The children were from Benin, Mali, and Togo, and headed to Gabon. There was a need for countries in West Africa to harmonize their anti-trafficking laws to protect children.[192]

GAMBIA

Up to 64 sex workers were deported. The victims were from Senegal, Nigeria, and Sierra Leone.[193]

GHANA

Mentioned in Sr. Maura O'Donohue's 1994 report which found that young nuns were seen as targets for sex by Catholic priests, and in some cases, the priests impregnated the nuns and then encouraged them to have abortions.

---

[192] Anti-Slavery – News, *'Slave Ship' anniversary highlights plight of Africa's Trafficked Children,* April 15, 2002.

[193] Kamara, Foday, The Daily Observer (Gambia), *Over 60 Prostitutes Deported,* June 6, 2002.

GUINEA

Guinea has a well-established aid program in their refugee camps. Aid workers from more than 40 agencies and over 65 named workers involved in using the very food they were providing for sexual favors.

Most of the girls were between 13 and 18 years of age, but children as young as four years of age were also targeted. Children in **Sierra Leone and Liberia** were also target for aid in exchange for sexual favors to the aid workers.[194]

KENYA

Mentioned in Sr. Maura O'Donohue's 1994 report which found that young nuns were seen as targets for sex by Catholic priests, and in some cases, the priests impregnated the nuns and then encouraged them to have abortions.

A Study released in 1991 found that 300,000 school age children were not attending school. During the 1980s there was an increase in children on the streets, children, in the commercial sex industry, and as illegal migrant workers on plantations and in domestic work.[195]

In 2001, nine people, including three employees of the United Nations High Commission for Refugees were arrested on criminal charges of demanding sex in exchange for humanitarian aid.

LESOTHO

Mentioned in Sr. Maura O'Donohue's 1994 report which found that young nuns were seen as targets for sex by Catholic priests, and in some cases, the priests impregnated the nuns and then encouraged them to have abortions.

LIBERIA

Liberia has a well-established aid programme in their refugee camps. Aid workers for more than 40 agencies and over 65 named workers were involved in using the

---

[194] Millar, Kate, Agence France Presse, *UN Probes Child Refugee Sex Abuse Claims in West Africa*, February 27, 2002.

[195] Onyango, Ms. Philista, Regional Chairperson, African Network for the Prevention and Protection of Child Abuse and Neglect (ANPPCAN, Kenya) 1999.

very food they were providing for sexual favors. Most of the girls were between 13 and 18 years of age, but children as young as four years of age also were targeted.[196]

MALAWI

Mentioned in Sr. Maura O'Donohue's 1994 report which found that young nuns were seen as targets for sex by Catholic priests, and in some cases, the priests impregnated the nuns and then encouraged them to have abortions.

In 1994, this information was presented to Rome. In 1988, a team of a diocesan women's congregation was dismissed by a local bishop after it complained that 29 nuns were impregnated by diocesan priests.

MALI

The city of Gao in northwestern Mali is a starting ground of trafficking of victims to Europe. From Gao, some Nigerians and Ghanaians risked the treacherous trek across the desert headed for Europe. They headed north to Morocco and from there, their entry point into Europe was Spain. The network was organized in Spain. The Chief of Police in Gao, Abdoullaye Danfaga, claimed that the biggest industry in Gao is human trafficking.[197]

MOZAMBIQUE

The Mozambique government and the International Organization for Migration (IOM) hosted a trafficking in persons workshop in Maputo, Mozambique for the 14-member state of Southern Africa Development Community (SADC) in October 2002. Although the trafficking in persons issue was not well-documented, the IOM suggests the trafficking of persons for sexual purposes was pervasive. South Africa was a destination country for those in more impoverished African countries in the region and served as a transit country for those going to Europe, North America, and Southeast Asia.[198]

---

[196] Gillian, Audrey, and Peter Moszynski, The Guardian, *Aid Workers in food for Child Sex Scandal,* February 27, 2002.

[197] Baxter, Joan, BBC World News, *Mali's Dangerous Desert Gateway,* June 25, 2002.

[198] International Organization for Migration, *Mozambique – MIDSA Workshop on Trafficking in Persons,* October 4, 2002.

NIGERIA

Mike Mku, Special Adviser to President Olusegun Obasanjo on Human Trafficking and Child Labor reported that 90 percent of foreign prostitutes in Italy were from Nigeria. From 2000 – 2002, 1,098 Nigerian trafficked victims across Europe and North America were deported to Nigeria. More than 98% were female. Only 17 were male.

The highest figure for deportation to Nigeria came from Italy, followed by Spain. The rest of the deportees came from Germany, South Africa, Saudi Arabia, Switzerland, and the United States. Combating trafficking from Nigeria was hampered by the absence of a strong punishing law. Mrs. Titi Atiku Abubakar, wife of the then Vice-President, and Chairwoman of Trafficking and Child Labor Eradication Foundation (WOTCLEF) initiated the trafficking bill which awaited passage during this time.[199]

In May of 2202, Mrs. Atiku made a call upon the Vatican with Cardinal Francis Arinze, urging the Vatican to add its moral authoritative voice to the crusade against the social malaise of human trafficking.[200]

In the Spring of 2002, a Nigerian boy's headless body was found floating in the Thames River. After consulting with experts, it was suggested that the boy may have been a victim of the ancient ritual of Obeh. This ritual involves drinking the blood from the head of a pre-pubescent child and washing with the blood. Obeh is a ritual which sacrifices to a Nigerian sea goddess in worship.[201]

Mentioned in Sr. Maura O'Donohue's 1994 report which found that young nuns were seen as targets for sex by Catholic priests, and in some cases, the priests impregnated the nuns and then encouraged them to have abortions.

---

[199] United Nations Integrated Regional Information Networks, (allAfrica.com), *Some 1,098 Victims of Trafficking Deported in Three Years,* June 26, 2002.

[200] Odivwri, Eddy, allAfrica.com, *Atiku's Wife Tasks Catholic Church on Human Trafficking,* May 29, 2002.

[201] Dynes, Michael, British News, *Torso Boy 'Sacrificed to Sea Goddess,'* April 19, 2002.

RWANDA

Rwanda is a predominantly Catholic country where 75% of the population call themselves Catholic even if they did not practice in 2002.

In 1994, almost one million men, women, and children were slaughtered and hacked to death with machetes and guns over a 100-day reign of terror. It was the worst genocide since World War II.

In 2000, an international panel created by the Organization of African Unity concluded that the UN Security Council, the United States, France, and the Roman Catholic Church failed to prevent the genocide. At the time of the report's release, the Vatican had "no comment" on the report. The panel concluded that the Catholic Church, as well as the Anglican Church, failed to use "their unique moral position among the overwhelmingly Christian population to denounce ethnic hatred and human rights abuses."

Not only was the Catholic Church implicated, but several Catholic priests, including Bishop Augustin Misago, and several nuns were implicated and prosecuted for their direct involvement in the murders of innocent victims. Two priests were found guilty and put to death. Some of them had even been moved from Rwanda to other locations to protect them from prosecution in Italy and Belgium.

Athanase Seromba, who now by 2002 used the alias of Don Anastasio Sumba Bura lived in Florence, Italy. Seromba, a Hutu, was a deputy Catholic priest at Nyange, Rwanda in April 1994. He had been stationed in Nyange for about six months. During the genocide of the Tutsis, Seromba sided with the Hutus.

As the killing began, Seromba encouraged Tutsis to come to his church for protection. Approximately 2,500 sought protection carrying knives, guns, stones, and traditional weapons. Seromba was not an innocent bystander in their slaughter. He was intricately involved with the Gregoire Ndaimana, the Hutu Mayor, in meetings where they and others planned the refugees' fatal fates.

Days after they were secured in the church, Hutus confiscated most of the Tutsis' weapons leaving them virtually defenseless. According to a police officer who attended the meetings, Seromba agreed to the killings. Witnesses saw Seromba firing into the crowd. After a couple of days of fighting, Seromba and Ndaimana decided that the church needed to be destroyed, and bulldozers were used to smash down the church with the remaining refugees inside.

As the church was collapsing, Hutu militia moved into the church to kill the remaining survivors. Father Jean Francois Kayirang and Edouard Nkurikiye, two of Seromba's priests were indicted in a Rwandan court in 1998 and found guilty of crimes against humanity for their participation in the Nyange massacre and were sentenced to death. Seromba left Rwanda and passed through Kenya before he landed in Florence, Italy.

African Rights, a London human rights organization, which investigated the genocide for years, presented a letter regarding Seromba to Pope John Paul II. African Rights received no response. Bishop Augustin Misago of Gikongoro also was indicted and tried for his collaboration with officials who exterminated Tutsis. Misago allegedly sent three priests and dozens of schoolchildren to their deaths after denying them shelter. They were hacked to death by a mob.

In mid-May 2000, Pope John Paul II sent a letter of support to Misago after the prosecutor sought the death penalty. African Rights released another report on the involvement of the nuns in the Rwandan genocide. They called upon the Belgian courts to prosecute Sister Gertrude Mukangango and Sister Julienne Kizito residing at the Benedictine Convent in Maredret, Belgium after the Rwandan genocide. African Rights alleged that both nuns were involved in the deaths of 6,000 Tutsis in Sovu, Rwanda from April to July 1994. There were testimonies from 34 witnesses, including other nuns.[202]

SENEGAL

In August 2001, Senegalese authorities busted a sex network trafficking Senegalese victim to Libya. At the airport, several hundred women showed up and claimed that they were models heading to Tripoli to participate in a modeling event.[203]

SIERRA LEONE

Mentioned in Sr. Maura O'Donohue's 1994 report which found that young nuns were seen as targets for sex by Catholic priests, and in some cases, the priests impregnated the nuns and then encouraged them to have abortions.

---

[202] Reuters, *Rwandan Genocidal Clergy Hearts of Darkness,* February 28, 2000, London Times, November 21, 2000; Associated Press, *Blame Shared for Rwandan Genocide,* July 7, 2000.

[203] Doyle, Mark, World Africa, *African Sex Ring Busted,* August 30, 2001.

Guinea has a well-established aid program in their refugee camps. Aid workers from more than 40 agencies and over 65 named workers were involved in using the very food they were providing for sexual favors. Most of the girls were between 13 and 18, but children as young as four years of age were also targeted. Children in **Sierra Leone and Liberia** were also target for aid in exchange for sexual favors to the aid workers.[204]

SOUTH AFRICA

In May 2001, Wilfrid Cardinal Napier of Durban, and President of the South African Catholic Bishop's Conference, expressed "shock, disappointment and condemnation" of the reported sexual abuse of nuns and children. There are about a dozen reported cases of priests having sex with children. Napier claims that the incidences happened years ago.

Auxiliary Bishop Reginald Cawcutt of Cape Town, Spokesman for the South African Bishops' Conference said in *The Southern Cross* that the code of conduct "must be issued to every candidate priest and religious in southern Africa from the very outset." Cawcutt was a regular contributor to the St. Sebastian's Angel sexually explicit website for gay clergy. On the website, Cawcutt wrote that *he looked forward to the deaths of Pope John Paul II and Joseph Cardinal Ratzinger.*[205]

During the June 2002 US Bishop's Conference in Dallas, Texas, Roman Catholic Faithful, which is run by Stephen Brady, released copies of the St. Sebastian's Angel website to the media.

Juan Miguel Petit, Special Rapporteur on the sale of Children, Child Prostitution, and Child Pornography of the United Nations Commission on Human Rights, called for an urgent effort to recognize the increase in sexual violence against children in South Africa. In an onsite investigation while in South Africa in September 2002, Petit concluded that there is an overall increase of rape cases involving incredibly young children and babies as well as a significant increase in

---

[204] Millar, Kate, Agence France Presse, *UN Probes Child Refugee Sex Abuse Claims in West Africa*, February 27, 2002.

[205] National Catholic Reporter, *South African Bishops Denounce Abuse,* May 4, 2001.

the prostitution of incredibly young children. In the case of baby rapes, the ratio between girls and boys was 50:50.

Petit's full Report was be presented to the UN in Geneva during the UN Commission on Human Rights in March 2003.[206]

Dr. Rachel Jewkes of the Medical Research Council in Pretoria, South Africa found that 1/3 of the child rapes in South Africa were committed by teachers and researchers.

"Our findings confirm that rape of girls, especially in schools, is a substantial public health problem."

In 2001, 21,000 child rape cases were reported in South Africa. According to South African Police Service, 41% of all rapes and attempted rapes were on children. Over 15% of all reported rapes were on children under 11, and 26 percent against children 12-17 years of age. In 2000 alone, some 58 daily rapes against children occurred.

During the fall of 2001, South Africa was rocked when newspapers splashed across their front pages the rape of a nine-month-old baby girl. Six men were initially charged, but the charges were later dropped after DNA tests could not link them to the crime. In February 2002, a two-month-old infant girl was raped. One predator was 76 years of age; the other was 26 years of age. In March 2002, a 23-year-old man was arrested for raping a nine-month-old baby girl. Some believed that the increase in infant rapes was fueled by the belief that a man with AIDS would be cured if he had sex with a virgin or that sex with a virgin would protect him from AIDS. About 25% of the adult population in South Africa had AIDS at that time. [207]

---

[206] United Nations, *United Nations Rights Expert Calls for Measures Aimed at Child Victims of Sexual Violence in South Africa,* October 4, 2002.

[207] Reaney, Patricia, Reuters, *Teachers Commit Many South Africa Child Rapes-Study,* January 24, 2002; Swarns, Rachel L., The New York Times, *Child Rape Increasing at Alarming Rate in South Africa,* January 29, 2002, Reuters, *South Africa Police Arrest 23-Year-Old for Baby Rape,* March 7, 2002; BBC, *SA Catholics Admit Abuse,* April 26, 2002; Singer, Rena, Boston Globe, *In South Africa, Painful Past Reclaimed,* May 4, 2002; Cauvin, Henri E., The New York Times, *H.I.V. Survey in*

South Africa was mentioned in Sr. Maura O'Donohue's 1994 report which found that young nuns were seen as targets for sex by Catholic priests, and in some cases, the priests impregnated the nuns and then encouraged them to have abortions.

SUDAN

More than two million people had died because of the 18-year-old civil war and repeated famines in Sudan by 2002. President George W. Bush appointed John Danforth to lead an international commission to investigate slavery in Sudan and it found that Sudan has done little to control the slavery practice which had historical roots.

"They burn villages, loot cattle, rape and kill civilians, and abduct and enslave men, women, and children. The record is clear: the government arms and directs marauding raiders who operate in the south, destroying villages and abducting women and children to serve as chattel servants, herders, and field hands," stated their findings.

Although this commission did not give figures on the number of slaves, other reports had figures ranging from 10,000 to 100,000. Several Christian groups had travelled to Sudan and paid up to $50 to get individuals out of slavery. Many of the Christians in southern Sudan were targeted for abduction.[208]

TANZANIA

Significant numbers of women and children were abducted or coerced into sex slavery from the rural areas to the urban areas. Tanzanian victims were trafficked to South Africa, the Middle East, Asia, and Europe to work as prostitutes. Tanzania's efforts to prevent this slavery were hampered by "severe financial constraints,

---

South Africa Suggests Plateau in Infections, June 10, 2002; LoBaido, Anthony C., WorldNetDaily.com, *Child-Rape Epidemic in South Africa, Fueled by Widespread Belief that Sex with Virgin Cures AIDS,* December 26, 2001; Chang, Kenneth, The New York Times, *South Africa's Bounty,* September 19, 2002.

[208] Lacey, Marc, The New York Times, *U.S.-Led Panel Condemns Sudan for Allowing Slavery to Flourish,* May 22, 2002;Morahan, Lawrence, CNSNews.com, *'Dan Rather Was Duped,' Say Critics of Report on Sudanese Slavery,* May 30, 2002.

pervasive corruption and porous borders." Trafficking was considered a crime both inside Tanzania and outside of the country, but penalties were "relatively light."[209]

Tanzania was mentioned in Sr. Maura O'Donohue's 1994 report which found that young nuns were seen as targets for sex by Catholic priests, and in some cases, the priests impregnated the nuns and then encouraged them to have abortions.

TOGO

See Gabon note.

UGANDA

"Tens of thousands" of women and children have been abducted by the Lord's Resistance Army during the last 15 years. The government had "limited resources, a civil conflict and continued kidnapping raids" which hampered the fight against the exploitation of children by 2002. [210]

Uganda was mentioned in Sr. Maura O'Donohue's 1994 report which found that young nuns were seen as targets for sex by Catholic priests, and in some cases, the priests impregnated the nuns and then encouraged them to have abortions.

ZAMBIA

Zambia was highlighted in Sr. Maura O'Donohue's 1994 report which found that young nuns were seen as targets for sex by Catholic priests, and in some cases, the priests impregnated the nuns and then encouraged them to have abortions.

ZIMBABWE

Zimbabwe was also noted in Sr. Maura O'Donohue's 1994 report which found that young nuns were seen as targets for sex by Catholic priests, and in some cases, the priests impregnated the nuns and then encouraged them to have abortions.

---

[209] Kelley, Kevin J., The East African (Nairobi), *US Accuses Kampala, TZ of Slavery*, June 10, 2002.

[210] Kelley, Kevin J., The East African (Nairobi), *US Accuses Kampala, TZ of Slavery*, June 10, 2002.

AUSTRALIA

A bishop in Ballarat was forced to resign in 1997 after being accused of covering up sexual abuse of another priest. The bishop moved him from parish to parish instead of reporting him to police.

In 1998, an Australian official committee comprised of federal, state and territory legal advisors, submitted a report, "Non-Fatal Offenses Against the Person." They recommended that "significant emotional harm" inflicted by religious groups be classified as criminal offenses.

"It [the committee] is concerned that the criminal offense proposed catches the causing of significant psychological harm to people, accompanied with criminal intention. If a religious organization does that, it, like anyone else, should be guilty of the appropriate criminal offense," read the report.

The committee's findings were supported by a ruling cited from the California Supreme Court that "…coercive persuasion…" by religious sects may cause" …serious physical and psychiatric disorders." From this and other historical and current examples, the report identifies "…the techniques involved may include isolation, manipulation of time and attention, positive and negative reinforcement, peer group pressure, prohibition of dissent, deprivation of sleep and protein and the inducement of fear, guilt and emotional dependence."

Furthermore, it stated, "Freedom of religion is not freedom, for example to defraud, nor is it freedom to cause significant psychological or psychiatric harm to any person,"[211]

On March 26, 1998, Father Morrie Crocker, 60, a Catholic priest, former rugby player, boxer, soldier, and teacher, was found hanging by a chain in a gym in Wollongong, Australia. He was a whistleblower. He came forward and reported on his fellow clergymen who abused children. In 1989, three men told Crocker that they had been abused by Fr. Peter Comensoli and Brother Michael Evans. Crocker told Bishop William Murray and the police about the abuse. Murray failed to act, and the police claimed that there was not enough evidence to launch an investigation because so much time had elapsed.

---

[211] Bita, Natasha, The Australian, *Australia Getting Tough on Cults,* October 14, 1998.

Frustrated with inaction, Crocker went to the press in 1993. There were sworn statements from six men. In the end, Comensoli was charged, convicted, and sentenced to 18 months in jail. Comsensoli pled guilty to assaulting two boys aged 11 and 17, and admitted that he used alcohol, pornography, and gifts to seduce the boys. Brother Evans fled Wollongong and committed suicide before he was charged. Father Crocker's efforts led to the Woods Royal Commission inquiry into pedophilia.

Church officials ostracized Father Crocker. Peter Cullen, a newspaper editor at the time, stated, "[The Church] treated him like a leper, preferring to sing the praises of the accused and the jailed rather applaud the courage of the priest who cut the pedophile clergy off at the knees."

After Crocker's death, it was discovered that his notebooks with information leading to allegations of three other priests as abusers was missing. [212]

In 1999, 17 women, who were orphans at Nazareth House Orphanage in Brisbane in the 1940s and 1950s sued The Poor Sisters of Nazareth. The victims claimed sexual and physical abuse by the nuns while in the orphanage. Most of the nuns had died. The Order paid up to US$41,400 to 13 of the women but would not admit any guilt. Lizzie Walsh, a victim, claimed that she was raped with a flagstick to "get the devil out of her."

Bobbie Ford, another victim, claimed that she and other girls were stripped naked, thrown on the bed on their stomachs and whipped with straps. Ford claimed that the children were abused like that every night. Sister Breen said that the victims received payments for their "unhappy memories."[213]

In 2001, The Child Sex Trade Report – a 10-year international study, conducted by the charity Child Wise – revealed that thousands of Australians were involved in the child sex industry. It found an alarming rate of Australian men

[212] New Zealand Herald, *Clergy Heroes Fighting Priest Loses Last Round, Fr. Morrie Crocker, Australian Whistle-Blower Apparently Commits Suicide*, March 1998.

[213] Reuters, Sydney, Australia, *Australian Nuns in Sex Abuse Spotlight*, August 28, 2002.

involved in pedophilia, child pornography and sex tourism overseas. Many Cambodian children had been bought for sex and brought to Australia.[214]

The report called for the reopening of a special police unit to investigate Australians who travel overseas to have sex with children. [215] In 1994, Australia passed child sex tourism laws that provided for jail terms of up to 17 years for Australians found guilty of sex with children overseas.

In January 1999, Stephen John Brown, a 49-year-old former church camp caretaker, was accused of 170 charges related to 27 boys between the ages of 11 – 17 years of age – the highest number of victims ever attributed to date at that time to a single alleged offender by New South Wales police. The alleged offenses occurred between 1977 to 1998 at 18 locations in Sydney and on the south coast, central coast, southern highlands, and central west during youth camps and skiing trips. [216]

In May 1998, Philip Newell, the Anglican Bishop of Tasmania, offered apologies to victims of sexual abuse by the clergy following the publication of a report, which he commissioned. The report criticized him for caring more about a predator than a victimized boy at a church camp.

The Report uncovered 40 years of systematic sexual abuse by Tasmanian clergy. Newell announced that most of the Report's recommendations would be implemented. The report gave the bishop the power to suspend or dismiss a priest against whom a case of sexual misconduct had been established.[217]

In February 1999, an Anglican minister was charged and arrested for sexual molestation of two sisters in 1976, who were seven and eight years of age at the time.[218]

---

[214] Mercer Phil, BBC, *Australia Child Sex Trade 'Growing,'* December 16, 2001.

[215] Mercer, Phil, BBC, *Australia Child Sex Trade 'Growing,'* December 16, 2001.

[216] Australian Associated Press, Sydney Morning Herald, *Former Church Worker to Face New Child Sex Charges,* January 19, 1999.

[217] Australian Associated Press, *Bishop Apologizes for Church's Sex Abuse,* May 8, 1998.

[218] Australian Associated Press, *Anglican Minister Charged with Sex Offenses,* February 19, 1999.

In 1964, 12-year-old Dominic Ganino, a Catholic schoolboy walked his dog and disappeared. Fifteen days later, his body was found, and police believed that he was assaulted and that the case had the trappings of a homosexual murder. What was withheld at that time of this crime was another unsolved murder and that Robert Charles Blunden – known as Bert Blunden – was known by Church officials to have abused children.

Blunden was interviewed at the time of the murder. Information about his sex abuse was withheld. Police only learned about Blunden's sex abuse when a victim came forward in 1996.

In that 1996 statement, Father Arthur Kevin Ryan, told police that he learned of Blunden's abuse of children in 1968. Ryan banned Blunden from his parish and informed then Archbishop James Knox, who did not tell police about Blunden. In 1997, at the age of 80, Blunden was jailed for four years after pleading guilty to 27 charges of indecent assault and buggery on males between 1964 and 1970.

Blunden was a church volunteer during fund-raising activities and used to transport altar boys to Smith's Beach, Phillip Island, which was the same camp connected with sex abuse allegations against Sydney Archbishop George Pell. Blunden died in 1998.[219]

In 1999, Victoria's largest class action suit was filed. More than 100 former orphans sued for sexual, psychological, and physical abuse in orphanages across rural and metropolitan Victoria which was run mostly by Catholic nuns. Some cases originated from 1955 to 1965. Children were allegedly flogged, used as labor and sex slaves, and in some cases, shared by their abusers. The children included both boys and girls. They were allegedly forced to engage in sodomy, rape, intercourse, and anal sex. [220]

Between 1993 and 1997, according to Broken Rites, a victims' support organization claimed that 35 Catholic priests and religious brothers were sentenced, and

---

[219] Miller, Wayne, Martin Daly, *Church Accused of Hindering Murder Case,* August 27, 2002.

[220] Sunday Age, June 13, 1999.

five others died before their cases reached trial. Eight others awaited trial. And 12 others were charged for molestation.[221]

In 1995, *The Sydney Morning Herald* reported that from 1987 to 1995 100 Christian Brothers from Sydney, Wollongong, Toowoomba, Perth, and Darwin, were accused of sexually abusing children.[222]

In 1996, 260 men claiming they were sexually molested in boarding schools in Western Australia run by Christian Brothers – dating as far back as 1930s – settled with the Order. The Christian Brothers agreed to pay $3.5 million.[223]

In 1998, the Catholic Church and the Sisters of Mercy reached an out-of-court settlement with more than 60 former Neerko Orphanage residents between 1924 and 1971. The victims claimed that they were sexually abused and, in some cases, imprisoned.

Vincent Keirin Kiss, 70, a former Catholic priest, pled guilty to sex offences against four teen-age boys from 1966 to 1973, and was sentenced to 10 ½ years. He used to take the boys on sailing trips. He had already served time in prison for stealing $990,000 from a charitable trust.[224]

NEW ZEALAND

By 2002, *The New Zealand Herald* had reported that the Catholic Church in New Zealand, had been embroiled in 38 sexual cases of pedophilia by priests within its six dioceses going back to the 1950s. The complaints involved priests, brothers, lay members of the church and involved children, teenagers, and adults who were in pastoral counselling. The hierarchy in New Zealand admitted by 2002 that the way they handled the offenders was wrong and harmful to the victims.

Under new policies, they claimed they would remove any priests from ministry if they were known pedophiles and they urged victims to take their complaints to law enforcement.

---

[221] The Secular Review, July 1997.

[222] The Sydney Morning Herald, July 22, 1995.

[223] Eros Foundation, *Hyprocrites,* April 2000.

[224] Associated Press, *Ex-Priest Sentenced in Australia,* September 13, 2002.

"The Church has come to understand the need for openness and transparency so that people can be empowered to come forward with complaints and the healing process can take place," said Lyndsay Freer, the Catholic Communications Director.

In the past, the Church had prohibited details of any settlements. The Society of Mary, the largest Catholic Order in New Zealand, explicitly stated that they would not act against victims who spoke out. Offenders in New Zealand were sent to Australia for treatment.[225]

In August 2002, the Action for Children and Youth Aotearoa, an umbrellas group of child advocates, released a report which claimed that New Zealand had yet to comply with recommendations made by the U.N. Committee on the Rights of the Child. Spokesman, Ian Hassall, said that violence towards children was too high and that help for abused victims was inadequate.[226]

Brother Rodger Maloney, who ran Maryland Special School in Christchurch for disadvantaged in the 1970s had been suspended from his duties in Australia after new allegations surfaced that he had abused boys while at Maryland. Maloney was a member of the Order of St. John of God in Australia. Eleven complaints were lodged against Maloney. In Australia alone, the Order of St. John of God had already paid out $4 million to victims.[227]

Alan Woodcock, a former New Zealand priest, had been arrested for child sexual abuse in Great Britain. He had served as a priest in Manawatu and Wellington regions and as a teacher at an Upper Hutt Catholic college. One of his victims alleged that Woodcock abused him between 1982 and 1985. Woodcock resigned from the Order of the Society of Mary in 1991.[228]

---

[225] The Zealand Herald, *Catholic Church in NZ Admits to Sex Abuse Payouts,* June 22, 2002.

[226] www.onenews.nzoom.com, *Shameful Child Abuse Report,* August 8, 2002.

[227] www.onenews.nzoom.com, June 27, 2002.

[228] www.onenews.nzoom.com. August 2002.

EAST ASIA

In February 2002, in Bali, Indonesia, there was a three-day conference on illegal immigration. Thirty-seven nations from Asia, the Middle East, and the Pacific were represented.

The delegates agreed to examine proposals regarding human smuggling and trafficking and improvement on law enforcement training.

"The most important achievement is that countries in the Asia-Pacific region agreed that people-smuggling and related transnational crimes are international issues that require a collective response," stated the Indonesian Foreign Minister Hassa Wirayuda.[229]

CAMBODIA

Mary Robinson, while still the top United Nations Human Rights Chief, slammed the male Cambodian culture for allowing it to be culturally acceptable that men have sex with girls as young as 8, 9, 10 years of age. Robinson said that Cambodia "needs to undergo a cultural change as rapidly as possible."

Cambodia was in the past and still is today viewed as a Mecca for human trafficking of children and a haven for local and foreign pedophiles.[230]

In May 2002, 10 Vietnamese children, ranging from 12 to 18, were trafficked to Cambodia and forced to work as sex slaves. They were rescued from a brothel by children's rights' activists. A month later, the activists were arrested and imprisoned for entering Cambodia illegally. They were sentenced up to three months in jail in Cambodia and upon release were to be deported to Vietnam. The traffickers were not prosecuted. As many as 20,000 underage prostitutes were working in

---

[229] Lekic, Slobodan, The Associated Press, *Illegal Immigration Conference Closes, International Forum Recommends Stiffer Laws, Police Cooperation to Combat People Smuggling,* February 28, 2002.

[230] BBC World News, *UN Rights Chief Rebukes Cambodian Men for Child Sex Trade,* August 22, 2002.

Cambodia and US State Department estimated at the time that 100,000 sex workers were working against their will in Cambodia. There was anywhere up to four
million trafficked sex slaves entered into the arena of human trafficking in 2001.[231]

With a cease-fire in 1998, the trade and tourism exchange between Cambodia
and Thailand has flourished. So, had a new feeding ground for trafficking children
from Cambodia to Thailand under the false hope of a job in Thailand.[232]

Crackdowns on sex slaves in Thailand and Vietnam were pushing sex predators
to Cambodia. Girls as young as 12 or 13 years of age were sold into slavery as
virgins, for a price anywhere from US$300 to US$1,000.

Most Cambodians survived on less than one dollar a day in 2002. Although
sex with those 14 years or younger carried a penalty of up to 20 years in prison,
prostitution was thriving in massage parlors, karaoke bars, brothels and on the
streets. [233]

CHINA

"Thirty-five children, aged 1 to 7 years of age, were rescued from being sold, while
28 persons suspected of trafficking children were arrested. Chen Qifu, an inhabit-
ant of Xisui, and members of his family had embarked on child trafficking in 1995.
The police of Guizou Province succeeded in rescuing children from the sales to
buyers in Guangdong by a group having made an estimated amount of RMB 1
million. Chen Qifu and members of the group admitted to kidnapping more than
60 children, but the police believed the number to be larger."[234]

---

[231] BBC World News, *Cambodia Jails Vietnamese Brothel Victims*, August 5, 2002;
WOMENSENEWS, *Cambodia Prosecutes 10 Women for Being Abducted*, August 17, 2002.

[232] BBC World News, *Cambodia's Trade in Children*, December 12, 2001.

[233] Associated Press, *Child Sex Abuse Tests Cambodia*, August 25, 2002; Doyle, Kevin, The Cambodia
Daily, *Trafficking Victim Challenges Court Decision*, August 17, 2002.

[234] Sinopolis.com, January 13, 2000.

HONG KONG

Hong Kong had a population of about seven million in 2002, and of that, 250,000 were Catholic. There were about 300 Catholic priests in Hong Kong at that time. Cardinal John Baptist Wu had been the Bishop of Hong Kong for over 27 years.

Michael Lau, 42, was defrocked as a priest in 1995. He was one of eight priests who had been accused of sexually abusing as many as 10 children over the past 30 years. Lau's criminal charges involved a teenaged boy whom he sexually molested in a dormitory in 1991 and 1992 while a seminarian.

The victim reported the abuse to the Church in 1994. The Church found Lau guilty and subsequently defrocked him. Lau was criminally charged in 2002. After the diocese handled Lau's case in 1995, they found another priest guilty of child sexual abuse and he was suspended from the ministry while he underwent therapy and then was reassigned to Australia. Another was sent to Canada.

The Hong Kong diocese chose not to report the cases to law enforcement and justified their silence by claiming that they did not have to under Hong Kong law and that the victims' families asked them not to report them. Hong Kong police set up a 24-hour hotline in May 2002. The archdiocese's position then was one of "zero tolerance" since the abuse cases were not made public. BBC's Damian Grammaticas in Hong Kong said that the Church in Hong Kong had been criticized for not acknowledging the cases sooner.[235]

Police Superintendent Shirley Chu, who investigated all eight cases, complained that Church officials refused to turn over written confessions made by priests during the Church's internal investigations, which led to the protection of its own reputation and that of the priests. Hong Kong Church officials admitted that their internal investigations confirmed pedophilia crimes by these priests. The Church refused to turn over documents to law enforcement, which the Church

---

[235] Lyn, Tan Ee, Reuters, *Defrocked HK Priest Charged with Sexual Abuse,* June 6, 2002; BBC News, *HK Investigates New Child Abuse Claims,* May 15, 2002; Reuters, *Three Catholic Priests in HK accused of Child Abuse,* May 2, 2002.

admitted to were confessions. Church officials argued that they would not turn them over because by doing so would violate the sanctity of the confessions.[236]

INDONESIA

According to the International Labour Organisation, at least one million children worked as informal or formal prostitutes across Asia. Child prostitution was on the rise back in 2002. Bali was a Mecca for pedophiles. One of its poorest regions had become extremely popular.

In the Buleleng regency of North Bali, pedophiles looked for children in villages such as Lovina Beach, Kalibukbuk, Kaliasem, Kay Putih, Selata and Anturan. The Yayasan Anak Kita Foundation, which had conducted a thorough investigation into pedophilia since 1998, reported that the first pedophile discovered was around 1973. Ever since then the number of pedophiles either operating or visiting had skyrocketed.

The first ones were disguised as German tourists. In the 1980s Kuta was a major destination for European pedophiles, especially German and French. Karangasem was their next target. They disguised themselves as "foster fathers" for needy children. The pedophiles bribed parents with money, food, household goods, and police and village councils received donations, improvement projects, rental cars, and health and education training. A baby-selling syndicate smuggled teenage girls from Kalimantan in Indonesia to produce babies. The police were investigating whether the girls were also used for prostitution.[237]

JAPAN

The number of foreigners entering Japan on visas is increased to approximately 118,000 in 2001. Sixty percent of them were from the Philippines. About 14, 000 involved in illegal work and 40% of them were bar hostesses – "prostitutes." Foreign workers were absorbed into the sex industry and in some cases, several of

---

[236] Luk, Helen, Associated Press, *Hong Kong Police Complain Roman Catholic Church Shielded Pedophile Priests*, May 16, 2002.

[237] Straits Times Interactive (Singapore), *"Baby Factory' Busted in Sarawak*, June 24, 2002; Juniartha, I Wayan, The Jakarta Post, *Immediate Steps Urged Against Pedophilia*, July 27, 2002; Sharma, Sushil, BBC News, *Regional Police for South Asia*, August 30, 2002.

them had murdered owners of bars where they worked because of abusive treatment. Other victims who were trafficked to Japan had arrived from Thailand and Colombia.

Japan had no law prohibiting human trafficking at that time and because of their anti-prostitution law, although women were coerced and kidnapped into trafficking for sex, the trafficked victims were often prosecuted.[238]

KOREA

Over 5,000 victims from Philippines and the former Soviet Union had been trafficked into South Korea for sex since the mid-1990s by 2002. The September 2002 IOM Report, which reported this finding, was authored by Dr. June Lee, who was the former head of the International Organization of Migration office in Seoul. The Filipino victims had been trafficked to bars located near the U.S. military bases.

THE PHILIPPINES

The Philippines had been mentioned in Sr. Maura O'Donohue's 1994 report which found that young nuns were seen as targets for sex by Catholic priests, and in some cases, the priests impregnated the nuns and then encouraged them to have abortions.

By 2002, there were some 50 million Catholics in The Philippines. Archbishop Orlando Quevedo, president of the Catholic Bishops Conference, said that some 200 Catholic priests had been investigated for sexual misconduct over the past 20 years. Some of the 200 had been dismissed and most had resigned voluntarily.[239]

In July 2002, The Philippine Bishops Conference announced that it would tighten the screening process for applicants for the seminary. Bishop Quevedo announced that 38% of seminary applicants had either sexual abuse experiences as victims or were facing sexual abuse charges.[240]

---

[238] Hara, Shin, Kyodo News, *Trafficking of Female Foreign Workers Increasing,* July 19, 2002.

[239] Reuter, *200 Priests Investigated for Sexual Abuses in Philippine, July* 19, 2002.

[240] Dancel, Joshua, The Manila Times, *CBCP Tries to Salvage Image: Tightens Screening for Seminarians,* July 9, 2002; Gomez, Jim, Associated Press, *Filipino Catholics Address Sex Abuse,* July 8, 2002.

Father Polienta Bernabe, 61, was accused of sexually abusing an eight-year-old girl more than 20 years ago in the United States in Florida. There was a no statute of limitation for having sex with a child under the age of 12 in The Philippines. There was an arrest warrant from a Florida court for Bernabe.

"He [Bernabe] should be apprehended and put on trial. And once proven guilty, he must be penalized with the full force of the law in the country where he committed the crime," Archbishop Oscar Cruz of the Archdiocese of Lingayen-Dagupan announced.

Bishop Cruz also ordered all his priests not to give Bernabe any sanctuary.

"He should be dismissed from the clerical state," the bishop added.

Melissa Price, a Bernabe victim, said that Bernabe had been a visiting priest when he began the abuse in 1978 at the Holy Name Catholic Church in Gulfport and the Holy Family Catholic Church in Petersburg in the 1970s and 1980s. She claimed that she had sex hundreds of times with Bernabe.[241]

Father Apolinario "Jing" Mejorada, a former rector of the Basilica Minore del Nanta Nine in Cebu City, had been accused of sexually molesting four teenaged boys ranging in age from 15 to 17. He molested them between 1995 and 2000 when they were serving as altar boys at the Basilica.

Although the priest was sent to a treatment center near Manila, the boys had demanded that the priest be expelled and threatened to bring legal action if the Order of Saint Augustine did not act. Father Mario Mejorada claimed that church officials paid the boys each $7,157 for their silence.

In Cebu, children of priests with their mistresses were living with priests in rectories. One monsignor had his own basketball team of young boys. Another monsignor had a wife who used his name. A third monsignor was allegedly having an affair with a separated woman who sought pastoral counseling.[242]

---

[241] Cruz, Maricel V., The Manila Times, 'Pain, Shame' for Bishop Over Priest's Sex Raps, July 19, 2002.

[242] Yahoo.com, Philippine Priest Accused of Sexually Molesting Altar Boys, July 22, 200; Stinus-Remonde, Marit, The Manial Times, Another Erring Priest, July 23, 2002.

THAILAND

One-third of Thailand's prostitutes in 2002 were minors, and the sex industry then earned 10-14% of the country's gross domestic product.[243]

In April 2002, Nicholas Bredimus, a wealthy Dallas American businessman was indicted in Dallas for allegedly traveling to Thailand to have sex with minors. Bredimus was arrested by Thai officials in November 2001.

Children told the Thai police that Bredimus paid them to have their pictures taken in the nude and filmed videos of Bredimus having sex with the children. Thai police seized a digital camera, video camera and tape which appeared to show children having sex with a man who appeared to be Bredimus.

After his arrest, Bredimus posted a bond and was released. He then went to the U.S. Embassy in Bangkok and told them that he lost his passport, needed a replacement, and left Thailand. In February 2002, U.S. officials found Bredimus in Hawaii and arrested him.[244]

Bredimus was a wealthy tech businessman, on his second marriage and had a son, who was in his mid-30s. He tried to concoct a wild story for his defense but in the end he was convicted in the U.S. for having sex with a minor abroad.

Before Bredimus' indictment in the U.S., according to prosecutors, only two other American men had been convicted in the U.S. of having sex abroad with minors. He was sentenced to 5 and half years in prison and a $30,000 fine.

In May 2002, Michael Rostoker, a Silicon Valley executive millionaire and top patent attorney in California, was convicted of traveling to Vietnam to have sex with a minor and using the internet to induce a minor to commit sex acts. He paid a 13-year-old girl and her family more than $150,000 and arranged falsified immigration papers to bring her into the U.S.

Two years before that, Marvin Hersch, a professor at Florida Atlantic University, whose pedophilic history went back almost 20 years, was sentenced to 105 years in prison. He molested four Honduran siblings between 10-18 years of age.

---

[243] Ashayagachat, Achara, and Bhanravee Tansubhapol, Bangkok Post, *Legalise It?*, September 3, 2002.

[244] The Nation, *US Indicts Citizen for Thai 'Sex Trip,'* April 25, 2002.

Hersch smuggled the 15-year-old Honduran brother into the U.S. Hersch pretending he was his son, but he was his lover. Hersch was the first American to be convicted under the 1994 statute making it illegal to travel abroad for underage sex.

These cases are called "sex tourism" cases.

Musician Eric Rosser, who is an American from Bloomington, Indiana and who had been living in Bangkok, was the first-ever pedophile to appear on the FBI's Ten Most Wanted Fugitives' list.

On August 19, 2002, the Bangkok Criminal Court approved Rosser's extradition to the U.S. where he is wanted on six counts of producing and distributing child pornography. Rosser allegedly molested an unknown number of girls in Bangkok and Bloomington, Indiana – many of them between seven and 11 years of age.

Rosser filmed himself having sex with an 11-year-old. In 2000, he wrote a letter to a Bangkok newspaper in which he stated, "Yes, I am a pedophile." [245]

BALTIC/NEW INDEPENDENT STATES/CENTRAL ASIA

"A network of Baltic states is working closely with the aim to follow the trafficker all the way back from the destination of the cargo to the country of origin."[246]

KAZAKHSTAN

By 2002, the Kazakhstan state orphanages released children literally on the streets when they turned 16 years of age.

When a child reached 16, they are no longer considered to be an orphan that will be taken care of by the state government. They are turned out on the streets with nowhere to go. Many of the girls end up in prostitution and addicted to drugs. The boys became members of criminal gangs. [247]

---

[245] Perrin, Andrew, TIME, *Shame – Asia's Child-Sex Industry is Booming, despite Tougher Laws and a Few High-Profile Deportation Cases,* September 2, 2002.

[246] BBC, *Tackling the Human Traffickers,* September 9, 2002.

[247] Green, Randy and Sandra, *Letter to Solicitors for Money for "The Light House,"* January 20, 2002.

LITHUANIA

The country passed an anti-trafficking law in 1998, but it was uninspiring at best. By 2002, only 35 cases had been investigated and only three convictions had been successful.[248]

UKRAINE

In August 2002, law enforcement busted a criminal gang who used to ship Ukrainian girls and women into United Arab Emirate brothels. The victims were sold like slaves for $2,000 each. At least, 120,000 young girls and women were sold in 2001. According to the Ukrainian Ministry of Internal Affairs, up to 450,000 victims were sold in recent years. In addition to being shipped to UAE, the victims were sent to Türkiye, Italy, Greece, and Spain. The victims were shipped from the Dnipropetrovsk railway station in Ukraine. Since 1999, up to 125 criminal trials were prosecuted against traffickers in Ukraine.[249]

MIDDLE EAST AND NORTH AFRICA

LEBANON

In the town of Bhamdoun in 2002, there were nightclubs with signs hanging outside – "Super Night Club," "Swing," "Cobra," "White Nights," and "Excalibur." Inside was evidence of women who knowing and some unwillingly are trafficked for prostitution from Russia, Belarus, and Ukraine.

In the late 1990s, victims were from the Republic of Czech and Hungary. Some had agreed to come and do the stripping and sex trade because there was no economy in their countries after the Fall of Communism – no free schools, no free universities, no free apartments, and no jobs to enable them to put a roof over their heads and put food on the table.[250]

---

[248] Jaskunas, Paul, Pittsburg Post-Gazette, *Activists Combat Sex Trafficking in East Europe,* July 1, 2002.

[249] BBC Monitoring Service, *Women-Trafficking Gang Caught in Eastern Ukraine,* August 22, 2002.

[250] Fisk, Robert, The Independent, *A Nation's Worst-Kept Secret: The Women Lured to Lebanon with a One-Way Ticket into Slavery,* July 6, 2002.

MOROCCO

According to Moroccan Government statistics in 2002, 538,000 children under the age of 15 were exploited as cheap labour in this country and did not attend school.[251]

QATAR

By 2002, it was well known that South Asian and African children were trafficked to Qatar to be used as camel jockeys. Most of the children were trafficked from Sudan. The children were strapped to the camels and in some instances, had been severely injured and crushed to death.

"I agree this has sullied Qatar's image abroad and this is also a part of the discussions going on. We do not like it, but we are looking for alternatives," said Sheikh Hamad bin Jassin Faisal al-Thani, President of Qatar's racing organization and a member of the royal family. [252]

SAUDI ARABIA

In 2002, the U.S. State Department revealed that there were 46 known cases of 92 children being held captive in Saudi Arabia. Congressman Richard Burton (R-Ind.) urged President Bush to instruct the State Department to withhold visas of the kidnappers and their extended family members who were holding US citizens against their will.

"If Saudi Arabia is not willing to recognize the importance of American law and the rights of American citizens, it is difficult to see how Saudi Arabia will fully cooperate with the U.S. in the war on terror."

Pat Roush, mother of two daughters had fought for 16 years to bring her daughters back to the US. They were taken from her when they were 3 and 7 years of age.

---

[251] BBC News, June 19, 2001.

[252] Hussein, Kristin Alynn, CNSNews.com, *Illegally Trafficked Children Used as Camel Jockeys in Qatar*, February 26, 2001.

"They are grown women who have been stripped of all their rights as human beings for 16 years and now have been sold into arranged marriages and impregnated by Saudi men. It amazes me to see the lengths to which Washington will go to protect the Saudis and disavow my American daughters" said Roush.

Roush said that the State Department had told her that her youngest daughter would be sole and married in retaliation for her testimony before Burton's committee.

Roush testified that Saudi Arabia "is ruled by a single family of corrupt, degenerative, greedy princes. The prize, of course, is the oil, and the stakes are high. High enough for the government of the United States to sacrifice any ideals and scruples they might have to keep this totalitarian regime operating."

After the hearing, Richard Boucher, State Department Spokesperson, referred to these international parental kidnapping cases as "civil cases."[253]

UNITED ARAB EMIRATES (UAE)

See Bangladesh and Qatar notes.

Even though the trafficking of children for use as camel jockeys is prohibited by the United Nations' Convention of the Rights of the Child (CRC) and by the International Labour Organization's (ILO) Conventions – all which has been ratified by UAE, and even though the Emirates Camel Racing Federation forbids the use of riders under 14 years of age, or weighing less than 100 pounds, there was a strong evidence that children under 14 years of age were still being used as camel jockeys in 2002. The UAE government was not taking adequate measures to tackle this situation.

The victims were usually boys less than 10 years old. [254] In May 2001, some 100 children demonstrated in front of the Embassy of the Arab Emirates in Dhaka against children being sent as camel jockeys.

---

[253] Maier, Timothy W., Insight Magazine, *Kids Held Captive in Saudi Arabia,* June 21, 2002.

[254] Anti-Slavery Organization, www.anti-slavery.org., United Nations Commission on Human Rights, Sub-Commission on Promotion and Protection of Human Rights Working Group on Contemporary Forms of Slavery, 26th Session, Geneva, Switzerland, June 2001.

SOUTHERN ASIA

AFGHANISTAN

In 1999, the London Sunday Telegraph reported that bin Laden paid rifles to Ugandan rebels for African children he trafficked into Afghanistan to work in the drug fields that the Al-Qaeda ran.

BANGLADESH

Children – as young as two years old - were kidnapped in Bangladesh and trafficked to United Arab Emirates as illegal camel jockeys. The children were treated as slaves and lived in harsh conditions.[255] There were many trafficked children in Pakistan and India. Others were trafficked further to UAE.

A 7-year-old boy was rescued from a house by the Mirpur police in conjunction with the Bangladesh National Women Lawyers Association (BNWLA) after discovering that the child's parents thought that the boy was going abroad for an education, but instead was trafficked to Dubai as a camel jockey. Five traffickers were arrested.[256]

INDIA

India was highlighted in Sr. Maura O'Donohue's 1994 report which found that young nuns were seen as targets for sex by Catholic priests, and in some cases, the priests impregnated the nuns and then encouraged them to have abortions.

There were 400,000 to 500,000 child prostitutes in India in 2002.

NEPAL

According to an International Labor Organization (ILO) report circa 2002, the porous 1,000-mile border between India and Nepal, where border crossings then did not require passports, served as an entry point for human slavery.

---

[255] Llewellyn Smith, Julia, The Sunday Telegraph, *Boys of Two Kidnapped to be Camel Jockeys,* November 30, 1997.

[256] The Independent, *Kidnapped Boy Rescued, Five Traffickers Arrested,* January 11, 2002.

Some 12, 000 Nepalese girls and women were trafficked from Nepal into India's sex industry on an annual basis. Indian brothel owner scoured Nepalese festivals scouting for victims. They sold the victims for $200. Girls as young as nine were trafficked with promises of a "better life." Sometime the girls were sold by family members for a few hundred to a thousand dollars.

Girls were forced to have sex with an average of 14 clients daily – minimum of 3 to a maximum of 40 clients. Clients paid more for younger girls. If the girls were tested for pregnancies, and often were found to be infected with HIV/AIDS. In 2000, when Nepalese victims under the age of 18 were tested, 72% of them were infected with AIDS. Consequently, there was a higher demand for victims between the ages of 8 to 12.[257]

PAKISTAN

By 2002, the Human Rights Commission of Pakistan estimated that a woman was raped every two hours in Pakistan. In Punjab, a woman was raped every six hours, and a woman was gang-raped every four days. On June 22, 2002, a 30-year-old woman was raped repeatedly for one hour by four men after a village jury of elders convicted her because her young brother had sex with a girl of a high-class tribe. The woman received an $8,200 check from the government which vowed to pursue the case.

In October 2002, President General Pervez Musharraf under the Prevention and Control of Human Trafficking Ordinance, set different punishments for human trafficking offenses recognizing that human trafficking is a serious offense. The Ordinance extended to all of Pakistan.[258]

SRI LANKA

Large scale trafficking from Sri Lanka was rare in 2002, but when it did happen, it occurred by sea or air. In Sri Lanka, the trafficking route moved from the rural areas to the towns. In the 1980s, Sri Lanka's parents were lured by the promises to take care of their little boys in the Gulf States. In many instances, the boys were trafficked as again as camel jockeys. "Baby farms" on the west coast flourished and

---

[257] Babu, Kausalya Mohan, The Washington Times, *Nepal's Sex-Trade Victims*, October 2, 2002.

[258] F.P. Report, *Two More Ordinances Come into Force*, October 3, 2002.

served as a haven for the illegal adoptions trade. In the last 1980s Japanese men sought brides by mail in Sri Lanka and advertised for virgins. A Catholic convent was responsible for sending these mail orders brides to Japan. [259]

MEXICO/CENTRAL AMERICA/LATIN AMERICA

In a U.N. report issued by the International Labour Organisation circa 2002, some 17.4 million children in Latin America between the ages of 5 and 17 must work to contribute to their families' income to survive. There are approximately 180 million children in the world. One in eight is a child.

Latin America then represented approximately 30% of the world's Roman Catholics. It was a region, where there seemed to be less cases of pedophile priests reported as in other parts of the world. Few doubted though that those cases were rampant even though they were unreported..

The infrastructure may have insulated the fact that there were fewer reports of pedophile priests. The priests were treated like gods in society where they had enormous social power. The region's bankrupt judicial systems, the fact that the culture exudes an excessive distain for homosexuality, and the acceptance that a victim was somehow responsible for such acts also added to the prohibitive nature of witnesses coming forth and hence, no prosecutions.

Individual cases had been reported in Bolivia, Colombia, and Venezuela though. Three priests in Chile had been sued.

Former Mexican students of Reverend Marcial Maciel, the Founder of the Legions of Christ, whose Order was headquartered in Rome, had been accused by 2002. Some of the grievances went back to the 1940s. Some were filed in Rome with Cardinal Ratzinger office. He later became Pope Benedict XVI. Ratzinger chose not to investigate these cases. It would take years before the Vatican acknowledged the profound depth and breadth of Maciel not only abusing children, but fathering at least three children. Many of his priests were fanned out across the

---

[259] Report of South Asian Workshop on Trafficking in Women and Children Formulating Strategies of Resistance, Organized by UBINIG, (Policy Research for Development Alternative), October 9-10, 1996, Tangaiil, Bangladesh.

world and many identified as abusers. The Church released a document in 2023.
[260]

MEXICO

In April 2002, "Assassination of a Cardinal," by Jorge Carpizo, a former Attorney General and co-author Julian Andrade, went on sale in bookstores. Once again, it ignited the ongoing feud between Carpizo and Catholic Cardinal Juan Sandoval Iniguez over the investigations into the May 24, 1993, slaying of Sandoval's predecessor, Cardinal Juan Jesus Posadas Ocampo. The book suggested that Mexican churchmen acted as intermediaries between the government and a major narcotics network. [261]

"The young women sexually exploited in the el Pijuyal zone are mostly illegal immigrants, and based on the information gathered, it can be asserted that a high percentage of them are minors. They are *more than 300 in the high season,* reports say, adding that it is the owners of the *bars* who seek this condition. *The owners of the places prefer the young ones, to increase the prestige of their business and get more visitors.*[262]

In May 2002, John Hopkins University released a Report on 190 countries on human trafficking. It identified that the Mexican "Titanium," which recruits and kidnaps individuals for human slavery as domestic and/or sex slaves is one of the largest criminal rings.

By 2024, Mexico is the trafficking route that leads to the U.S. southern border. Since the Biden-Harris administration began in January 2021, over 10 million illegals have come through the Mexican-U.S. border. Of that, by the time of this

---

[260] Miller, Christian, The Los Angeles Times, *In Latin America, Abuse by Priests Hidden in Shadows, Culture: Reverence for the Clergy, Machismo, and Distrust of Judges Make Speaking Out Difficult,* July 31, 2002; ABC's 20/20, Report by Brian Ross on Fr. Marcial Maciel and the Legion of Christ, April 2002.

https://legionariesofchrist.org

[261] The Associated Press, *Book Alleges Church, Drug Ties,* April 30, 2002.

[262] Negrete, Norma Elena, Casa Alianza and ECPAT, *Investigation on the Trafficking, Sex Tourism, Pornography, and Prostitution of Children in Central America and Mexico,* December 2001.

publication, the U.S. federal agency I.C.E. has admitted that nearly 300,000 un-accompanied minors are not accounted for inside the U.S. They have gone missing Catholic charities are partners with the Biden Harris administration in the trafficking operation at the U.S. border and for placements in the U.S. [263]

ARGENTINA

In August 2002, Olga Wornat's book, Nuestra Santa Madre, was released. Her book linked decades old rumors of sexual abuse by Archbishop Edgardo Gabriel Storni against children. Storni had become archbishop in 1984. Shortly thereafter, the rumors became rampant. In the book, Storni was accused of abusing at least 47 seminarians.

Wornat interviewed victims who were forced to have sex with Storni when they were 15- and 16-years old seminarians at Seminario duce Nuestra Senora, where Storni taught up until 2001.

The author also investigated the complicity between the church and the military dictatorship, which had been blamed for killing an estimated 30,000 people.

In August 2002, the U.S. State Department released about 4,000 documents compiled by U.S. Embassy in Argentina. They outlined the systematic killings, kidnapping, and torture of leftists by the military dictatorship which ruled Argentina from 1976 until 1983.

Shortly before the releases of the book and the documents – in July 2002 - General Leopoldo Galtieri, Argentine's former military dictator, and 30 more officers, were arrested on charges of human rights violations.

Wornat's book rocked the archdiocese of Santa de la Vera Cruz (Sante Fe), which included 88 parishes in one of Argentine's wealthiest provinces.

Judge Eduardo Alberto Giovannini was the lead investigator of Storni's case. Judges in Argentine lead investigations and another body determines guilt and imposes sentences.

By September 2002, Storni, 66, left Argentina for a scheduled meeting at the Vatican. Storni had been investigated by the Vatican well before 2002.

---

[263] https://www.heritage.org, Who is Helping Biden Facilitate America's Border Crisis?

In 1994, the Vatican investigated Storni for sexual allegations. The results of that report were never made public.

A second judge also was investigating charges against five priests, two deacons, and a notary public for allegedly coercing, intimidating, and threatening Reverend Jose Guntern, 82, to sign an affidavit denying statements which he had made against Storni.

"At any moment you could die," on priest threated Father Guntern if he did not sign the document.

By 2002, Father Guntern was under police protection. Approximately 1,500 citizens had gathered outside of Guntern's home to show him their support. In 1992, Guntern wrote a letter to Storni about his contact with seminarian students. Another priest wrote a letter to Storni in 1994 urging him to step down because of his "sickness."

Another group protested against Guntern at a Mass officiated by Reverend Hugo Cappello, who had allegedly tried to intimidate Guntern.

After Cappello blessed the crowd, one protestor shouted, "And may He not bless you, Mafioso." [264]

Storni resigned on October 1, 2002, but said his resignation was not an admission of guilt.

BRAZIL

Brazil was also mentioned in Sr. Maura O'Donohue's 1994 report which found that young nuns were seen as targets for sex by Catholic priests, and in some cases, the priests impregnated the nuns and then encouraged them to have abortions.

By 2002, Church officials admitted that pedophilia was a problem in Brazil.

"The problem of sexual appetite is one that afflicts every human being, said Bishop Angelico Sandalo Bernardino in 2002.

---

[264] Moore, Leslie, Boston Globe, *Sex Abuse Allegations Rock Bastion of Catholicism,* September 15, 2002; Dao, James, New York Times, *U.S. Releases 1980's Files on Repression in Argentina,* August 21, 2002.

In 2002, Father Paulo Sergio Maya Barbosa was arrested after police discovered him sexually abusing a 15-year-old in a parked car in Sao Paolo. Upon arrest, police discovered child pornography, child photos, and condoms in the car as well. In just 2002 alone, 11 Brazilian priests had been accused of abusing children and young people.[265]

COLOMBIA

Colombia too was mentioned in Sr. Maura O'Donohue's 1994 report, which found that young nuns were seen as targets for sex by Catholic priests, and in some cases, the priests impregnated the nuns and then encouraged them to have abortions.

By December 2001, Bogota Mayor Antanas Mockus, had imposed a curfew on minors and a fine of $1,000 for anyone selling alcohol to minors. If the children were out past 11pm, they were to be arrested. This was in reaction to the UNICEF Report on sex trafficking. The report found that many of the same traffickers who sold and bought humans were the same as those who bought and sold drugs. Colombia then produced more than 80% of the world's cocaine and supplied more heroin to the U.S. than any other country. [266]

COSTA RICA

"There is no rigid profile of sexual exploiters. They include adult men, both local national and foreigners who, according to our sources, are mainly from the USA, Canada, Italy, China, Nicaragua, Europe, and South America. The age range of these foreign adults is broad, varying from 30 to 65 years," read a December 2001 NGO report.

Elderly foreign adults have frequently been observed in shopping centers accompanied by incredibly young women, including adolescents, buying them clothing, jewelry, and other articles. Many have been seen visiting massage parlors, bars or being visited in their hotels by girls and adolescents, generally paying high tips in dollars. The reports on the commercialization of sex tourism in Costa Rica

---

[265] BBC World Service, *Brazil Priest Arrested for Child Sex Abuse, September 2002.*

[266] BBC, *Bogota Curfew Aims at Child Sex,* December 13, 2001,

demonstrated that many of these foreigners come to the country motivated or seduced by publications promoting Costa Rica as a sex tourism destination.

The internet played a fundamental role in trafficking even then. Among the
tourists who visited massage parlors or bars and approached minors to sexually
exploit them, key informants stated many were American men older than 60.
These men had great economic solvency to pay for services, invitations, gifts and,
as some of the children mentioned being paid in dollars with large tips.

Other nationalities mentioned by included: Chinese, South Americans, Cana-
dians, and Europeans such as Italians and German.

Some of them also sought out the minors for pictures and videos, but the children were not aware of the purpose of the pictures and videos. When the predators
were detained, law enforcement had confiscated the pornographic material. One
television newscast reported that one of the predators had contacted many adolescents for pictures and videos." [267]

In 1999, two Americans were arrested in Costa Rica. When law enforcement
arrested Arthur Kanev, 55, a Boston dentist and Joe Curtis Baker, 50 a vet from
Oklahoma, a largess of child pornography was confiscated.

In June 2001, Kanev jumped bail. In December 2000, Kanev had stated in an
ABC's 20/20 report that he believed it was "morally acceptable" to have sex with
a 13-year-old girl. Baker, 50, had allegedly raped girls as young as 10 and 11 years
of age.

By February 2002, they were put on trial for having sex with dozens of minors
and possession of child pornography. Several of their victims were allegedly offered
money not to testify in the trial. Unfortunately, the trial was suspended after 11
victims testified to being given drugs before they were raped. [268]

---

[267] Retana, Viviana, and Inti Ardon, Alcides Conejo, Adina Castro, Casa Alianza and ECPAT,
*Investigation on the Trafficking, Sex Tourism, Pornography, and Prostitution of Children in Central
America and Mexico,* December 2001.

[268] Caza Alianza, owner-rapid-response@casa-alianza.org, Trial Against American Suspended in
Costa Rica, February 22, 2002.

Casa Alianza, an NGO, had been speaking out about the trafficking of young girls from the Dominican Republic, The Philippines, Bulgaria, and Russia to Costa Rica.[269]

In February 2002, Casa Alianza filed a criminal lawsuit against five members of the Board of the Patronato Nacional de la Infacia (PANI) – the national welfare system for children - because they had neglected to fulfill their legal obligations to protect the country's most vulnerable children. In San Jose alone, there were 500 homeless children.

In March 2001, Costa Rica's Constitutional Court ruled in favor of a petition by Casa Alianza that the government should be required to pay the 7% of taxes collected to the PANI that the law required. This debt, which amounted to over US $42 million had not then been paid. The PANI Board was responsible for negotiating those funds, but it had not taken the necessary actions to insist that the government provide the funds. [270]

In early March 2002, the Court ruled once again that the payment of 7% of the tax income to the PANI must be included in the country's annual budget. The Court also confirmed the violation of the law by the different Ministers of Finance since 1998 who have not respected the law.[271]

Muritizio Giordano Lanza was arrested in Costa Rica on March 1, 2002. He had been wanted on charges of sexually abusing an 11-year-old in 1997. His arrest warrant had been issued by a Waterbury, Connecticut court.

By March 27, 2002, President Miguel Angel Rodriquez signed into law changes in the criminal code which allowed for intervention of personal communications in cases of trafficking of persons, production of child pornography, commercial sexual exploitation of children, and the trafficking of human organs.

---

[269] Caza Alianza, owner-rapid-response@casa-alianza.org., Trafficker of Children to Costa Rica Jailed, February 25, 2002.

[270] Caza Alianza, owner-rapid-response@casa-alianza.org., Criminal Charges Against PANI, February 27, 2002.

[271] Caza Alianza, owner-rapid-response@casa-alianza.org., Court Rules Against Costa Rican Minister, March 1, 2002.

In a report issued by the International Labor Organization, 147,000 Costa Rican children – 15% of the total population of children – worked in "agriculture, fishing, street selling and child prostitution." The children of Costa Rica represented 13% of the workforce and received only 37% of the minimum wage for those who were working.

EL SALVADOR

By December 2001, Casa Alianza was reporting that the trafficking of boys, girls, and adolescents for commercial sexual exploitation purposes, occurred mainly from rural, departmental capitals, ports and cities like San Miguel and San Salvador. It also occurred over the borders and in "Blind Spots" between Guatemala, Honduras, Nicaragua, and El Salvador.

Honduran, Nicaraguan, and Salvadoran girls were trafficked into Guatemala, and Guatemalans, Hondurans, and Nicaraguans into El Salvador. This type of traffic was carried out by organized networks (frequently linked to drug, stolen car, or human traffic to the USA), or could be in a more informal, "independent" form.

The archbishop of Guatemala had denounced the existence of a network of traffickers of girls for sex tourism from this country to Panama and in the zones bordering on Mexico. But, Guatemalan little girls had been kidnapped and found in El Salvadoran brothels, where they had been raped and drugged." [272]

According to the U.N.'s International Labour Organisation Report, 17% of all children had to work to financially support their families.

In early 2002, William Hernandez, 31, an openly gay activist, accused Father Luis Recinos publicly of sexually abusing him 15 years earlier in Apopa. He claimed that the abuse started with hugs and kissing, and eventually led to oral sex. Hernandez claimed that if he refused, Recinos would beat him. After a year of the abuse, Hernandez ran away to escape the abuse. Two years later, Hernandez reported Recinos to church officials because a friend told him that he had also been abused by Recinos. Before coming to Apopa, Recinos had been accused of molesting boys at another parish.

---

[272] Dominguez, Liza, Casa Alianza and ECPAT, *Investigation on the Trafficking, Sex Tourism, Pornography, and Prostitution of Children in Central America and Mexico,* December 2001.

The Church initially responded by sending Father Recinos to Rome to "study" for a year. Upon his return from that trip, Recinos began abusing Hernandez again. In 1998, additional abuse stories surfaced and Recinos was sent to Rome again. Later, he was assigned to another parish in El Salvador. Hernandez again reported Recinos' abuses to the Bishop in 2000. Nothing happened. Then Hernandez complained again in 2002. This time the Church opened a formal ecclesiastical tribune investigation. Recinos continued to deny the charges although the charges seem credible to church officials.

Bishop Rafael Urisote claimed that the Church was open to investigating reports of abuse but suggested that there may be only a few Latin priests who abuse children. One Church official claimed that there were only three other priests in El Salvador who may have abused children. None of these men had been reported to law enforcement.

Judge Melida Rivera, a former prosecutor, tried to investigate a US Catholic priest who worked at a children's home in El Salvador in 2000, but the priest left El Salvador soon after the accusations were made.[273]

GUATEMALA

In November 2001, Julio Arango Escobar, Guatemala's Human Rights Ombudsman, received accusations about three Catholic priests abusing two young girls and two male theology students. These were the first cases of pedophile priests in the country. The girls were aged seven and nine. The theology students were under 16 years of age.

The three priests were Hugo Portillo, head of a pastoral unit in the town of Quetzaltenaggo, Cesar Isaias Coroy and Luis Fernando Oliva Ponce, clerics in a village outside of Guatemala City. Escobar concluded his investigation in April 2002 and passed on the information to church officials and the Attorney General's office. Both offices were to do their own investigations.[274]

---

[273] Miller, Christian, The Los Angeles Times, *In Latin America, Abuse by Priests Hidden in Shadows, Culture: Reverence for the Clergy, Machismo, and Distrust of Judges Make Speaking Out Difficult,* July 31, 2002.

[274] Reuters, *Guatemala Accuses Three Priests of Sex Abuse,* August 20, 2002.

"In the report *The Forgotten Children of Guatemala,* Human Rights Watch asserts that there are from 1,500 to 5,000 minors in Guatemala who are homeless. According to Infomundi, millions of street boys and girls who work, traffic, steal and prostitute themselves out of need for money and due to marginalization by their societies, are between five and seventeen years old. *Some 12-yar old girls would visit this place by going through a barber shop that worked as a front (its back door led to the bar). In the morning, these girls sold quesadilla and in the evening they would go to the bar. These girls were also filmed. The videos were more expensive, and they were sold outside the place – abroad, I think...*

The Sister who was the coordinator of the House of Women, run by the Order of Oblate Sisters, was also very clear concerning the existence of the [trafficking] networks...*They [the networks] do exist, and the girls can openly witness to it – girls who have been victims and have suffered from this kind of abuse, who have been deceived in situations where third parties are involved. Someone is responsible for contacting them, someone else takes care of transportation to the place, and someone else sells them. The owner of the bar travels all over Central America, looking for young girls of only 14 years old. She brings them over no matter how – under deception or by force. I remember a girl named Thelma, who was a virgin. She was offered there to a rich man. She was a slave; she took care of cleaning and occupied herself.* [275]

According to the UN's International Labour Organisation Report, 33% of all children had to work to financially help themselves or their families

HONDURAS

Cardinal Oscar Rodriguez Maradiaga – sometime mentioned as a successor to Pope John Paul II – had told the Italian Catholic monthly *Thirty Days,* that the American media was acting with "a fury which reminds me of the times of Diocletian and Nero and more recently, Stalin and Hitler. The church should be free of this kind of treatment."

He accused CNN's Founder Ted Turner and AOL of being "openly anti-Catholic," and insisted that "newspapers like *The New York Times, The Washington*

[275] Villareal, Eugenia, Casa Alianza and ECPAT, *Investigation on the Trafficking, Sex Tourism, Pornography, and Prostitution of Children in Central America and Mexico,* December 2001.

Post and *The Boston Globe* were protagonists of what he did not hesitate to define as a "persecution against the church" for reporting on the sex scandals in 2002.

Rodriquez viewed the investigation of Cardinal Bernard Law as akin to a "witch-hunt" and referred to it as "the dark days of Stalinist trials of churchmen of Eastern Europe."

"It would be a tragedy to reduce the role of pastor to that of cop…I would be prepared to go to jail rather than harm one of my priests," said the Cardinal during a press conference. [276]

Four Honduran nationalists were arrested in Texas for trafficking girls and women to the U.S. from Honduras following raids in Fort Worth, Texas. According to court documents, the "Molina Organisation" used residences and other establishments to harbor victims – many of whom were minors. The girls were trafficked to the U.S. under the deception that they would work in hotels and bars. Once in the U.S., their documents were confiscated, and they were told that they owed the traffickers money and had to work in "bars" as strippers. [277]

Honduras was a young country in 2002. Most of its population consisted of boys, girls, adolescents, which meant that, when speaking of children's rights being violated that was about most of the country's population. Honduras was then one of the poorest country in Latin America.

In each of the Honduran child pornography investigations back in 2002, the predators were foreigners. In six of the cases, the predators were U.S. citizens. Whether reproduced in video form or on the internet, Honduran child pornography did not then seem to have much of a local market. Most of the child pornography was distributed to an international market. Only three of the victims received an explanation of the purpose of the photos and video sessions.

Two were told that they were "adult movies."

"Some Americans had photographed and filmed me, they said they were with the Playboy magazine. We were in the Hotel Partenon Beach, we spent, like two months doing that. The American was only called "Jenny." He filmed my girlfriend and I

---

[276] Thirty Days, June 2002.

[277] Casa Alianza, *4 Hondurans Charged with Trafficking of Girls,* Mary 29, 2002.

having orgies with him and his friend. He said he would come back in three months," reported the 15-year-old girl.

In terms of sexual exploitation of children, sex tourism was the human trafficking market in Comayagua, and, in almost all cases, it was engaged near U.S. troops on the "Palmerola" military base.

"I charge 1,500, in dollars, it depends on the client and the place, sometimes they have parties on the base, and they come get us in Comayagua to take us to the base all night, we charge more at these parties, I like them because they pay in dollars, but they always want sex from behind and one time they gang raped me," said a 17-year-old girl during an interview in October 2000.

Honduras had a genuine problem of commercial sexual exploitation of children expressed through all its various human trafficking faces, albeit in different degrees: child prostitution, sex tourism, trafficking of boys, girls and adolescents for sexual purposes, and child pornography. Because of the absence of a state policy for children, they were culturally vulnerable. Children were fertile grounds for exploitation. The exploiters ranged from hooker, pimp, establishment owner, client, migrations contact, and even family members.

Criminal organizations in the country were dedicated to commercial sexual exploitation of children, oriented especially toward trafficking boys, girls, and adolescents for sexual purposes, and for servicing the sex tourism sector. After child prostitution, sex tourism was the most frequently trafficking face in Honduras. The clients were manly adult males from developed countries, especially the U.S, and Europe, who indulged in child pornography. At this point in time, Honduran pedophiles were not necessarily focused on child pornography. [278]

According to the UN's International Labour Organisation Report, 21% of all children had work to financially help themselves or their families. Between January 1998 and 2002. more than 1,300 children had been murdered in Honduras.[279]

---

[278] Bahr, Sergio Fernando, and Julio Nunex, Misaela Mejia, and margarita Puerto Gomez, Casa Alianza and ECPAT, *Investigation on the Trafficking, Sex Tourism, Pornography, and Prostitution of Children in Central America and Mexico,* December 2001.

[279] Casa Alianza, *Children Dead and Dying on the Streets of Honduras,* January 14, 2002; Casa Alianza, *From Murders to Massacres – Child Killings Accelerate in Honduras,* September 17, 2002.

NICARAGUA

"According to testimonies and press reports, Nicaragua served as a principal sup-
plier of victims of commercial sexual exploitation for the other countries of Central
America where sexual exploitation venues operated." [280]

---

[280] Lang, Rosamaria Sanchez, and Danilo Medrano, Sylvia Hernandez, and Johnny Mua, Casa
Alianza and ECPAT, *Investigation on the Trafficking, Sex Tourism, Pornography, and Prostitution of
Children in Central America and Mexico*, December 2001.

Acknowledgements

There are numerous individuals who opened the doors for me and agreed to be interviewed during this investigation. For security reasons, I cannot name them all. You know who you are – my warmest heartfelt gratitude!

I owe the deepest appreciation to those who put up with me as we labored over this investigation, supported me, and have prayed for me over two decades and continue to for the protection of children. I am blessed. What I have learned is I could not do these investigations without your prayers. Thank you from the bottom of my heart.

I honor my dearest best friends in the earliest days.

Anne, my late mother, who passed away in March 2002, asked me, "Does your father *know* what you are doing? and then said to me before she died, "You do know, My Darling, you are rocking the boat and the powers that be will come after you? Be strong and never give up!"

My late father, Buddy, who was a relentless advocate for the protection of children, and earnestly stated repeatedly to anyone who would listen as the Boston diocese imploded in 2002, especially within the Catholic Church, "It is the responsibility of every adult to protect every child!"

To my dear late friend and news mentor, Ed Turner, who always said, "Just tell the story and it will wake up the audience but get the whole damn story!"

To Linda MacDonald and Jeanne Sarson, so many thanks are not enough for putting this horror into the right words – yes, this is *ritual abuse torture*!

To my dearest friend, Homayra Sellier, riding this rollercoaster with you made it fun to go after the bad guys!

To Jan Eliasson, former Swedish Ambassador to the U.S., and former Deputy Secretary of the United Nations - "They were right – we are obsessed with protecting children!"

To my friend and colleague, Dr. Richard Sezibera, former Rwandan Ambassador to the U.S., "I am honored to be your friend. You have taught me so much!"

To Father Tom Doyle, whose Irish wit kept me going through this "ordeal" years ago, and whose wise counsel kept me focused – "a truly compassionate and courageous crusader for children!"

To Jeffrey Anderson, so many thanks for your commitment to helping victims and their families for decades. Tom Doyle and you deserve a Medal of Honor.

To Tim Conlon, who went the distance not just for me, but for the victims!

To Marcy Jackson, Kurt Schwartz and Tom Reilly, the Boston prosecutors I met with in January 2002. You believed and stood tall morally as prosecutors.

To Mike Tario, the late Judith Reisman, Helen, Hank, Mike, and their friends in Chicago! Thank you for your hours of educating me.

To Jason Berry and all those authors who went before me, whose books I read and reread, thank you for laying the trail!

To Michael Skinner, one of the bravest survivors I know, who endured the most unspeakable and despicable acts by his parents and their pedophile friends –

Michael, *Your candor, and leadership have shown truth overcomes evil.*

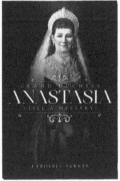